Regular Expression Recipes for Windows Developers

A Problem-Solution Approach

NATHAN A. GOOD

Regular Expression Recipes for Windows Developers: A Problem-Solution Approach

Copyright © 2005 by Nathan A. Good

ISBN (pbk): 1-59059-497-5

9 8 7 6 5 4 3 2 1

Lead Editor: Chris Mills
Technical Reviewer: Gavin Smyth
Editorial Board: Steve Anglin, Dan Appleman, Ewan Buckingham, Gary Cornell, Tony Davis,
     Jason Gilmore, Jonathan Hassell, Chris Mills, Dominic Shakeshaft, Jim Sumser
Assistant Publisher: Grace Wong
Project Manager: Beth Christmas
Copy Manager: Nicole LeClerc
Copy Editor: Kim Wimpsett
Production Manager: Kari Brooks-Copony
Production Editor: Ellie Fountain
Compositor: Dina Quan
Proofreader: Patrick Vincent
Indexer: Nathan A. Good
Cover Designer: Kurt Krames
Manufacturing Manager: Tom Debolski

Distributed to the book trade in the United States by Springer-Verlag New York, Inc., 233 Spring Street, 6th Floor, New York, NY 10013, and outside the United States by Springer-Verlag GmbH & Co. KG, Tiergartenstr. 17, 69112 Heidelberg, Germany.

In the United States: phone 1-800-SPRINGER, fax 201-348-4505, e-mail orders@springer-ny.com, or visit http://www.springer-ny.com. Outside the United States: fax +49 6221 345229, e-mail orders@springer.de, or visit http://www.springer.de.

For information on translations, please contact Apress directly at 2560 Ninth Street, Suite 219, Berkeley, CA 94710. Phone 510-549-5930, fax 510-549-5939, e-mail info@apress.com, or visit http://www.apress.com.

The source code for this book is available to readers at http://www.apress.com in the Downloads section.

Contents at a Glance

Contents

About the Author

NATHAN A. GOOD lives in the Twin Cities area in Minnesota. As a contractor, he does software development, software architecture, and systems administration for a variety of companies.

When he's not writing software, Nathan enjoys building PCs and servers, reading about and working with new technologies, and trying to get all his friends to make the move to open-source software. When he's not at a computer, he spends time with his family, with his church, and at the movies. Nathan can be reached by e-mail at mail@nathanagood.com.

About the Technical Reviewer

GAVIN SMYTH is a professional software engineer with more years of experience in development than he cares to admit, ranging from device drivers to multihost applications, from real-time operating systems to Unix and Windows, from assembler to C++, and from Ada to C#. He has worked for clients such as Nortel, Microsoft, and BT, among others; he has written a few pieces as well (EXE and Wrox, where are you now?), but finds criticizing other people's work much more fulfilling. Beyond that, when he's not fighting weeds in the garden, he tries to persuade LEGO robots to do what he wants them to do (it's for the kids' benefit, honest).

Acknowledgments

I'd like to first of all thank God. I'd also like to thank my wonderful and supportive wife and kids for being patient and sacrificing while I was working on his book. I couldn't have done this work if it wasn't for my wonderful parents and grandparents.

Also, I'd like to thank Jeffrey E. F. Friedl for both editions of his stellar book, *Mastering Regular Expressions*.

Introduction

This book contains recipes for regular expressions that you can use in languages common on the Microsoft Windows platform. It provides ready-to-go, real-world implementations and explains each recipe. The approach is right to the point, so it will get you off and using regular expressions quickly.

Who Should Read This Book

This book was written for Web and application programmers and developers who might need to use regular expressions in their .NET applications or Windows scripts but who don't have the time to become entrenched in the details. Each recipe is intended to be useful and practical in real-world situations but also to be a starting point for you to tweak and customize as you find the need.

I also wrote this for people who don't know they should use regular expressions yet. The book provides recipes for many common tasks that can be performed in other ways besides using regular expressions but that could be made simpler with regular expressions. Many methods that use more than one snippet of code to replace text can be rewritten as one regular expression replacement.

Finally, I wrote this book for programmers who have some spare time and want to quickly pick up something new to impress their friends or the cute COBOL developer down the hall. Perhaps you're in an office where regular expressions are regarded as voodoo magic—cryptic incantations that everyone fears and nobody understands. This is your chance to become the Grand Wizard of Expressions and be revered by your peers.

This book doesn't provide an exhaustive explanation of how regular expression engines read expressions or do matches. Also, this book doesn't cover advanced regular expression techniques such as optimization. Some of the expressions in this book have been written to be easy to read and use at the expense of performance. If those topics are of interest to you, see *Mastering Regular Expressions*, Second Edition, by Jeffrey E. F. Friedl (O'Reilly, 2002).

Conventions Used in This Book

Throughout this book, changes in typeface and type weight will let you know if I'm referring to a regular expression recipe or a string. The example code given in recipes is in a fixed-width font like this:

```
This is sample code.
```

The actual expression in the recipe is called out in bold type.

```
Here is an expression.
```

When expressions and the strings they might match are listed in the body text, they look like `this`.

Recipes that are related because they use the same metacharacters or character sequences are listed like this at the end of some recipes:

▪**See Also** 4-9, 5-1

How This Book Is Organized

This book is split into sets of examples called *recipes*. The recipes contain different versions of expressions to do the same task, such as replacing words. Each recipe contains examples in JavaScript, VBScript, VB .NET, and C# .NET (or any other .NET language, since their regular expressions are common to all languages). In recipes that do only matching, I've included examples in ASP.NET that use the RegularExpressionValidator control.

After the examples in each recipe, the "How It Works" section breaks the example down and tells you why the expression works. I explain the expression character by character, with text explanations of each character or metacharacter. When I was first learning regular expressions, it was useful to me to read the expression aloud while I was going through it. Don't worry about your co-workers looking at you oddly—the minute you begin wielding the awesome power of regular expressions, the joke will be on them.

At the end of some recipes, you'll see a "Variations" section. This section highlights some common variations of expressions used in some of the recipes.

The code samples in this book are simple and are for the most part identical for two reasons. First, each example is ready to use and complete enough to show the expression working. Second, at the same time, the focus of these examples is the expression, not the code.

The recipes are split into common tasks, such as working with comma-separated-value (CSV) files and tab-delimited files or working with source code. The recipes aren't organized from simple to difficult, as there's little point in trying to rate expressions in their difficulty level. The tasks are as follows:

Words and text: These recipes introduce many concepts in expressions but also show common tasks used in replacing and searching for words and text in regular blocks of text.

URLs and paths: These recipes are useful when operating on filenames, file paths, and URLs. In the .NET Framework, you can use many different objects to deal safely with paths and URLs. Remember that it's often better for you to use an object someone has already written and tested than for you to develop your own object that uses regular expressions to parse paths.

CSV and tab-delimited files: These recipes show how to change CSV records to tab-delimited records and how to perform tasks such as extracting single fields from tab-delimited records.

Formatting and validating: These recipes are useful for writing routines in applications where the data is widely varying user input. These expressions allow you to determine if the input is what you expect and deal with the expressions appropriately.

HTML and XML: These recipes provide examples for working with HTML and XML files, such as removing HTML attributes and finding HTML attributes. Just like URLs and paths, many objects come with the .NET Framework that you can use to manipulate XML and well-formed HTML. Using these objects instead may be a better idea, depending on what you need to do. However, sometimes regular expressions are a better way to go, such as when the HTML and XML is in a form where the object won't work.

Source code: This final group of recipes shows expressions that you can use to find text within comments or perform replacements on parameters.

What Regular Expressions Are

My favorite way to think about regular expressions is as being just like mathematical expressions, except they operate on sequences of characters or on strings instead of numbers.

Understanding this concept will help you understand the best way to learn how to use regular expressions. Chances are, when you see $4 + 3 = 7$, you think "four plus three equals seven." The goal of this book is to duplicate that thought process in the "How It Works" sections, where expressions are broken down into single characters and explained. An expression such as ^$ becomes "the beginning of a line followed immediately by the end of a line" (in other words, a completely empty line).

The comparison to mathematical expressions isn't accidental. Regular expressions find their roots in mathematics. For more information about the history of regular expressions, see http://en.wikipedia.org/wiki/Regular_expression.

Regular expressions can be very concise, considering how much they can say. Their brevity has the benefit of allowing you to say quite a lot with one small, well-written expression. However, a drawback of this brevity is that regular expressions can be difficult to read, especially if you're the poor developer picking up someone else's uncommented work. An expression such as ^['^']*?'['^']*?' can be difficult to debug if you don't know what the author was trying to do or why the author was doing it that way. Although this is a problem in all code that isn't thoroughly documented, the concise nature of expressions and the inability to debug them make the problem worse. In some implementations, expressions can be commented, but realistically that isn't common and therefore isn't included in the recipes in this book.

What Regular Expressions Aren't

As I mentioned previously, regular expressions aren't easy to read or debug. They can easily lead to unexpected results because one misplaced character can change the entire meaning of the expression. Mismatched parentheses or quotes can cause major issues, and many syntax-highlighting IDEs currently released do nothing to help isolate these in regular expressions.

Not everyone uses regular expressions. However, since they're available in the .NET Framework and are supported by scripting languages such as JavaScript and VBScript, I expect more and more people will begin using them. Just like with anything else, be prudent and consider the skills of those around you when writing the expressions. If you're working with a staff unfamiliar with regular expressions, make sure to comment your code until it's painfully obvious exactly what's happening.

When to Use Regular Expressions

Use regular expressions whenever there are rules about finding or replacing strings. Rules might be "Replace this *but only when it's at the beginning of a word*" or "Find this *but only when it's inside parentheses*." Regular expressions provide the opportunity for searches and replacements to be really intelligent and have a lot of logic packed into a relatively small space.

One of the most common places where I've used regular expressions is in "smart" interface validation. I've had clients with specific requests for U.S. postal codes, for instance. They wanted a five-number code such as 55555 to work but also a four-digit extension, such as 55555-4444. What's more, they wanted to allow the five- and four-digit groups to be separated by a dash, space, or nothing at all. This is something that's fairly simple to do with a regular expression, but it takes more work in code using things such as conditional statements based on the length of the string.

When Not to Use Regular Expressions

Don't use regular expressions when you can use a simple search or replacement with accuracy. If you intend to replace *moo* with *oink*, and you don't care where the string is found, don't bother using an expression to do it. Instead, use the string method supported in the language you're using.

Particularly in the .NET platform, you can use objects to work with URLs, paths, HTML, and XML. I'm a big fan of the notion that a developer shouldn't rewrite something that already exists, so use discernment when working with regular expressions. If something quite usable already exists that does what you need, use it rather than writing an expression.

Consider not using expressions if in doing so it will take you longer to figure out the expression than to filter bad data by hand. For instance, if you know the data well enough that you already know you might get only three or four false matches that you can correct by hand in a few minutes, don't spend 15 minutes writing an expression. Of course, at some point you have to overcome a learning curve if you're new to expressions, so use your judgment. Just don't get too expression-happy for expressions' sake.

Syntax Overview

This book contains .NET and other Microsoft technologies as opposed to open-source technologies such as Perl and PHP, which were used in another version of this book, *Regular Expression Recipes: A Problem-Solution Approach* (Apress, 2005).

The following sections give an overview of the syntax of regular expressions as used in C#, Visual Basic .NET, ASP.NET, VBScript, and JavaScript. The regular expression engine is the same for all the languages in the .NET Framework as opposed to different support between Perl and PHP, so using regular expressions with Microsoft technologies can be a little easier. The value of having the different languages listed in this book is that it allows you to use the expression easily without getting caught up in syntax differences between the different languages.

Expression Parts

The terminology for various parts of an expression hasn't ever been as important to me as knowing how to use expressions. I'll touch briefly on some terminology that describes each part of an expression and then get into how to put those parts together.

An expression can either be a single atom or be the joining of more than one atom. An *atom* is a single character or a metacharacter. A *metacharacter* is a single character that has special meaning other than its literal meaning. An example of both an atom and a character is a; an example of both an atom and a metacharacter is ^ (a metacharacter that I'll explain in a minute). You put these atoms together to build an expression, like so: ^a.

You can put atoms into groups using parentheses, like so: (^a). Putting atoms in a group builds an expression that can be captured for back referencing, modified with a qualifier, or included in another group of expressions.

(starts a group of atoms.

)   ends a group of atoms.

You can use additional modifiers to make groups do special things, such as operate as *look-arounds* or give captured groups names. You can use a *look-around* to match what's before or after an expression without capturing what's in the look-around. For instance, you might want to replace a word but only if it isn't preceded or followed by something else.

(?=   starts a group that's a positive look-ahead.

(?!   starts a group that's a negative look-ahead.

(?<=   starts a group that's a positive look-behind.

(?<!   starts a group that's a negative look-behind.

)   ends any of the previous groups.

A *positive look-ahead* will cause the expression to find a match only when what's inside the parentheses can be found to the right of the expression. The expression \.(?=), for instance, will match a period (.) only if it's followed immediately by two spaces. The reason for using a look-around is because any replacement will leave what's found inside the parentheses alone.

A *negative look-ahead* operates just like a positive one, except it will force an expression to find a match when what's inside the parentheses *isn't* found to the right of the expression. The expression \.(?!), for instance, will match a period (.) that *doesn't* have two spaces after it.

Positive look-behinds and *negative look-behinds* operate just like positive and negative look-aheads, respectively, except they look for matches to the left of the expression instead of the right. Look-behinds have one ugly catch: many regular expression implementations don't allow the use of variable-length look-behinds. This means you can't use qualifiers (which are discussed in the next section) inside look-behinds.

Another feature you can use with groups is the ability to name a group and use the name later to insert what was captured in the group into a replacement or to simply extract what was captured in the group. The "Back References" section covers the syntax for referring to groups.

To name a group, use (?<*myname*> where *myname* is the name of the group.

(?<...>   the start of a named group, where . . . is substituted with the name . . .

)   the end of the named group.

Qualifiers

Qualifiers restrict the number of times the preceding expression may appear in a match. The common single-character qualifiers are ?, +, and *.

?   means "zero or one," which matches the preceding expression found zero or one time.

◾See Also 1-4, 2-2, 2-3, 2-5, 2-8, 2-9, 2-10, 4-1, 4-2, 4-3, 4-10, 4-12, 4-13, 4-15, 4-17, 4-18, 4-22, 4-23, 5-7

+   means "one or more." An expression using the + qualifier will match the previous expression one or more times, making it required but matching it as many times as possible.

◾See Also 1-3, 1-10, 1-11, 1-14, 1-15, 2-3, 2-4, 2-5, 2-6, 2-7, 2-8, 2-9, 3-1, 3-2, 3-5, 3-6, 4-4, 4-5, 4-7, 4-11, 4-12, 4-19, 4-20, 4-21, 5-2, 5-3, 5-5, 5-6, 5-7

---

*   means "zero or more." You should use this qualifier carefully; since it matches zero occurrences of the preceding expression, some unexpected results can occur.

See Also 1-1, 1-7, 1-9, 1-11, 1-17, 1-25, 1-27, 2-2, 2-3, 2-5, 2-9, 3-1, 3-3, 3-4, 3-5, 3-6, 4-8, 4-19, 4-20, 4-21, 5-5, 5-6

Ranges

Ranges, like qualifiers, specify the number of times a preceding expression can occur in the string. Ranges begin with { and end with }. Inside the brackets, either a single number or a pair of numbers can appear. A comma separates the pair of numbers.

When a single number appears in a range, it specifies exactly how many times the preceding expression can appear. If commas separate two numbers, the first number specifies the least number of occurrences, and the second number specifies the most number of occurrences.

{   specifies the beginning of a range.

}   specifies the end of a range.

{n}   specifies the preceding expression is found exactly *n* times.

{n,}   specifies the preceding expression is found at least *n* times.

{n,m}   specifies the preceding expression is found at least *n* but no more than *m* times.

Line Anchors

The ^ and $ metacharacters are line anchors. They match the beginning of the line and the end of the line, respectively, but they don't consume any real characters. When a match consumes a character, it means the character will be replaced by whatever is in the replacement expression. The fact that the line anchors don't match any real characters is important when making replacements, because the replacement expression doesn't have to be written to put the ^ or $ back into the string.

^   specifies the beginning of the line.

$ specifies the end of the line.

An Escape

You can use the escape character \ to precede atoms that would otherwise be metacharacters but that need to be taken literally. The expression \+, for instance, will match a plus sign and doesn't mean a backslash is found one or many times.

\   indicates the escape character.

■See Also 2-2, 2-10, 4-5, 4-8, 4-11, 4-12, 4-16, 4-21, 6-10, 6-13, 6-16, 6-24, 6-25

Saying "Or"

You use the | metacharacter as an "or" operator in regular expressions. You use it between expressions, which can consist of a single atom or an entire group.

| indicates "or."

■See Also 1-3, 1-16, 1-18, 2-1, 2-4, 2-6, 2-9, 2-11, 2-12, 3-1, 3-3, 3-5, 4-2, 4-10, 4-12, 4-16, 4-17, 5-1, 5-4, 6-1, 6-2, 6-8, 6-9, 6-14, 6-18

Character Classes

Character classes are defined by square brackets ([and]) and match a single character, no matter how many atoms are inside the character class. A sample character class is [ab], which will match a or b.

You can use the - character inside a character class to define a range of characters. For instance, [a-c] will match *a*, *b*, or *c*. It's possible to put more than one range inside brackets. The character class [a-c0-2] will not only match *a*, *b*, or *c* but will also match *0*, *1*, or *2*.

[indicates the beginning of a character class.

-        indicates a range inside a character class (unless it's first in the class).

^   indicates a negated character class, if found first.

]   indicates the end of a character class.

To use the - character literally inside a character class, put it first. It's impossible for it to define a range if it's the first character in a range, so it's taken literally. This is also true for most of the other metacharacters.

The ^ metacharacter, which normally is a line anchor that matches the beginning of a line, is a negation character when it's used as the first character inside a character class. If it isn't the first character inside the character class, it will be treated as a literal ^.

A character class can also be a sequence of a normal character preceded by an escape. One example is \s, which matches whitespace (either a tab or a space).

The character classes \t and \n are common examples found in nearly every implementation of regular expressions to match tabs and newline characters, respectively. Listed in Table 1 are the character classes supported in the .NET Framework.

Table 1. *.NET Framework Character Classes*

Character Class	Description
\d	This matches any digit such as 0–9.
\D	This matches any character that isn't a digit, such as punctuation and letters *A–Z* and *a–z*.
\p{...}	This matches any character that's in the Unicode group name supplied inside the braces.
\P{...}	This matches any character that *isn't* in the Unicode class where the class name is supplied inside the braces.
\s	This matches any whitespace, such as spaces, tabs, or returns.
\S	This matches any nonwhitespace.
\u*n*	This matches any Unicode character where *n* is the Unicode character expressed in hexadecimal notation.
\w	This matches any word character. Word characters in English are 0–9, *A–Z*, *a–z*, and _.
\W	This matches any nonword character.

You can find out the name of a character's Unicode class by going to http://www.unicode.org/Public/UNIDATA/UCD.html or by using the GetUnicodeCategory method on the Char object.

Matching Anything

The period (.) is the wildcard in regular expressions—it matches anything. Using .* will match anything, everything, or nothing.

.   indicates any character.

◼**See Also** 2-4, 2-6, 2-7, 2-8, 2-9, 2-10, 2-11, 2-12, 3-5, 3-6, 4-1, 4-9, 4-19, 4-20, 4-21, 5-7, 6-2, 6-5, 6-8, 6-9, 6-10, 6-11, 6-12, 6-18, 6-19, 6-20, 6-21, 6-22

Back References

Back references provide a way of referring to the results of a capture. The back reference \1, for instance, refers to the first capture in a regular expression. Back references allow search expressions to search for repeated words or characters by saying to the regular expression engine, "Whatever you found in the first group, look for it again here." One common use in this book for back references in searching is parsing HTML or XML, where the closing and ending tags have the same name, but you might not know at search time what the names will be.

The sequences \1 through \9 are interpreted by the regular expression engine to be back references automatically. Numbers higher than nine are assumed to be back references if they have corresponding groups but are otherwise considered to be octal codes.

If the groups are named with the (?<...> syntax, you can refer to the named groups by using \k<...>. As an example, (?<space>\s)\k<space> finds doubled spaces. (This is just an example—there are easier ways to do this particular one.)

.NET Framework Classes

The classes and methods listed in the following sections are provided with the .NET Framework for use with regular expressions. Since all classes inherit certain methods, not all of them are listed here. Each class, for example, has an Equals method. In the following sections, the primary concern is the methods that will be used throughout this book.

Regex

The Regex class is located in the System.Text.RegularExpressions namespace. It's an immutable class and is thread safe, so you can use a single Regex class in a multithreaded parser if you want. The Regex class allows you to define a single regular expression and exposes methods that can be used to search through strings and hold results of searches.

■**Note** An *immutable class* is a class that can't be modified once it has been created.

See the C# and Visual Basic .NET examples later in this section that show how to use the Regex class. Table 2 shows the Regex public properties, and Table 3 shows the Regex public methods.

Table 2. Regex *Public Properties*

Public Property Name	What It Does
Options	This property returns the options that were given to the Regex constructor.
RightToLeft	This property returns true if the regular expression searches from right to left.

Table 3. Regex *Public Methods*

Public Method Name	What It Does
CompileToAssembly	Compiles the regular expression to an assembly and saves it to disk.
Escape	This static method escapes the metacharacters \, *, +, ?, |, {, [, (,), ^, $, ., #, and whitespace. The result of Regex.Escape("+") is \+.
GetGroupNames	This method returns an array of capturing group names. In the expression ^(?<proto>[a-z]+)://(?<hostname>[a-z0-9][a-z0-9_]+)$ the array will contain three elements: the first with the string 0, the second with the string proto, and the third with the string hostname; the zero group will contain the complete expression.

Public Method Name	What It Does
GetGroupNumbers	This method returns an array of capturing group numbers. Using the expression shown in the example next to GetGroupNames, the array will be a three-element array that will contain the numbers (as integers) 0, 1, and 2.
GetNameFromNumber	This method returns the group name given the group's number.
GetNumberFromName	This method returns the group number given the group's name.
IsMatch	Returns true if the regular expression finds a match in the string.
Match	This method returns the exact result of the search as a Match object. See "Match" later in this section.
Matches	This method returns all occurrences of successful matches found in the string. It's a collection of Match objects.
Replace	This method replaces the search expression with another string. No replacement is made if there's no successful match in the expression.
Split	This method slices a string into parts defined by the regular expression and returns the result as an array of strings.
ToString	This method returns the original expression that was given to the Regex object's constructor. Remember that since the Regex class is immutable, this means that the original expression can't be changed once the object has been created.
Unescape	This static method removes the escape for any escaped characters in the string. The result of Result.Unescape(@"\\+") is \+.

The Regex object accepts options in the constructor that determine how the regular expression finds matches. You can tweak case sensitivity and behavior such as ignoring whitespace by setting the options in the constructor. The RegexOption enumeration contains values that can be used in the constructor. Table 4 shows the Regex options.

Table 4. Regex *Options*

Regex Option	What It Does
None	None of the options has been set.
Compiled	Although a compiled regular expression has slower startup time, it can be beneficial for performance to use compiled expressions when many objects are using the expression or when the expression is used many times in the same class, such as when looping line by line through a large file.
CultureInvariant	The engine will ignore culture differences.
ECMAScript	If this option is used, the regular expression engine exhibits ECMA-compliant behavior. Note that it can be used only with two other tags—IgnoreCase and Multiline. Otherwise, an exception will be thrown. ECMAScript doesn't support Unicode.
ExplicitCapture	Only groups that are named are evaluated. This means all the groups must be named using the (?<name> syntax, or they won't be considered capturing groups. For instance, if ExplicitCapture is enabled with the regular expression (\w)\1, an exception will actually be thrown because the group referenced by \1 is undefined.

Continued

Table 4. *Continued*

Regex **Option**	**What It Does**
IgnorePatternWhitespace	Whitespace inside the regular expression is ignored. The most important thing to remember when enabling this option is that you should use the character class \s to match a space.
Multiline	The ^ and $ metacharacters are modified to be line anchors that match each line, not just the beginning and end of the entire string
Singleline	This options tells the engine to assume the string is a single line. The . wildcard matches every character, including \n.

Capture

The Capture class contains the results of a single expression capture. Table 5 lists its public properties, and Table 6 lists its public methods.

Table 5. Capture *Public Properties*

Public Property Name	**What It Contains**
Index	This contains the position in the string where the first character of the capture can be found.
Length	This property contains the length of the captured string.
Value	This stores the string value of what has been captured.

Table 6. Capture *Public Methods*

Method Name	**What It Does**
ToString	This returns a string representation of the Capture object. In this case, it's the same as the string returned by the Value property.

Group

A Group contains the results from one capturing group. (A GroupCollection object contains the results of more than one capturing group.) Table 7 lists its public properties, and Table 8 lists its public methods.

Table 7. Group *Public Properties*

Public Property Name	**What It Contains**
Captures	This property contains a collection of Capture objects that are matched by the capturing group.
Index	This property contains the position in the string in which the match begins.

Public Property Name	What It Contains
Length	This property contains the length of the captured string.
Success	This property is true if the match was successful.
Value	This property contains the string value of the match.

Table 8. Group *Public Methods*

Public Method Name	What It Does
ToString	This returns the same value as the Value property.

Match

This object contains the results of a successful regular expression search. Table 9 lists its public properties, and Table 10 lists its public methods.

Table 9. Match *Public Properties*

Public Property Name	What It Contains
Captures	This contains a collection of Capture objects that are matched by the capturing group.
Empty	This contains an empty match set that's the result of failed matches.
Groups	This contains a collection of Group objects that are matched by the expression.
Index	This contains the position in the string in which the first match was made.
Length	This contains the length of the matched part of the string.
Success	This contains a value of true if the search was successful in finding a match.
Value	This contains the matched value found in the string.

Table 10. Match *Public Methods*

Public Method Name	What It Does
NextMatch	This returns a new Match object that contains the result of the next match in the string.
Result	This returns the value of the passed-in replacement pattern.
Synchronized	This returns a Match object that's thread safe.
ToString	This returns the same string as the Value property.

Scripting

The objects used in VBScript and JavaScript for scripting are different from the .NET Framework classes. The `RegExp` object provides support in VBScript and JavaScript. It's a global object that's available and ready for use—it doesn't need to be created, and no other statements are required to begin using it.

One added note with JavaScript: you can use two different objects—the Regular Expression object and the `RegExp` object. The Regular Expression object is a single instance of a regular expression. Table 11 lists the `RegExp` object properties in JavaScript, Table 12 lists the Regular Expression object properties in JavaScript, and Table 13 lists the Regular Expression object methods in JavaScript.

Table 11. `RegExp` *Object Properties in JavaScript*

Property Name	Description
index	The read-only index at which the first successful match was found in the string.
input	This read-only property contains the value of the original string against which the search was performed.
lastIndex	The position in the string where the next match begins, containing -1 if no match is found.
lastMatch	A read-only property that contains the last match found in the string.
lastParen	A read-only property that contains the last submatch found in the string.
leftContext	A read-only property that contains a substring that begins at the beginning of the original string and ends at the lastIndex position.
rightContext	A read-only property that contains a substring that starts at the lastIndex position and goes to the end of the string.
$1...$9	Each number contains the match found in the string that corresponds with the number. For example, $1 returns the first match found, $2 returns the second match found, and so on.

Table 12. *Regular Expression Object Properties in JavaScript*

Property Name	Description
global	A read-only property that returns true if the g flag was used with the expression.
ignoreCase	A read-only property that returns true if the i flag was used with the expression.
multiline	A read-only property that returns a boolean true if the m flag was used with the regular expression.
source	This returns the regular expression as a string.

Table 13. *Regular Expression Object Methods in JavaScript*

Method Name	Description
compile	This method compiles the regular expression, making the execution faster.
exec	This runs the regular expression against the provided string and returns an array that contains the result of the search.
test	This returns true if a match was found in the supplied string.

String methods in JavaScript can be called on the strings directly, such as calling Match on a value property of a field in an HTML form. Table 14 lists the string methods in JavaScript.

Table 14. *String Methods in JavaScript*

Method Name	Description
match	This method can accept either a literal regular expression or a Regular Expression object. If a match isn't found, it returns null. If a match is found, it returns with an object with an index, the input, [0] (which contains the portion of the string that was matched last), and [1] and higher to correspond with capturing groups if there are any.
replace	This method accepts the regular expression, which can be a literal expression, and the replacement string.
search	The search method returns a true if a match is found in the string on which the method is called; otherwise, it returns false.
split	This method can be passed a regular expression that will be used to carve the string up into substrings that were separated by the regular expression in the original string. Passing /,/ into the method on a string containing 1,2,3,4 will return an array with the first element being 1, the second being 2, and so on.

The methods and properties listed in the following tables belong to the RegExp object in VBScript, which is much like the Regular Expression object in JavaScript. Table 15 lists the properties, and Table 16 lists the methods.

Table 15. RegExp *Properties in VBScript*

Property Name	Description
Global	This sets or returns true if the object should match every occurrence in the string or just the first occurrence.
IgnoreCase	This can be set to or return true if the expression should ignore case in matching.
Pattern	This sets or returns the regular expression.

Table 16. Regexp *Methods in VBScript*

Method Name	Description
Execute	This executes the regular expression against the supplied string.
Replace	This replaces the string matched by the regular expression with another supplied string.
Test	This returns true if the regular expression finds a match in the supplied string.

Using the Examples

The examples in this book are all ready to use as they're listed in the book. Optionally, you can download the code from the Downloads section at the Apress Web site (http://www.apress.com) and just compile or run those.

You'll need to compile the C# and Visual Basic .NET examples before you can use them. To make this a little easier, I've included a file called Makefile with the code available for download so you can compile all the code in each chapter at one shot using the nmake command.

You can use the ASP.NET examples, VBScript, and JavaScript examples without compiling them. They're ready to run as long as you have the required software, which is outlined for each language in the following sections.

C#

The C# examples in this book require the C# compiler, which comes with the .NET Framework Software Development Kit (SDK). You can download the SDK at http://www.microsoft.com/netframework/downloads/updates/default.aspx.

The command used to compile each of the C# examples in this book is csc.exe. You can run it at the command line by typing this:

```
csc.exe /target:exe /out:runrecipe.exe Recipe.cs
```

Each regular expression class is also testable with the NUnit testing framework, which you can read more about at http://www.nunit.org. If you want to run the executable on the command line, you can type this:

```
runrecipe.exe filename
```

where *filename* is the name of the file that contains the text you want to search or replace using the regular expression given in the recipe.

Visual Basic .NET

The Visual Basic .NET examples in this book are also ready-to-compile, complete classes that you can compile and execute at the command line. The Visual Basic .NET compiler also comes with the .NET Framework SDK (http://www.microsoft.com/netframework/downloads/updates/default.aspx). This is the command used to compile all the classes in this book:

```
vbc.exe /r:System.dll /target:exe /out:runrecipe.exe Recipe.vb
```

You can run the recipes from the command line by typing this:

```
runrecipe.exe filename
```

and replacing *filename* in the previous line with the name of the file that contains the strings you want to search or replace.

ASP.NET

The ASP.NET examples shown in this book showcase the RegularExpressionValidator control. With the exception of the validator control, the regular expression syntax is the same as that shown in the C# and Visual Basic .NET examples.

The ASP.NET examples require that you have IIS installed and running on your computer. To keep yourself organized, I suggest you create a directory under the document root, which is by default C:\Inetpub\Wwwroot. Name the directory something like Regex, and then put all the ASP.NET code in .aspx files under that directory. As long as you have IIS running on your computer, you can navigate to the recipe by typing http://localhost/Regex/*filename* (where *filename* is the name of the file with the example code in it).

VBScript

The VBScript examples in this book are best run using the cscript.exe program that's included with the Windows Scripting Host (WSH). The reason it's better to use that program than simply double-clicking the file is because most of the scripts have multiple lines of output, and this can get tedious pretty quickly when they're all printed as message boxes. WSH comes standard on Windows XP. If you have an earlier version of Windows, you can download WSH from http://msdn.microsoft.com/downloads/list/webdev.asp.

The VBScript files are ready to be used and don't need to be compiled.

JavaScript

You can easily embed the JavaScript examples in this book into ASP.NET pages (as you can the VBScript examples). You can also run the JavaScript examples in this book in standard HTML pages, as long as your browser has JavaScript turned on.

■**Note** If you develop a lot on the Microsoft platform, you may find the inclusion of JavaScript in this book instead of JScript a little out of place. I've used JavaScript instead of JScript for a couple of reasons—one is that theoretically the scripts in this book will run fine as JScript. The other reason is that JavaScript has better support on different browsers, and I think more readers will be able to take advantage of the JavaScript examples.

Tools

When writing this book, I used a few helpful (and free!) tools to assist me with writing, running, and testing code. I've listed the tools in the following sections in case you might find them useful, and I've also provided a short description of each tool along with the URL where you can download it.

#develop

My hat goes off to the team working on this wonderful product. It's an open-source .NET Framework IDE that I've used to work on my C# and VB .NET code. This IDE has a feature that's particularly useful in writing this book—if you're using it, under the Tools menu you'll find Regular Expression Toolkit. This allows you to test expressions and get information about the matches such as the number of groups found and the character positions of each match.

You can find more information about #develop at `http://www.icsharpcode.com/OpenSource/SD/Default.aspx`.

ASP.NET Web Matrix

This product is a Microsoft community-developed product that's available for free download. It supports syntax highlighting for ASP.NET and offers some useful features such as the ability to visually design ASP.NET Web pages. You can read more about ASP.NET Web Matrix at `http://www.asp.net/webmatrix/default.aspx`.

Vim

Alas, old habits are hard to break. I'm a big fan of Vim and use it whenever I have to do any major text editing. I use the visual Windows version available at `http://www.vim.org`.

NUnit

This unit testing tool works wonderfully for testing code written in the .NET Framework. You can test each class included in the code samples in this book using NUnit. You can find more information about NUnit at `http://www.nunit.org`.

CHAPTER 1

■■■

Words and Text

This chapter includes recipes for doing some of the basics of regular expressions, such as finding and replacing words and certain special characters such as tabs and trademark characters.

Although this book isn't organized into levels of difficulty, this first chapter includes many basic concepts that will make the rest of the book easier to follow. You won't have to go through this chapter to understand later ones, but it may help if you're new to regular expressions to make sure all the recipes in this chapter are easy to understand.

1-1. Finding Blank Lines

You can use this recipe for identifying blank lines in a file. Blank lines can contain spaces or tabs, or they can contain a combination of spaces and tabs. Variations on these expressions can be useful for stripping blank lines from a file.

.NET Framework

ASP.NET

```
<%@ Page Language="vb" AutoEventWireup="false" %>
<!DOCTYPE HTML PUBLIC "-//W3C//DTD HTML 4.0 Transitional//EN">
<html>
<head><title></title>
</head>
<body>
    <form Id="Form1" RunAt="server">
    <asp:TextBox id="txtInput" runat="server"></asp:TextBox>
    <asp:RegularExpressionValidator Id="revInput" RunAt="server"
        ControlToValidate="txtInput"
        ErrorMessage="Please enter a valid value"
        ValidationExpression="\s*"></asp:RegularExpressionValidator>
    <asp:Button Id="btnSubmit" RunAt="server" CausesValidation="True"
        Text="Submit"></asp:Button>
    </form>
</body>
```

C#

```csharp
using System;
using System.IO;
using System.Text.RegularExpressions;

public class Recipe
{
    private static Regex _Regex = new Regex( @"^\s*$" );

    public void Run(string fileName)
    {
        String line;
        int lineNbr = 0;
        using (StreamReader sr = new StreamReader(fileName))
        {
            while(null != (line = sr.ReadLine()))
            {
                lineNbr++;
                if (_Regex.IsMatch(line))
                {
```

```
                    Console.WriteLine("Found match '{0}' at line {1}",
                        line,
                        lineNbr);
                }
            }
        }
    }

    public static void Main( string[] args )
    {
        Recipe r = new Recipe();
        r.Run(args[0]);
    }
}
```

Visual Basic .NET

```
Imports System
Imports System.IO
Imports System.Text.RegularExpressions
Public Class Recipe

    Private Shared _Regex As Regex = New Regex("^\s*$")

    Public Sub Run(ByVal fileName As String)
        Dim line As String
        Dim lineNbr As Integer = 0
        Dim sr As StreamReader = File.OpenText(fileName)
        line = sr.ReadLine
        While Not line Is Nothing
            lineNbr = lineNbr + 1
            If _Regex.IsMatch(line) Then
                Console.WriteLine("Found match '{0}' at line {1}", _
                    line, _
                    lineNbr)
            End If
            line = sr.ReadLine
        End While
        sr.Close()
    End Sub

    Public Shared Sub Main(ByVal args As String())
        Dim r As Recipe = New Recipe
        r.Run(args(0))
    End Sub
End Class
```

VBScript

```
Dim fso,s,re,line,lineNbr
Set fso = CreateObject("Scripting.FileSystemObject")
Set s = fso.OpenTextFile(WScript.Arguments.Item(0), 1, True)
Set re = New RegExp
re.Pattern = "^\s*$"
lineNbr = 0
Do While Not s.AtEndOfStream
    line = s.ReadLine()
    lineNbr = lineNbr + 1
    If re.Test(line) Then
        WScript.Echo "Found match: '" & line & "' at line " & lineNbr
    End If
Loop
s.Close
```

JavaScript

```
<html>
<head>
<title></title>
</head>
<body>
<form name="form1">
    <input type="textbox" name="txtInput" />
    <script type="text/javascript">
    function validate() {
        if (! document.form1.txtInput.value.match(/^\s*$/)) {
            alert("Please enter valid value!")
        } else {
            alert("Success!")
        }
    }
    </script>
    <input type="button" name="btnSubmit" onclick="validate()" value="Go" />
</form>
</body>
</html>
```

How It Works

In addition to completely blank lines, this expression also matches lines that have only tabs or spaces in them. It does this by using the \s character class, which matches a tab or a space.

Here's the expression broken down into parts:

^   starts the beginning of the line, followed by . . .

\s   any whitespace character (a tab or space) . . .

*   zero or more times, followed by . . .

$ the end of the line.

1-2. Finding Words

You can use this recipe for finding single words in a block of text. The expression will find only complete words surrounded by spaces or other word delimiters, such as punctuation or the beginning or end of a line.

.NET Framework

ASP.NET

```
<%@ Page Language="vb" AutoEventWireup="false" %>
<!DOCTYPE HTML PUBLIC "-//W3C//DTD HTML 4.0 Transitional//EN">
<html>
<head><title></title>
</head>
<body>
    <form Id="Form1" RunAt="server">
    <asp:TextBox id="txtInput" runat="server"></asp:TextBox>
    <asp:RegularExpressionValidator Id="revInput" RunAt="server"
        ControlToValidate="txtInput"
        ErrorMessage="Please enter a valid value"
        ValidationExpression=".*\bsomething\b.*"></asp:RegularExpressionValidator>
    <asp:Button Id="btnSubmit" RunAt="server" CausesValidation="True"
        Text="Submit"></asp:Button>
    </form>
</body>
```

C#

```
using System;
using System.IO;
using System.Text.RegularExpressions;

public class Recipe
{
    private static Regex _Regex = new Regex( @"\bsomething\b" );

    public void Run(string fileName)
    {
        String line;
        int lineNbr = 0;
        using (StreamReader sr = new StreamReader(fileName))
        {
            while(null != (line = sr.ReadLine()))
            {
                lineNbr++;
                if (_Regex.IsMatch(line))
                {
```

```
                Console.WriteLine("Found match '{0}' at line {1}",
                    line,
                    lineNbr);
            }
        }
    }
}

public static void Main( string[] args )
{
    Recipe r = new Recipe();
    r.Run(args[0]);
}
}
```

Visual Basic .NET

```
Imports System
Imports System.IO
Imports System.Text.RegularExpressions
Public Class Recipe

    Private Shared _Regex As Regex = New Regex("\bsomething\b")

    Public Sub Run(ByVal fileName As String)
        Dim line As String
        Dim lineNbr As Integer = 0
        Dim sr As StreamReader = File.OpenText(fileName)
        line = sr.ReadLine
        While Not line Is Nothing
            lineNbr = lineNbr + 1
            If _Regex.IsMatch(line) Then
                Console.WriteLine("Found match '{0}' at line {1}", _
                    line, _
                    lineNbr)
            End If
            line = sr.ReadLine
        End While
        sr.Close()
    End Sub

    Public Shared Sub Main(ByVal args As String())
        Dim r As Recipe = New Recipe
        r.Run(args(0))
    End Sub

End Class
```

VBScript

```
Dim fso,s,re,line,lineNbr
Set fso = CreateObject("Scripting.FileSystemObject")
Set s = fso.OpenTextFile(WScript.Arguments.Item(0), 1, True)
Set re = New RegExp
re.Pattern = "\bsomething\b"
lineNbr = 0
Do While Not s.AtEndOfStream
    line = s.ReadLine()
    lineNbr = lineNbr + 1
    If re.Test(line) Then
        WScript.Echo "Found match: '" & line & "' at line " & lineNbr
    End If
Loop
s.Close
```

JavaScript

```
<html>
<head>
<title></title>
</head>
<body>
<form name="form1">
    <input type="textbox" name="txtInput" />
    <script type="text/javascript">
    function validate() {
        if (! document.form1.txtInput.value.match(/\bsomething\b/)) {
            alert("Please enter valid value!")
        } else {
            alert("Success!")
        }
    }
    </script>
    <input type="button" name="btnSubmit" onclick="validate()" value="Go" />
</form>
</body>
</html>
```

How It Works

A special character class, \b, allows you to easily search for whole words. This is an advantage because without doing a whole bunch of extra work you can make sure that a search for *something*, for example, doesn't yield unexpected matches such as *somethings*.

You can break the regular expression shown here into the following:

\b	a word boundary (a space, beginning of a line, or punctuation) . . .
something	*s, o, m, e, t, h, i, n,* and *g* . . .
\b	a word boundary at the end of the word.

This expression differs just slightly from the C# and Visual Basic .NET examples because the RegularExpressionValidator control assumes that the expression is to match the entire value (there's an implied ^ at the beginning of the expression and $ at the end of the expression). The combination .* has been added before and after the word boundary \b so the full word can float around inside the line.

1-3. Finding Multiple Words with One Search

You can use this recipe for finding one of a list of words in a line. This recipe assumes both words are whole words surrounded by whitespace and that the list is a short one containing the words *moo* and *oink*.

.NET Framework

ASP.NET

```
<%@ Page Language="vb" AutoEventWireup="false" %>
<!DOCTYPE HTML PUBLIC "-//W3C//DTD HTML 4.0 Transitional//EN">
<html>
<head><title></title>
</head>
<body>
    <form Id="Form1" RunAt="server">
    <asp:TextBox id="txtInput" runat="server"></asp:TextBox>
    <asp:RegularExpressionValidator Id="revInput" RunAt="server"
        ControlToValidate="txtInput"
        ErrorMessage="Please enter a valid value"
        ValidationExpression=".*\s+(moo|oink)\s+.*">
    </asp:RegularExpressionValidator>
    <asp:Button Id="btnSubmit" RunAt="server" CausesValidation="True"
        Text="Submit"></asp:Button>
    </form>
</body>
```

C#

```csharp
using System;
using System.IO;
using System.Text.RegularExpressions;

public class Recipe
{
    private static Regex _Regex = new Regex( @"\s+(moo|oink)\s+" );

    public void Run(string fileName)
    {
        String line;
        int lineNbr = 0;
        using (StreamReader sr = new StreamReader(fileName))
        {
            while(null != (line = sr.ReadLine()))
            {
                lineNbr++;
                if (_Regex.IsMatch(line))
```

```
            {
                Console.WriteLine("Found match '{0}' at line {1}",
                    line,
                    lineNbr);
            }
        }
    }
}

    public static void Main( string[] args )
    {
        Recipe r = new Recipe();
        r.Run(args[0]);
    }
}
```

Visual Basic .NET

```
Imports System
Imports System.IO
Imports System.Text.RegularExpressions
Public Class Recipe

    Private Shared _Regex As Regex = New Regex("\s+(moo|oink)\s+")

    Public Sub Run(ByVal fileName As String)
        Dim line As String
        Dim lineNbr As Integer = 0
        Dim sr As StreamReader = File.OpenText(fileName)
        line = sr.ReadLine
        While Not line Is Nothing
            lineNbr = lineNbr + 1
            If _Regex.IsMatch(line) Then
                Console.WriteLine("Found match '{0}' at line {1}", _
                    line, _
                    lineNbr)
            End If
            line = sr.ReadLine
        End While
        sr.Close()
    End Sub

    Public Shared Sub Main(ByVal args As String())
        Dim r As Recipe = New Recipe
        r.Run(args(0))
    End Sub

End Class
```

VBScript

```
Dim fso,s,re,line,lineNbr
Set fso = CreateObject("Scripting.FileSystemObject")
Set s = fso.OpenTextFile(WScript.Arguments.Item(0), 1, True)
Set re = New RegExp
re.Pattern = "\s+(moo|oink)\s+"
lineNbr = 0
Do While Not s.AtEndOfStream
    line = s.ReadLine()
    lineNbr = lineNbr + 1
    If re.Test(line) Then
        WScript.Echo "Found match: '" & line & "' at line " & lineNbr
    End If
Loop
s.Close
```

JavaScript

```
<html>
<head>
<title></title>
</head>
<body>
<form name="form1">
    <input type="textbox" name="txtInput" />
    <script type="text/javascript">
    function validate() {
        if (! document.form1.txtInput.value.match(/\s+(moo|oink)\s+/)) {
            alert("Please enter valid value!")
        } else {
            alert("Success!")
        }
    }
    </script>
    <input type="button" name="btnSubmit" onclick="validate()" value="Go" />
</form>
</body>
</html>
```

How It Works

Starting outside working in, this expression searches for something that's surrounded by whitespace. For example:

\s	whitespace . . .
+	found one or more times . . .
(...)	followed by something . . .
\s	followed by whitespace . . .
+	that occurs one or more times.

The *something* here is another expression, moo|oink. This expression is as follows:

m	an *m*, followed by . . .
o	an *o*, then . . .
o	an *o* . . .
|	or . . .
o	an *o*, followed by . . .
i	an *i*, then . . .
n	an *n*, followed by . . .
k	a *k*.

Variations

A useful variation of this recipe is to replace the \s+ combination, which matches specifically whitespace, with the word boundary character class \b.

1-4. Finding Variations on Words (*John, Jon, Jonathan*)

You can use this recipe for finding variations on a word with one search. This particular recipe searches for the strings *Jon Doe, John Doe,* or *Jonathan Doe.*

.NET Framework

ASP.NET

```
<%@ Page Language="vb" AutoEventWireup="false" %>
<!DOCTYPE HTML PUBLIC "-//W3C//DTD HTML 4.0 Transitional//EN">
<html>
<head><title></title>
</head>
<body>
    <form Id="Form1" RunAt="server">
    <asp:TextBox id="txtInput" runat="server"></asp:TextBox>
    <asp:RegularExpressionValidator Id="revInput" RunAt="server"
        ControlToValidate="txtInput"
        ErrorMessage="Please enter a valid value"
        ValidationExpression=".*\bJoh?n(athan)?➥
Doe\b.*"></asp:RegularExpressionValidator>
    <asp:Button Id="btnSubmit" RunAt="server" CausesValidation="True"
        Text="Submit"></asp:Button>
    </form>
</body>
```

C#

```
using System;
using System.IO;
using System.Text.RegularExpressions;

public class Recipe
{
    private static Regex _Regex = new Regex( @"\bJoh?n(athan)? Doe\b" );

    public void Run(string fileName)
    {
        String line;
        int lineNbr = 0;
        using (StreamReader sr = new StreamReader(fileName))
        {
            while(null != (line = sr.ReadLine()))
            {
                lineNbr++;
                if (_Regex.IsMatch(line))
```

```csharp
            {
                Console.WriteLine("Found match '{0}' at line {1}",
                    line,
                    lineNbr);
            }
        }
    }
}

    public static void Main( string[] args )
    {
        Recipe r = new Recipe();
        r.Run(args[0]);
    }
}
```

Visual Basic .NET

```vbnet
Imports System
Imports System.IO
Imports System.Text.RegularExpressions
Public Class Recipe

    Private Shared _Regex As Regex = New Regex("\bJoh?n(athan)? Doe\b")

    Public Sub Run(ByVal fileName As String)
        Dim line As String
        Dim lineNbr As Integer = 0
        Dim sr As StreamReader = File.OpenText(fileName)
        line = sr.ReadLine
        While Not line Is Nothing
            lineNbr = lineNbr + 1
            If _Regex.IsMatch(line) Then
                Console.WriteLine("Found match '{0}' at line {1}", _
                    line, _
                    lineNbr)
            End If
            line = sr.ReadLine
        End While
        sr.Close()
    End Sub

    Public Shared Sub Main(ByVal args As String())
        Dim r As Recipe = New Recipe
        r.Run(args(0))
    End Sub

End Class
```

VBScript

```
Dim fso,s,re,line,lineNbr
Set fso = CreateObject("Scripting.FileSystemObject")
Set s = fso.OpenTextFile(WScript.Arguments.Item(0), 1, True)
Set re = New RegExp
re.Pattern = "\bJoh?n(athan)? Doe\b"
lineNbr = 0
Do While Not s.AtEndOfStream
    line = s.ReadLine()
    lineNbr = lineNbr + 1
    If re.Test(line) Then
        WScript.Echo "Found match: '" & line & "' at line " & lineNbr
    End If
Loop
s.Close
```

JavaScript

```html
<html>
<head>
<title></title>
</head>
<body>
<form name="form1">
    <input type="textbox" name="txtInput" />
    <script type="text/javascript">
    function validate() {
        if (! document.form1.txtInput.value.match(/\bJoh?n(athan)? Doe\b/)) {
            alert("Please enter valid value!")
        } else {
            alert("Success!")
        }
    }
    </script>
    <input type="button" name="btnSubmit" onclick="validate()" value="Go" />
</form>
</body>
</html>
```

How It Works

This expression works by finding the common and optional parts of a word and searching based on them. *John, Jon,* and *Jonathan* are all similar. They start with *Jo* and have an *n* in them. The rest is the *h* in *John* or the *athan* ending in *Jonathan*. For example:

\b	a word boundary . . .
J	followed by . . .
o	then . . .
h	that is . . .
?	optional, followed by . . .
n	followed by . . .
(...)	a group of characters . . .
?	that may appear once but isn't required, followed by . . .
<space>	a space, followed by . . .
D	then . . .
o	and finally . . .
e	an *e*, then . . .
\b	another word boundary.

This group of characters is *athan*, which will let the expression match *Jonathan*. It may or may not appear as a whole part, so that's why it's grouped with parentheses and followed by ?.

Variations

One variation on this recipe is using instead an expression such as that found in recipe 1-3, like ((Jon)|(John)|(Jonathan)) Doe. Depending on the skills of your peers, this may be easy to use because it may be easier to read by someone else. Another variation on this is ((Jon(athan)?)|(John)) Doe. Writing an elegant and fast regular expression is nice, but these days processor cycles are often cheaper than labor. Make sure whatever path you choose will be the easiest to maintain by the people in your organization.

1-5. Finding Similar Words (*bat, cat, mat*)

Slightly different from the previous recipe, this recipe focuses on using a character class to match a single letter.

.NET Framework

ASP.NET

```
<%@ Page Language="vb" AutoEventWireup="false" %>
<!DOCTYPE HTML PUBLIC "-//W3C//DTD HTML 4.0 Transitional//EN">
<html>
<head><title></title>
</head>
<body>
    <form Id="Form1" RunAt="server">
    <asp:TextBox id="txtInput" runat="server"></asp:TextBox>
    <asp:RegularExpressionValidator Id="revInput" RunAt="server"
        ControlToValidate="txtInput"
        ErrorMessage="Please enter a valid value"
        ValidationExpression=".*\b[bcm]at\b.*"></asp:RegularExpressionValidator>
    <asp:Button Id="btnSubmit" RunAt="server" CausesValidation="True"
        Text="Submit"></asp:Button>
    </form>
</body>
```

C#

```
using System;
using System.IO;
using System.Text.RegularExpressions;

public class Recipe
{
    private static Regex _Regex = new Regex( @"\b[bcm]at\b" );

    public void Run(string fileName)
    {
        String line;
        int lineNbr = 0;
        using (StreamReader sr = new StreamReader(fileName))
        {
            while(null != (line = sr.ReadLine()))
            {
                lineNbr++;
                if (_Regex.IsMatch(line))
                {
                    Console.WriteLine("Found match '{0}' at line {1}",
```

```
                        line,
                        lineNbr);
                }
            }
        }
    }

    public static void Main( string[] args )
    {
        Recipe r = new Recipe();
        r.Run(args[0]);
    }
}
```

Visual Basic .NET

```
Imports System
Imports System.IO
Imports System.Text.RegularExpressions
Public Class Recipe

    Private Shared _Regex As Regex = New Regex("\b[bcm]at\b")

    Public Sub Run(ByVal fileName As String)
        Dim line As String
        Dim lineNbr As Integer = 0
        Dim sr As StreamReader = File.OpenText(fileName)
        line = sr.ReadLine
        While Not line Is Nothing
            lineNbr = lineNbr + 1
            If _Regex.IsMatch(line) Then
                Console.WriteLine("Found match '{0}' at line {1}", _
                    line, _
                    lineNbr)
            End If
            line = sr.ReadLine
        End While
        sr.Close()
    End Sub

    Public Shared Sub Main(ByVal args As String())
        Dim r As Recipe = New Recipe
        r.Run(args(0))
    End Sub

End Class
```

VBScript

```vbscript
Dim fso,s,re,line,lineNbr
Set fso = CreateObject("Scripting.FileSystemObject")
Set s = fso.OpenTextFile(WScript.Arguments.Item(0), 1, True)
Set re = New RegExp
re.Pattern = "\b[bcm]at\b"
lineNbr = 0
Do While Not s.AtEndOfStream
    line = s.ReadLine()
    lineNbr = lineNbr + 1
    If re.Test(line) Then
        WScript.Echo "Found match: '" & line & "' at line " & lineNbr
    End If
Loop
s.Close
```

JavaScript

```html
<html>
<head>
<title></title>
</head>
<body>
<form name="form1">
    <input type="textbox" name="txtInput" />
    <script type="text/javascript">
    function validate() {
        if (! document.form1.txtInput.value.match(/\b[bcm]at\b/)) {
            alert("Please enter valid value!")
        } else {
            alert("Success!")
        }
    }
    </script>
    <input type="button" name="btnSubmit" onclick="validate()" value="Go" />
</form>
</body>
</html>
```

How It Works

The key to the expressions in these recipes finding whole words, even those that have no spaces around them and are on lines all by themselves, is the \b character class, which specifies a word boundary. A word boundary can be any whitespace that sets a word apart from others and can also include the beginning of a line and the end of a line. The other character class that's in this expression is [bcm], which matches a single character that can be one of b, c, or m. So, you can break the entire expression down like this:

\b	is a word boundary, followed by . . .
[bcm]	one of *b*, *c*, or *m*, followed by . . .
a	then . . .
t	and finally . . .
\b	a word boundary.

Variations

A few variations on this expression exist, the most common of which is to use grouping and the "or" operator (|) instead of a character class to specify *b*, *c*, or *m*, as in \b(b|c|m)at\b.

1-6. Replacing Words

This recipe focuses on replacing complete words. It takes advantage of word anchors, which allow you to easily make sure you get an entire match.

.NET Framework

C#

```
using System;
using System.IO;
using System.Text.RegularExpressions;

public class Recipe
{
    private static Regex _Regex = new Regex( @"\bfrick\b" );
    public void Run(string fileName)
    {
        String line;
        String newLine;
        using (StreamReader sr = new StreamReader(fileName))
        {
            while(null != (line = sr.ReadLine()))
            {
                newLine = _Regex.Replace(line, "frack");
                Console.WriteLine("New string is: '{0}', " +
                    "original was: '{1}'",
                    newLine,
                    line));
            }
        }
    }

    public static void Main( string[] args )
    {
        Recipe r = new Recipe();
        r.Run(args[0]);
    }
}
```

Visual Basic .NET

```
Imports System
Imports System.IO
Imports System.Text.RegularExpressions
Public Class Recipe

    Private Shared _Regex As Regex = New Regex("\bfrick\b")
```

```
    Public Sub Run(ByVal fileName As String)
        Dim line As String
        Dim newLine As String
        Dim sr As StreamReader = File.OpenText(fileName)
        line = sr.ReadLine
        While Not line Is Nothing
            newLine = _Regex.Replace(line, "frack")
            Console.WriteLine("New string is: '{0}', original was:➥
 '{1}'", _
             newLine, _
             line))
            line = sr.ReadLine
        End While
        sr.Close()
    End Sub

    Public Shared Sub Main(ByVal args As String())
        Dim r As Recipe = New Recipe
        r.Run(args(0))
    End Sub

End Class
```

VBScript

```
Dim fso,s,re,line,newstr
Set fso = CreateObject("Scripting.FileSystemObject")
Set s = fso.OpenTextFile(WScript.Arguments.Item(0), 1, True)
Set re = New RegExp
re.Pattern = "\bfrick\b"
Do While Not s.AtEndOfStream
    line = s.ReadLine()
    newstr = re.Replace(line, "frack")
    WScript.Echo "New string '" & newstr & "', original '" & line & "'"
Loop
s.Close
```

JavaScript

```
<html>
<head>
<title></title>
</head>
<body>
<form name="form1">
    <input type="text" name="txtInput" />
    <div id="lblResult"></div>
```

```
<script language="javascript">
    function replace() {
        document.getElementById('lblResult').innerHTML = ➥
document.form1.txtInput.value.replace(/\bfrick\b/, "frack");
    }
</script>
<input type="button" name="btnSubmit" onclick="replace()" value="Go" />
</form>
</body>
</html>
```

How It Works

This recipe has two expressions in it—the search expression and the replacement expression. Some extra characters in this expression make sure the match works on a whole word and not a partial word. The word *frickster* will be left alone, for instance. Let's break down the search recipe:

\b   is a word boundary . . .

frick   *f, r, i, c,* and *k* . . .

\b   a word boundary.

Both the .NET Framework and the VBScript regular expression objects provide a Replace method that allows you to pass in another expression as a substitute for whatever is found in the search expression, and both return a new string containing the results. The JavaScript replace method is a method on a string, not on the regular expression object.

The Visual Basic .NET example is as follows:

```
newLine = _Regex.Replace(line, "frack")
```

If the value of line is *Replace frick*, the value of newLine will become *Replace frack*.

Notice that the word boundary characters aren't replaced in the result. This is because they're *noncapturing*, which means they can match but can't be replaced.

1-7. Replacing Everything Between Two Delimiters

This recipe replaces everything inside double quotes with a different string (in this case, three asterisks). You can replace the double-quote delimiter with a different character to build expressions that will replace anything inside delimiters with another string.

.NET Framework

C#

```csharp
using System;
using System.IO;
using System.Text.RegularExpressions;

public class Recipe
{
    private static Regex _Regex = new Regex( "(?<=\")[^\"]*(?=\")" );
    public void Run(string fileName)
    {
        String line;
        String newLine;
        using (StreamReader sr = new StreamReader(fileName))
        {
            while(null != (line = sr.ReadLine()))
            {
                newLine = _Regex.Replace(line, "***");
                Console.WriteLine("New string is: '{0}', original was: '{1}'",
                    newLine,
                    line));
            }
        }
    }

    public static void Main( string[] args )
    {
        Recipe r = new Recipe();
        r.Run(args[0]);
    }
}
```

Visual Basic .NET

```vbnet
Imports System
Imports System.IO
Imports System.Text.RegularExpressions
Public Class Recipe
```

```vbnet
    Private Shared _Regex As Regex = New Regex("(?<="")[^""]*(?="")")

    Public Sub Run(ByVal fileName As String)
        Dim line As String
        Dim newLine As String
        Dim sr As StreamReader = File.OpenText(fileName)
        line = sr.ReadLine
        While Not line Is Nothing
            newLine = _Regex.Replace(line, "***")
            Console.WriteLine("New string is: '{0}', original was: '{1}'", _
             newLine, _
             line))
            line = sr.ReadLine
        End While
        sr.Close()
    End Sub

    Public Shared Sub Main(ByVal args As String())
        Dim r As Recipe = New Recipe
        r.Run(args(0))
    End Sub

End Class
```

VBScript

```vbscript
Dim fso,s,re,line,newstr
Set fso = CreateObject("Scripting.FileSystemObject")
Set s = fso.OpenTextFile(WScript.Arguments.Item(0), 1, True)
Set re = New RegExp
re.Pattern = """[^""]*"""
re.Global = true
Do While Not s.AtEndOfStream
    line = s.ReadLine()
    newstr = re.Replace(line, """***""")
    WScript.Echo "New string '" & newstr & "', original '" & line & "'"
Loop
s.Close
```

JavaScript

```html
<html>
<head>
<title></title>
</head>
<body>
<form name="form1">
```

```
<input type="text" name="txtInput" />
<div id="lblResult"></div>
<script language="javascript">
    function replace() {
        document.getElementById('lblResult').innerHTML = ➥
document.form1.txtInput.value.replace(/\"[^\"]*\"/g, "\"***\"");
    }
</script>
<input type="button" name="btnSubmit" onclick="replace()" value="Go" />
</form>
</body>
</html>
```

How It Works

This recipe shows off a simple version of the recipes in Chapter 3. Two versions of the regex in this recipe exist because the .NET Framework supports look-behinds, while the scripting languages here don't. The simple example, without using look-behinds, is as follows:

"	is a quote, followed by . . .
[	a character class . . .
^	that isn't . . .
"	another quote . . .
]	the end of the character class . . .
*	zero or more times . . .
"	another quote appears.

You might notice that missing from the previous list are the extra characters found in the code that escape the double quotes. That's because the escape characters are necessary for the programming language in which they appear, so the compilers or scripting engines know how to parse the code. Escape characters for quotes aren't used by the regular expression engine. In C# and JavaScript, the double quotes are escaped with a \, which yields the \" combination found in the code. In Visual Basic .NET and VBScript, double quotes are escaped by doubling them up, like this: "".

Now back to the expression—why not just use ".*" and be done with it? Well, that will work. Somewhat. The problem is that a quote (") is matched by . (which matches anything). If you have a string such as this:

```
my "string" is "water absorbent"
```

you'll end up with this:

```
my "***"
```

This is because of *greedy matching*, which means * (a *greedy qualifier*) will match as much as it possibly can. By contrast, *lazy qualifiers* will stop as soon as it can, matching as little as possible. Since lazy matching will match as little as possible, another way of writing this expression is (?<").*?(?="). The combination *? is a *lazy qualifier*.

When using look-arounds in the regex, the " character at the beginning and end of the regex are replaced by (?<=") on the left and (?=") on the right. The advantage that look-arounds offer is that the double quote doesn't have to be put back into the replacement.

1-8. Replacing Tab Characters

This recipe is for replacing tab characters in a string with a different character. In this recipe, I use a pipe (|) to replace the tab.

.NET Framework

C#

```csharp
using System;
using System.IO;
using System.Text.RegularExpressions;

public class Recipe
{
    private static Regex _Regex = new Regex( @"\t" );
    public void Run(string fileName)
    {
        String line;
        String newLine;
        using (StreamReader sr = new StreamReader(fileName))
        {
            while(null != (line = sr.ReadLine()))
            {
                newLine = _Regex.Replace(line, @"|");
                Console.WriteLine("New string is: '{0}', original was: '{1}'",
                    newLine,
                    line));
            }
        }
    }

    public static void Main( string[] args )
    {
        Recipe r = new Recipe();
        r.Run(args[0]);
    }
}
```

Visual Basic .NET

```vbnet
Imports System
Imports System.IO
Imports System.Text.RegularExpressions
Public Class Recipe

    Private Shared _Regex As Regex = New Regex("\t")
```

```
    Public Sub Run(ByVal fileName As String)
        Dim line As String
        Dim newLine As String
        Dim sr As StreamReader = File.OpenText(fileName)
        line = sr.ReadLine
        While Not line Is Nothing
            newLine = _Regex.Replace(line, "|")
            Console.WriteLine("New string is: '{0}', original was: '{1}'", _
             newLine, _
             line))
            line = sr.ReadLine
        End While
        sr.Close()
    End Sub

    Public Shared Sub Main(ByVal args As String())
        Dim r As Recipe = New Recipe
        r.Run(args(0))
    End Sub

End Class
```

VBScript

```
Dim fso,s,re,line,newstr
Set fso = CreateObject("Scripting.FileSystemObject")
Set s = fso.OpenTextFile(WScript.Arguments.Item(0), 1, True)
Set re = New RegExp
re.Pattern = "\t"
re.Global = true
Do While Not s.AtEndOfStream
    line = s.ReadLine()
    newstr = re.Replace(line, "|")
    WScript.Echo "New string '" & newstr & "', original '" & line & "'"
Loop
s.Close
```

JavaScript

```
<html>
<head>
<title></title>
</head>
<body>
<form name="form1">
    <input type="text" name="txtInput" />
    <div id="lblResult"></div>
```

```
<script language="javascript">
    function replace() {
        document.getElementById('lblResult').innerHTML = ➡
document.form1.txtInput.value.replace(/\t/g, "|");
    }
</script>
<input type="button" name="btnSubmit" onclick="replace()" value="Go" />
</form>
</body>
</html>
```

How It Works

Breaking the recipe down yields simply the following:

\t   is a tab, replaced by . . .

| a pipe character.

By default, the regular expression object in the .NET Framework replaces each occurrence of the text that matches the search regex. However, the VBScript and JavaScript regular expression objects work differently because an option must be specified to replace each match. You can find more about these options in the "Syntax Overview" section of this book.

Variations

Since this is such a simple recipe, it has an extensive number of variations. You could replace the character class representing a tab with other character classes, especially the \s character class. The JavaScript variation /\s/g would replace each instance of whitespace with |.

One variation on the previous recipe is to use a qualifier after the character class to replace more than one instance of a tab at once. For instance, if you want to replace two tabs, you could use something such as /\t{2}/g in the JavaScript recipe.

1-9. Testing the Complexity of Passwords

This recipe tests a string to make sure it has a combination of letters and numbers in the string. This recipe heavily uses look-arounds, which specify matches before and after the regex without consuming text.

.NET Framework

ASP.NET

```
<%@ Page Language="vb" AutoEventWireup="false" %>
<!DOCTYPE HTML PUBLIC "-//W3C//DTD HTML 4.0 Transitional//EN">
<html>
<head><title></title>
</head>
<body>
    <form Id="Form1" RunAt="server">
    <asp:TextBox id="txtInput" runat="server"></asp:TextBox>
    <asp:RegularExpressionValidator Id="revInput" RunAt="server"
        ControlToValidate="txtInput"
        ErrorMessage="Please enter a valid value"
        ValidationExpression="(?=.*[A-Z])(?=.*[a-z])(?=.*[0-➥
9]).{7,15}"></asp:RegularExpressionValidator>
    <asp:Button Id="btnSubmit" RunAt="server" CausesValidation="True"
        Text="Submit"></asp:Button>
    </form>
</body>
```

C#

```
using System;
using System.IO;
using System.Text.RegularExpressions;

public class Recipe
{
    private static Regex _Regex =
        new Regex( @"^(?=.*[A-Z])(?=.*[a-z])(?=.*[0-9]).{7,15}$" );

    public void Run(string fileName)
    {
        String line;
        int lineNbr = 0;
        using (StreamReader sr = new StreamReader(fileName))
        {
```

```
            while(null != (line = sr.ReadLine()))
            {
                lineNbr++;
                if (_Regex.IsMatch(line))
                {
                    Console.WriteLine("Found match '{0}' at line {1}",
                        line,
                        lineNbr);
                }
            }
        }
    }
}

    public static void Main( string[] args )
    {
        Recipe r = new Recipe();
        r.Run(args[0]);
    }
}
```

Visual Basic .NET

```
Imports System
Imports System.IO
Imports System.Text.RegularExpressions
Public Class Recipe

    Private Shared _Regex As Regex = _
        New Regex("^(?=.*[A-Z])(?=.*[a-z])(?=.*[0-9]).{7,15}$")

    Public Sub Run(ByVal fileName As String)
        Dim line As String
        Dim lineNbr As Integer = 0
        Dim sr As StreamReader = File.OpenText(fileName)
        line = sr.ReadLine
        While Not line Is Nothing
            lineNbr = lineNbr + 1
            If _Regex.IsMatch(line) Then
                Console.WriteLine("Found match '{0}' at line {1}", _
                    line, _
                    lineNbr)
            End If
            line = sr.ReadLine
        End While
        sr.Close()
    End Sub
End Sub
```

```
    Public Shared Sub Main(ByVal args As String())
        Dim r As Recipe = New Recipe
        r.Run(args(0))
    End Sub

End Class
```

VBScript

```
Dim fso,s,re,line,lineNbr
Set fso = CreateObject("Scripting.FileSystemObject")
Set s = fso.OpenTextFile(WScript.Arguments.Item(0), 1, True)
Set re = New RegExp
re.Pattern = "^(?=.*[A-Z])(?=.*[a-z])(?=.*[0-9]).{7,15}$"
lineNbr = 0
Do While Not s.AtEndOfStream
    line = s.ReadLine()
    lineNbr = lineNbr + 1
    If re.Test(line) Then
        WScript.Echo "Found match: '" & line & "' at line " & lineNbr
    End If
Loop
s.Close
```

JavaScript

```
<html>
<head>
<title></title>
</head>
<body>
<form name="form1">
    <input type="textbox" name="txtInput" />
    <script type="text/javascript">
    function validate() {
        if (! document.form1.txtInput.value.match(/^(?=.*[A-Z])(?=.*[a-z])➡
(?=.*[0-9]).{7,15}$/)) {
            alert("Please enter valid value!")
        } else {
            alert("Success!")
        }
    }
    </script>
    <input type="button" name="btnSubmit" onclick="validate()" value="Go" />
</form>
</body>
</html>
```

How It Works

The look-arounds in the expression make it seem more complicated than it really is. At the heart of the expression, without the look-arounds, is the following:

^	at the beginning of the line, followed by . . .
.	any character . . .
{7,15}	found anywhere from seven to fifteen times, followed by . . .
$	the end of the line.

Now let's add the look-arounds, which are grouped by the expressions (?= and). Three of them exist in this expression: (?=.*[A-Z]), (?=.*[a-z]), and (?=.*[0-9]). These look-arounds say, "This expression must appear somewhere to the right." In this case, that's to the right of ^, which is the line anchor that anchors the beginning of the line. The first look-ahead matches anything followed by a capital letter ([A-Z]), the second matches anything followed by a lowercase letter ([a-z]), and the third matches anything followed by a number ([0-9]).

Variations

This one has many variations, but probably the most notable is to make the expression more complicated by adding a fourth look-ahead group that matches punctuation characters, such as (?=.*[!@#$%^&*()]).

Another variation is to use a different character class for the number, such as \d if the flavor of regular expressions you're using supports it.

1-10. Finding Repeated Words

You can use this recipe to find words that appear more than once on a line, such as *the the*.

.NET Framework

ASP.NET

```
<%@ Page Language="vb" AutoEventWireup="false" %>
<!DOCTYPE HTML PUBLIC "-//W3C//DTD HTML 4.0 Transitional//EN">
<html>
<head><title></title>
</head>
<body>
    <form Id="Form1" RunAt="server">
    <asp:TextBox id="txtInput" runat="server"></asp:TextBox>
    <asp:RegularExpressionValidator Id="revInput" RunAt="server"
        ControlToValidate="txtInput"
        ErrorMessage="Please enter a valid value"
        ValidationExpression=".*\b(\w+)\s\1\b.*"></asp:RegularExpressionValidator>
    <asp:Button Id="btnSubmit" RunAt="server" CausesValidation="True"
        Text="Submit"></asp:Button>
    </form>
</body>
```

C#

```csharp
using System;
using System.IO;
using System.Text.RegularExpressions;

public class Recipe
{
    private static Regex _Regex = new Regex( @"\b(\w+)\s\1\b" );

    public void Run(string fileName)
    {
        String line;
        int lineNbr = 0;
        using (StreamReader sr = new StreamReader(fileName))
        {
            while(null != (line = sr.ReadLine()))
            {
                lineNbr++;
                if (_Regex.IsMatch(line))
                {
                    Console.WriteLine("Found match '{0}' at line {1}",
                        line,
```

```
                    lineNbr);
            }
        }
    }
}

    public static void Main( string[] args )
    {
        Recipe r = new Recipe();
        r.Run(args[0]);
    }
}
```

Visual Basic .NET

```
Imports System
Imports System.IO
Imports System.Text.RegularExpressions
Public Class Recipe

    Private Shared _Regex As Regex = New Regex("\b(\w+)\s\1\b")

    Public Sub Run(ByVal fileName As String)
        Dim line As String
        Dim lineNbr As Integer = 0
        Dim sr As StreamReader = File.OpenText(fileName)
        line = sr.ReadLine
        While Not line Is Nothing
            lineNbr = lineNbr + 1
            If _Regex.IsMatch(line) Then
                Console.WriteLine("Found match '{0}' at line {1}", _
                    line, _
                    lineNbr)
            End If
            line = sr.ReadLine
        End While
        sr.Close()
    End Sub

    Public Shared Sub Main(ByVal args As String())
        Dim r As Recipe = New Recipe
        r.Run(args(0))
    End Sub

End Class
```

VBScript

```
Dim fso,s,re,line,lineNbr
Set fso = CreateObject("Scripting.FileSystemObject")
Set s = fso.OpenTextFile(WScript.Arguments.Item(0), 1, True)
Set re = New RegExp
re.Pattern = "\b(\w+)\s\1\b"
lineNbr = 0
Do While Not s.AtEndOfStream
    line = s.ReadLine()
    lineNbr = lineNbr + 1
    If re.Test(line) Then
        WScript.Echo "Found match: '" & line & "' at line " & lineNbr
    End If
Loop
s.Close
```

JavaScript

```html
<html>
<head>
<title></title>
</head>
<body>
<form name="form1">
    <input type="textbox" name="txtInput" />
    <script type="text/javascript">
    function validate() {
        if (! document.form1.txtInput.value.match(/\b(\w+)\s\1\b/)) {
            alert("Please enter valid value!")
        } else {
            alert("Success!")
        }
    }
    </script>
    <input type="button" name="btnSubmit" onclick="validate()" value="Go" />
</form>
</body>
</html>
```

How It Works

The most important aspect of this regular expression is the *back reference*, which is \1 in all the previous recipes. The back reference is just a way of saying "whatever you found in the first group." The parentheses in the expression define the group. Here's a breakdown of the expression:

\b	is a word boundary, followed by . . .
(. . .)	a group (explained next), then . . .
\s	a space . . .
+	one or more times, then . . .
\1	whatever was found in the group, and lastly . . .
\b	a word boundary.

The group is simply (\w+), which is as follows:

\w	a word character . . .
+	found one or more times.

This will match a word. The expression begins and ends with a word boundary anchor. This is to prevent the expression from matching a string such as *quarterback backrub*. If the word boundary anchors are removed, the expression will start matching subsections of words.

1-11. Searching for Repeated Words Across Multiple Lines

Similar to recipe 1-10, this recipe allows you to search for repeated words that occur on more than one line. For example:

```
word
word
```

.NET Framework

C#

```csharp
using System;
using System.IO;
using System.Text.RegularExpressions;

public class Recipe
{
    private static Regex _Regex = new Regex( @"\b(\w+)(\s*$\s*|\s+)\1\b",
        RegexOptions.Multiline | RegexOptions.IgnoreCase );

    public void Run(string fileName)
    {
        String line;
        using (StreamReader sr = new StreamReader(fileName))
        {
            if(null != (line = sr.ReadToEnd()))
            {
                if (_Regex.IsMatch(line))
                {
                    foreach (Match myMatch in _Regex.Matches(line))
                    {
                        Console.WriteLine("Found match '{0}'", myMatch.ToString());
                    }
                }
            }
        }
    }

    public static void Main( string[] args )
    {
        Recipe r = new Recipe();
        r.Run(args[0]);
    }
}
```

Visual Basic .NET

```vbnet
Imports System
Imports System.IO
Imports System.Text.RegularExpressions
Public Class Recipe

    Private Shared _Regex As Regex = New Regex("\b(\w+)(\s*$\s*|\s+)\1\b", _
        RegexOptions.IgnoreCase Or RegexOptions.Multiline)

    Public Sub Run(ByVal fileName As String)
        Dim line As String
        Dim sr As StreamReader = File.OpenText(fileName)
        line = sr.ReadToEnd()
        If Not line Is Nothing
            If _Regex.IsMatch(line) Then
                For Each myMatch As Match In _Regex.Matches(line)
                    Console.WriteLine("Found match '{0}'", myMatch.ToString())
                Next
            End If
        End If
        sr.Close()
    End Sub

    Public Shared Sub Main(ByVal args As String())
        Dim r As Recipe = New Recipe
        r.Run(args(0))
    End Sub

End Class
```

How It Works

The "magic" part of this expression is the option given to the constructor of the Regex class, RegexOptions.Multiline, which allows the $ anchor to match the end of a line as well as the end of a string. The difference between the two is that when using the ReadToEnd() method of the StreamReader, the entire contents of the file will be loaded into one string, even though the contents span multiple lines in the file. Each word can have some space between it and the end of the line or between the beginning of the line and the word. The part of the expression that matches this is as follows:

\s	whitespace . . .
*	that's optional . . .
$	the end of the line (given the MultiLine option) . . .
\s	some more whitespace . . .
*	that's optional.

Since I wanted to match two repeated words on one line as well as two lines, the expression must also look for a space between the words. This is the same as in recipe 1-10, which is \s+.

Another option is passed in on the constructor to the Regex class: RegexOptions. IgnoreCase. When more than one option is specified, the | operator is used in C# and the Or keyword is used in Visual Basic .NET between the options. The option to ignore case in this expression is used so it will find matches such as *This this* or *The the*.

1-12. Searching for Lines Beginning with a Word

This recipe allows you to find whole words at the beginning of a line.

.NET Framework

ASP.NET

```
<%@ Page Language="vb" AutoEventWireup="false" %>
<!DOCTYPE HTML PUBLIC "-//W3C//DTD HTML 4.0 Transitional//EN">
<html>
<head><title></title>
</head>
<body>
    <form Id="Form1" RunAt="server">
    <asp:TextBox id="txtInput" runat="server"></asp:TextBox>
    <asp:RegularExpressionValidator Id="revInput" RunAt="server"
        ControlToValidate="txtInput"
        ErrorMessage="Please enter a valid value"
        ValidationExpression="Moo\b.*"></asp:RegularExpressionValidator>
    <asp:Button Id="btnSubmit" RunAt="server" CausesValidation="True"
        Text="Submit"></asp:Button>
    </form>
</body>
```

C#

```csharp
using System;
using System.IO;
using System.Text.RegularExpressions;

public class Recipe
{
    private static Regex _Regex = new Regex( @"^Moo\b" );

    public void Run(string fileName)
    {
        String line;
        int lineNbr = 0;
        using (StreamReader sr = new StreamReader(fileName))
        {
            while(null != (line = sr.ReadLine()))
            {
                lineNbr++;
                if (_Regex.IsMatch(line))
                {
                    Console.WriteLine("Found match '{0}' at line {1}",
                        line,
```

```
                                    lineNbr);
                }
            }
        }
    }

    public static void Main( string[] args )
    {
        Recipe r = new Recipe();
        r.Run(args[0]);
    }
}
```

Visual Basic .NET

```
Imports System
Imports System.IO
Imports System.Text.RegularExpressions
Public Class Recipe

    Private Shared _Regex As Regex = New Regex("^Moo\b")

    Public Sub Run(ByVal fileName As String)
        Dim line As String
        Dim lineNbr As Integer = 0
        Dim sr As StreamReader = File.OpenText(fileName)
        line = sr.ReadLine
        While Not line Is Nothing
            lineNbr = lineNbr + 1
            If _Regex.IsMatch(line) Then
                Console.WriteLine("Found match '{0}' at line {1}", _
                    line, _
                    lineNbr)
            End If
            line = sr.ReadLine
        End While
        sr.Close()
    End Sub

    Public Shared Sub Main(ByVal args As String())
        Dim r As Recipe = New Recipe
        r.Run(args(0))
    End Sub

End Class
```

VBScript

```
Dim fso,s,re,line,lineNbr
Set fso = CreateObject("Scripting.FileSystemObject")
Set s = fso.OpenTextFile(WScript.Arguments.Item(0), 1, True)
Set re = New RegExp
re.Pattern = "^Moo\b"
lineNbr = 0
Do While Not s.AtEndOfStream
    line = s.ReadLine()
    lineNbr = lineNbr + 1
    If re.Test(line) Then
        WScript.Echo "Found match: '" & line & "' at line " & lineNbr
    End If
Loop
s.Close
```

JavaScript

```
<html>
<head>
<title></title>
</head>
<body>
<form name="form1">
    <input type="textbox" name="txtInput" />
    <script type="text/javascript">
    function validate() {
        if (! document.form1.txtInput.value.match(/^Word\b/)) {
            alert("Please enter valid value!")
        } else {
            alert("Success!")
        }
    }
    </script>
    <input type="button" name="btnSubmit" onclick="validate()" value="Go" />
</form>
</body>
</html>
```

How It Works

The key to this expression is the line anchor metacharacter ^. You can break the expression down like this:

^	at the start of the line, followed immediately by . . .
W	then . . .
o	followed by . . .
r	then . . .
d	and lastly . . .
\b	a word boundary.

The \b character class is an anchor like the ^ line anchor. However, \b is a word anchor, and the ^ metacharacter is a line anchor.

1-13. Searching for Lines Ending with a Word

This recipe finds full words at the end of a line. For the purposes of this example, that word is *finale*.

.NET Framework

ASP.NET

```
<%@ Page Language="vb" AutoEventWireup="false" %>
<!DOCTYPE HTML PUBLIC "-//W3C//DTD HTML 4.0 Transitional//EN">
<html>
<head><title></title>
</head>
<body>
    <form Id="Form1" RunAt="server">
    <asp:TextBox id="txtInput" runat="server"></asp:TextBox>
    <asp:RegularExpressionValidator Id="revInput" RunAt="server"
        ControlToValidate="txtInput"
        ErrorMessage="Please enter a valid value"
        ValidationExpression=".*\bfinale"></asp:RegularExpressionValidator>
    <asp:Button Id="btnSubmit" RunAt="server" CausesValidation="True"
        Text="Submit"></asp:Button>
    </form>
</body>
```

C#

```
using System;
using System.IO;
using System.Text.RegularExpressions;

public class Recipe
{
    private static Regex _Regex = new Regex( @"\bfinale$" );

    public void Run(string fileName)
    {
        String line;
        int lineNbr = 0;
        using (StreamReader sr = new StreamReader(fileName))
        {
            while(null != (line = sr.ReadLine()))
            {
                lineNbr++;
                if (_Regex.IsMatch(line))
                {
                    Console.WriteLine("Found match '{0}' at line {1}",
```

```csharp
                            line,
                            lineNbr);
                }
            }
        }
    }

    public static void Main( string[] args )
    {
        Recipe r = new Recipe();
        r.Run(args[0]);
    }
}
```

Visual Basic .NET

```vbnet
Imports System
Imports System.IO
Imports System.Text.RegularExpressions
Public Class Recipe

    Private Shared _Regex As Regex = New Regex("\bfinale$")

    Public Sub Run(ByVal fileName As String)
        Dim line As String
        Dim lineNbr As Integer = 0
        Dim sr As StreamReader = File.OpenText(fileName)
        line = sr.ReadLine
        While Not line Is Nothing
            lineNbr = lineNbr + 1
            If _Regex.IsMatch(line) Then
                Console.WriteLine("Found match '{0}' at line {1}", _
                    line, _
                    lineNbr)
            End If
            line = sr.ReadLine
        End While
        sr.Close()
    End Sub

    Public Shared Sub Main(ByVal args As String())
        Dim r As Recipe = New Recipe
        r.Run(args(0))
    End Sub

End Class
```

VBScript

```
Dim fso,s,re,line,lineNbr
Set fso = CreateObject("Scripting.FileSystemObject")
Set s = fso.OpenTextFile(WScript.Arguments.Item(0), 1, True)
Set re = New RegExp
re.Pattern = "\bfinale$"
lineNbr = 0
Do While Not s.AtEndOfStream
    line = s.ReadLine()
    lineNbr = lineNbr + 1
    If re.Test(line) Then
        WScript.Echo "Found match: '" & line & "' at line " & lineNbr
    End If
Loop
s.Close
```

JavaScript

```html
<html>
<head>
<title></title>
</head>
<body>
<form name="form1">
    <input type="textbox" name="txtInput" />
    <script type="text/javascript">
    function validate() {
        if (! document.form1.txtInput.value.match(/\bfinale$/)) {
            alert("Please enter valid value!")
        } else {
            alert("Success!")
        }
    }
    </script>
    <input type="button" name="btnSubmit" onclick="validate()" value="Go" />
</form>
</body>
</html>
```

How It Works

The key to this expression is the use of character classes. Two of them are used, one to define the end of the line and one to define a word boundary, so you get only whole words when using the expression. You can break the regular expression down like this:

\b   is a word boundary, such as a space, tab, and so on, followed by . . .

finale   *f, i, n, a, l,* followed by *e* and lastly . . .

$ the end of the line.

The line anchor $ is like the line anchor ^ because both of them are supported in nearly every flavor of regular expression. The "Syntax Overview" section at the beginning of this book highlights the different character classes supported in the various sections of regular expressions.

Variations

You may be interested in matching lines where the word is the last word on the line, which means spaces may appear between the end of the word and the end of the line. To modify the expression to match lines with possible spaces, use the character class that matches spaces with the * qualifier, which matches none or many. The regular expression variation looks like this: \bfinale\s*$.

1-14. Finding Words Not Preceded by Other Words

This recipe finds a word *likely* in text but will skip over it if the word before it is *not*. It provides an example of how to use a negative look-behind.

.NET Framework

ASP.NET

```
<%@ Page Language="vb" AutoEventWireup="false" %>
<!DOCTYPE HTML PUBLIC "-//W3C//DTD HTML 4.0 Transitional//EN">
<html>
<head><title></title>
</head>
<body>
    <form Id="Form1" RunAt="server">
    <asp:TextBox id="txtInput" runat="server"></asp:TextBox>
    <asp:RegularExpressionValidator Id="revInput" RunAt="server"
        ControlToValidate="txtInput"
        ErrorMessage="Please enter a valid value"
        ValidationExpression=".*(?<!not\s+)likely\b.*">
    </asp:RegularExpressionValidator>
    <asp:Button Id="btnSubmit" RunAt="server" CausesValidation="True"
        Text="Submit"></asp:Button>
    </form>
</body>
```

C#

```csharp
using System;
using System.IO;
using System.Text.RegularExpressions;

public class Recipe
{
    private static Regex _Regex = new Regex( @"(?<!not\s+)likely\b" );

    public void Run(string fileName)
    {
        String line;
        int lineNbr = 0;
        using (StreamReader sr = new StreamReader(fileName))
        {
            while(null != (line = sr.ReadLine()))
            {
                lineNbr++;
                if (_Regex.IsMatch(line))
                {
```

```
                            Console.WriteLine("Found match '{0}' at line {1}",
                                line,
                                lineNbr);
                    }
                }
            }
        }

    public static void Main( string[] args )
    {
        Recipe r = new Recipe();
        r.Run(args[0]);
    }
}
```

Visual Basic .NET

```
Imports System
Imports System.IO
Imports System.Text.RegularExpressions
Public Class Recipe

    Private Shared _Regex As Regex = New Regex("(?<!not\s+)likely\b")

    Public Sub Run(ByVal fileName As String)
        Dim line As String
        Dim lineNbr As Integer = 0
        Dim sr As StreamReader = File.OpenText(fileName)
        line = sr.ReadLine
        While Not line Is Nothing
            lineNbr = lineNbr + 1
            If _Regex.IsMatch(line) Then
                Console.WriteLine("Found match '{0}' at line {1}", _
                    line, _
                    lineNbr)
            End If
            line = sr.ReadLine
        End While
        sr.Close()
    End Sub

    Public Shared Sub Main(ByVal args As String())
        Dim r As Recipe = New Recipe
        r.Run(args(0))
    End Sub

End Class
```

How It Works

This recipe uses a negative look-behind as it's searching through the string to make sure what you're looking for, `likely\b`, isn't preceded by `not\s+`. It breaks down like this:

`(?<!`	the negative look-behind that matches . . .
`not`	the characters *n*, *o*, and *t*, followed by . . .
`\s`	a space . . .
`+`	found one or more times . . .
`)`	the end of the look-behind . . .
`likely`	the letters *l*, *i*, *k*, *e*, *l*, and *y*, followed by . . .
`\b`	a word boundary character.

1-15. Finding Words Not Followed by Other Words

This recipe uses a negative look-ahead to find a word but only if it isn't followed by another one. In the example shown here, those words are *hello* and *world*, respectively.

.NET Framework

ASP.NET

```
<%@ Page Language="vb" AutoEventWireup="false" %>
<!DOCTYPE HTML PUBLIC "-//W3C//DTD HTML 4.0 Transitional//EN">
<html>
<head><title></title>
</head>
<body>
    <form Id="Form1" RunAt="server">
    <asp:TextBox id="txtInput" runat="server"></asp:TextBox>
    <asp:RegularExpressionValidator Id="revInput" RunAt="server"
        ControlToValidate="txtInput"
        ErrorMessage="Please enter a valid ZIP code"
        ValidationExpression="\bhello\b(?!\s+world\b)">
    </asp:RegularExpressionValidator>
    <asp:Button Id="btnSubmit" RunAt="server" CausesValidation="True"
        Text="Submit"></asp:Button>
    </form>
</body>
```

C#

```
using System;
using System.IO;
using System.Text.RegularExpressions;

public class Recipe
{
    private static Regex _Regex = new Regex( @"\bhello\b(?!\s+world\b)" );

    public void Run(string fileName)
    {
        String line;
        int lineNbr = 0;
        using (StreamReader sr = new StreamReader(fileName))
        {
            while(null != (line = sr.ReadLine()))
            {
                lineNbr++;
                if (_Regex.IsMatch(line))
                {
```

```
                Console.WriteLine("Found match '{0}' at line {1}",
                    line,
                    lineNbr);
            }
        }
    }
}

    public static void Main( string[] args )
    {
        Recipe r = new Recipe();
        r.Run(args[0]);
    }
}
```

Visual Basic .NET

```
Imports System
Imports System.IO
Imports System.Text.RegularExpressions
Public Class Recipe

    Private Shared _Regex As Regex = New Regex("\bhello\b(?!\s+world\b)")

    Public Sub Run(ByVal fileName As String)
        Dim line As String
        Dim lineNbr As Integer = 0
        Dim sr As StreamReader = File.OpenText(fileName)
        line = sr.ReadLine
        While Not line Is Nothing
            lineNbr = lineNbr + 1
            If _Regex.IsMatch(line) Then
                Console.WriteLine("Found match '{0}' at line {1}", _
                    line, _
                    lineNbr)
            End If
            line = sr.ReadLine
        End While
        sr.Close()
    End Sub

    Public Shared Sub Main(ByVal args As String())
        Dim r As Recipe = New Recipe
        r.Run(args(0))
    End Sub

End Class
```

How It Works

Here's the expression broken down:

\b	a word boundary, followed by . . .
hello	the letters *h, e, l, l,* and *o*, followed by . . .
\b	another word boundary, then . . .
(?!	a negative look-ahead that contains . . .
\s	a whitespace character . . .
+	found one or more times . . .
world	the letters *w, o, r, l,* and *d* . . .
\b	a word boundary, followed by . . .
)	the end of the negative look-ahead.

1-16. Filtering Profanity

You can use this recipe as a simple profanity filter. For the purpose of this recipe, let's pretend that *bleep*, *beep*, and *blankity* are naughty words. This recipe will show you how to replace those words with *$%&@#!* to print the original text with the profanity filtered out.

.NET Framework

C#

```csharp
using System;
using System.IO;
using System.Text.RegularExpressions;

public class Recipe
{
    private static Regex _Regex = new Regex( @"\b(bleep|beep|blankity)\b" );
    public void Run(string fileName)
    {
        String line;
        String newLine;
        using (StreamReader sr = new StreamReader(fileName))
        {
            while(null != (line = sr.ReadLine()))
            {
                newLine = _Regex.Replace(line, @"$%&@#!");
                Console.WriteLine("New string is: '{0}', original was: '{1}'",
                    newLine,
                    line));
            }
        }
    }

    public static void Main( string[] args )
    {
        Recipe r = new Recipe();
        r.Run(args[0]);
    }
}
```

Visual Basic .NET

```vbnet
Imports System
Imports System.IO
Imports System.Text.RegularExpressions
Public Class Recipe
```

```vbnet
    Private Shared _Regex As Regex = New Regex("\b(bleep|beep|blankity)\b")

    Public Sub Run(ByVal fileName As String)
        Dim line As String
        Dim newLine As String
        Dim sr As StreamReader = File.OpenText(fileName)
        line = sr.ReadLine
        While Not line Is Nothing
            newLine = _Regex.Replace(line, "$%&@#!")
            Console.WriteLine("New string is: '{0}', original was: '{1}'", _
             newLine, _
             line))
            line = sr.ReadLine
        End While
        sr.Close()
    End Sub

    Public Shared Sub Main(ByVal args As String())
        Dim r As Recipe = New Recipe
        r.Run(args(0))
    End Sub

End Class
```

VBScript

```vbscript
Dim fso,s,re,line,newstr
Set fso = CreateObject("Scripting.FileSystemObject")
Set s = fso.OpenTextFile(WScript.Arguments.Item(0), 1, True)
Set re = New RegExp
re.Pattern = "\b(bleep|beep|blankity)\b"
re.Global = true
Do While Not s.AtEndOfStream
    line = s.ReadLine()
    newstr = re.Replace(line, "$%&@#!")
    WScript.Echo "New string '" & newstr & "', original '" & line & "'"
Loop
s.Close
```

JavaScript

```html
<html>
<head>
<title></title>
</head>
<body>
<form name="form1">
```

```
<input type="text" name="txtInput" />
<div id="lblResult"></div>
<script language="javascript">
    function replace() {
        document.getElementById('lblResult').innerHTML = ➡
document.form1.txtInput.value.replace(/\b(bleep|beep|blankity)\b/, "$%&@#!");
    }
</script>
<input type="button" name="btnSubmit" onclick="replace()" value="Go" />
</form>
</body>
</html>
```

How It Works

For brevity, I won't break down the words into characters for this recipe. Here's the breakdown of the search expression:

\b	is a word boundary, followed by . . .
(	a group of expressions containing . . .
bleep	the word *bleep* . . .
|	or . . .
beep	the word *beep* . . .
|	or . . .
blankity	the word *blankity* . . .
)	followed by . . .
\b	a word boundary.

Variations

For a variation on this recipe, you could change the word match—you could condense it. Be careful about how much the expressions are condensed, though, because sometimes they can become unreadable and harder to maintain in the future.

Here's a condensed version of the three-word match:

```
b(l?eep|lankity)
```

1-17. Finding Strings in Quotes

You can use this recipe to find a set of words (a string) but that matches only if the string is inside quotes.

.NET Framework

ASP.NET

```
<%@ Page Language="vb" AutoEventWireup="false" %>
<!DOCTYPE HTML PUBLIC "-//W3C//DTD HTML 4.0 Transitional//EN">
<html>
<head><title></title>
</head>
<body>
    <form Id="Form1" RunAt="server">
    <asp:TextBox id="txtInput" runat="server"></asp:TextBox>
    <asp:RegularExpressionValidator Id="revInput" RunAt="server"
        ControlToValidate="txtInput"
        ErrorMessage="Please enter a valid value"
        ValidationExpression='[^\"]*\"[^\"]*\bneat➥
 saying\b.*'></asp:RegularExpressionValidator>
    <asp:Button Id="btnSubmit" RunAt="server" CausesValidation="True"
        Text="Submit"></asp:Button>
    </form>
</body>
```

C#

```
using System;
using System.IO;
using System.Text.RegularExpressions;

public class Recipe
{
    private static Regex _Regex =
        new Regex( "^[^\"]*\"[^\"]*\\bneat saying\\b" );

    public void Run(string fileName)
    {
        String line;
        int lineNbr = 0;
        using (StreamReader sr = new StreamReader(fileName))
        {
            while(null != (line = sr.ReadLine()))
            {
                lineNbr++;
                if (_Regex.IsMatch(line))
                {
```

```csharp
                    Console.WriteLine("Found match '{0}' at line {1}",
                        line,
                        lineNbr);
                }
            }
        }
    }

    public static void Main( string[] args )
    {
        Recipe r = new Recipe();
        r.Run(args[0]);
    }
}
```

Visual Basic .NET

```vbnet
Imports System
Imports System.IO
Imports System.Text.RegularExpressions
Public Class Recipe

    Private Shared _Regex As Regex = _
        New Regex("^[^""]*""[^""]*\bneat saying\b")

    Public Sub Run(ByVal fileName As String)
        Dim line As String
        Dim lineNbr As Integer = 0
        Dim sr As StreamReader = File.OpenText(fileName)
        line = sr.ReadLine
        While Not line Is Nothing
            lineNbr = lineNbr + 1
            If _Regex.IsMatch(line) Then
                Console.WriteLine("Found match '{0}' at line {1}", _
                    line, _
                    lineNbr)
            End If
            line = sr.ReadLine
        End While
        sr.Close()
    End Sub

    Public Shared Sub Main(ByVal args As String())
        Dim r As Recipe = New Recipe
        r.Run(args(0))
    End Sub

End Class
```

VBScript

```
Dim fso,s,re,line,lineNbr
Set fso = CreateObject("Scripting.FileSystemObject")
Set s = fso.OpenTextFile(WScript.Arguments.Item(0), 1, True)
Set re = New RegExp
re.Pattern = "^[^""]*""[^""]*\bneat saying\b"
lineNbr = 0
Do While Not s.AtEndOfStream
    line = s.ReadLine()
    lineNbr = lineNbr + 1
    If re.Test(line) Then
        WScript.Echo "Found match: '" & line & "' at line " & lineNbr
    End If
Loop
s.Close
```

JavaScript

```
<html>
<head>
<title></title>
</head>
<body>
<form name="form1">
    <input type="textbox" name="txtInput" />
    <script type="text/javascript">
    function validate() {
        if (! document.form1.txtInput.value.match➡
(/^[^\"]*\"[^\"]*\bneat saying\b/)) {
            alert("Please enter valid value!")
        } else {
            alert("Success!")
        }
    }
    </script>
    <input type="button" name="btnSubmit" onclick="validate()" value="Go" />
</form>
</body>
</html>
```

How It Works

This expression makes sure no quotes are found between the opening quote and the word. This will ensure that the expression is found in quotes. Here's the expression broken down:

^	the beginning of the line . . .
[^	a character class that doesn't match . . .
""	a double quote (escaped here for Visual Basic .NET) . . .
]	the end of the character class . . .
*	found zero or more times . . .
""	a double quote . . .
[^	a character class that doesn't match . . .
""	another double quote . . .
]	the end of the character class . . .
*	found zero or more times . . .
\b	a word boundary character . . .
. . .	the text, omitted here for brevity . . .
\b	a word boundary character.

1-18. Escaping Quotes

You can use this recipe to add an escape character in front of double quotes that already aren't escaped. It's ideal for preparing strings to be wrapped in quotes, where all the existing quotes must have an escape sequence added to them. For the purposes of this recipe, the escape character is \.

.NET Framework

C#

```
using System;
using System.IO;
using System.Text.RegularExpressions;

public class Recipe
{
    private static Regex _Regex = new Regex( "(?<!\\\\)\"" );
    public void Run(string fileName)
    {
        String line;
        String newLine;
        using (StreamReader sr = new StreamReader(fileName))
        {
            while(null != (line = sr.ReadLine()))
            {
                newLine = _Regex.Replace(line, "\\\"");
                Console.WriteLine("New string is: '{0}', original was: '{1}'",
                    newLine,
                    line));
            }
        }
    }

    public static void Main( string[] args )
    {
        Recipe r = new Recipe();
        r.Run(args[0]);
    }
}
```

Visual Basic .NET

```
Imports System
Imports System.IO
Imports System.Text.RegularExpressions
Public Class Recipe
```

```
Private Shared _Regex As Regex = New Regex("(?<!\\)""")

Public Sub Run(ByVal fileName As String)
    Dim line As String
    Dim newLine As String
    Dim sr As StreamReader = File.OpenText(fileName)
    line = sr.ReadLine
    While Not line Is Nothing
        newLine = _Regex.Replace(line, "\""")
        Console.WriteLine("New string is: '{0}', original was: '{1}'", _
         newLine, _
         line))
        line = sr.ReadLine
    End While
    sr.Close()
End Sub

Public Shared Sub Main(ByVal args As String())
    Dim r As Recipe = New Recipe
    r.Run(args(0))
End Sub

End Class
```

VBScript

```
Dim fso,s,re,line,newstr
Set fso = CreateObject("Scripting.FileSystemObject")
Set s = fso.OpenTextFile(WScript.Arguments.Item(0), 1, True)
Set re = New RegExp
re.Pattern = "(^|[^\\])"""
Do While Not s.AtEndOfStream
    line = s.ReadLine()
    newstr = re.Replace(line, "$1\""")
    WScript.Echo "New string '" & newstr & "', original '" & line & "'"
Loop
s.Close
```

JavaScript

```
<html>
<head>
<title></title>
</head>
<body>
<form name="form1">
    <input type="text" name="txtInput" />
```

```
<div id="lblResult"></div>
<script language="javascript">
    function replace() {
        document.getElementById('lblResult').innerHTML = ➥
document.form1.txtInput.value.replace(/(^|[^\\])\"/, '\1\\\"');
    }
</script>
<input type="button" name="btnSubmit" onclick="replace()" value="Go" />
</form>
</body>
</html>
```

How It Works

The recipes in this section are a little different from each other because of the features that different flavors of regular expressions support. The .NET regular expression implementation supports look-arounds, which provide the ability to define what comes before and after the expression. These come in handy in situations such as this one, where the expression is saying, "Show me quotes that don't have escape characters in front of them."

The grouped expression breaks down as follows:

(?<!   the beginning of a negative look-behind . . .

\\   an escaped \ . . .

)   the end of the negative look-behind.

The negative look-behind expression is defined by (?<!. Everything between that and the closing parenthesis,), is evaluated. So the recipe (?<!\\)\" will match a quote as long as it isn't preceded by a back slash (\).

The VBScript and JavaScript regexes are slightly different, replacing the negative look-behind (which isn't supported) with the expression (^|[^\\]). This expression looks for the beginning of the line (^) or a character class that isn't an escape.

1-19. Removing Escaped Sequences

This recipe removes escape characters such as \ unless they're escaped themselves. So, given a
string such as \slashes\\, this recipe will yield slashes\\.

.NET Framework

C#

```csharp
using System;
using System.IO;
using System.Text.RegularExpressions;

public class Recipe
{
    private static Regex _Regex = new Regex( @"(?<!\\)\\(?!\\)" );
    public void Run(string fileName)
    {
        String line;
        String newLine;
        using (StreamReader sr = new StreamReader(fileName))
        {
            while(null != (line = sr.ReadLine()))
            {
                newLine = _Regex.Replace(line, @"");
                Console.WriteLine("New string is: '{0}', original was: '{1}'",
                    newLine,
                    line));
            }
        }
    }

    public static void Main( string[] args )
    {
        Recipe r = new Recipe();
        r.Run(args[0]);
    }
}
```

Visual Basic .NET

```vbnet
Imports System
Imports System.IO
Imports System.Text.RegularExpressions
Public Class Recipe

    Private Shared _Regex As Regex = New Regex("(?<!\\)\\(?!\\)")
```

```
Public Sub Run(ByVal fileName As String)
    Dim line As String
    Dim newLine As String
    Dim sr As StreamReader = File.OpenText(fileName)
    line = sr.ReadLine
    While Not line Is Nothing
        newLine = _Regex.Replace(line, "")
        Console.WriteLine("New string is: '{0}', original was: '{1}'", _
         newLine, _
         line))
        line = sr.ReadLine
    End While
    sr.Close()
End Sub

Public Shared Sub Main(ByVal args As String())
    Dim r As Recipe = New Recipe
    r.Run(args(0))
End Sub

End Class
```

How It Works

You can break the regular expression down like this:

(?<!	is a look-behind expression that *doesn't* match . . .
\\	a character that's a slash . . .
)	(end of the look-behind expression) followed by . . .
\\	a slash, where . . .
(?!	a look-ahead expression that *doesn't* match . . .
\\	another slash . . .
)	(end of the look-ahead expression).

1-20. Adding Semicolons at the End of a Line

This recipe will add a semicolon to the end of each line. This recipe can come in handy to turn lines of regular text to lines of code. Variations on this recipe allow you to add a comma to the end of a line.

.NET Framework

C#

```csharp
using System;
using System.IO;
using System.Text.RegularExpressions;

public class Recipe
{
    private static Regex _Regex = new Regex( "(?<=[^;])$" );
    public void Run(string fileName)
    {
        String line;
        String newLine;
        using (StreamReader sr = new StreamReader(fileName))
        {
            while(null != (line = sr.ReadLine()))
            {
                newLine = _Regex.Replace(line, ";");
                Console.WriteLine("New string is: '{0}', original was: '{1}'",
                    newLine,
                    line));
            }
        }
    }

    public static void Main( string[] args )
    {
        Recipe r = new Recipe();
        r.Run(args[0]);
    }
}
```

Visual Basic .NET

```vbnet
Imports System
Imports System.IO
Imports System.Text.RegularExpressions
Public Class Recipe

    Private Shared _Regex As Regex = New Regex("(?<=[^;])$")
```

```
Public Sub Run(ByVal fileName As String)
    Dim line As String
    Dim newLine As String
    Dim sr As StreamReader = File.OpenText(fileName)
    line = sr.ReadLine
    While Not line Is Nothing
        newLine = _Regex.Replace(line, ";")
        Console.WriteLine("New string is: '{0}', original was: '{1}'", _
         newLine, _
         line))
        line = sr.ReadLine
    End While
    sr.Close()
End Sub

Public Shared Sub Main(ByVal args As String())
    Dim r As Recipe = New Recipe
    r.Run(args(0))
End Sub

End Class
```

VBScript

```
Dim fso,s,re,line,newstr
Set fso = CreateObject("Scripting.FileSystemObject")
Set s = fso.OpenTextFile(WScript.Arguments.Item(0), 1, True)
Set re = New RegExp
re.Pattern = "([^;])$"
Do While Not s.AtEndOfStream
    line = s.ReadLine()
    newstr = re.Replace(line, "\1;")
    WScript.Echo "New string '" & newstr & "', original '" & line & "'"
Loop
s.Close
```

JavaScript

```
<html>
<head>
<title></title>
</head>
<body>
<form name="form1">
    <input type="text" name="txtInput" />
    <div id="lblResult"></div>
    <script language="javascript">
```

```
        function replace() {
            document.getElementById('lblResult').innerHTML = ➡
document.form1.txtInput.value.replace(/([^;])$/, "\1;");
        }
    </script>
    <input type="button" name="btnSubmit" onclick="replace()" value="Go" />
</form>
</body>
</html>
```

How It Works

This recipe is fairly straightforward—it demonstrates the use of the $ metacharacter that matches the end of a line and a negative look-behind to make sure a semicolon isn't already there. You can break the match portion of the recipe down like this:

(?<!   a negative look-behind that doesn't match . . .

;   a semicolon . . .

)   the end of the negative look-behind . . .

$ marks the end of the line.

The replacement section is simply as follows:

;   is a semicolon.

Since VBScript doesn't support negative look-behinds, the recipe has to go about it from a little different angle. This recipe captures the character before the end of the line, making sure it isn't a semicolon, and then uses the back reference \1 to put whatever it found back into the replacement string. The rest of it breaks down like this:

(a group that contains . . .

[^   a character class that doesn't match . . .

;   a semicolon . . .

]   the end of the character class . . .

)   the end of the capturing group . . .

$ the end of the line.

1-21. Adding to the Beginning of a Line

Sometimes it's useful to add text at the beginning of a line. In the "real world," I've used this recipe along with recipe 1-20 to turn lines of a file into code statements. For example, you can turn the following:

```
This line
That line
```

into this:

```
string.Add( "This line" );
string.Add( "That line" );
```

In the variations at the end of this recipe, I'll show you how to do this in one expression instead of two.

.NET Framework

C#

```
using System;
using System.IO;
using System.Text.RegularExpressions;

public class Recipe
{
    private static Regex _Regex = new Regex( @"^" );
    public void Run(string fileName)
    {
        String line;
        String newLine;
        using (StreamReader sr = new StreamReader(fileName))
        {
            while(null != (line = sr.ReadLine()))
            {
                newLine = _Regex.Replace(line, @"line:  ");
                Console.WriteLine("New string is: '{0}', original was: '{1}'",
                    newLine,
                    line));
            }
        }
    }

    public static void Main( string[] args )
    {
        Recipe r = new Recipe();
```

WORDS AND TEXT

```
        r.Run(args[0]);
    }
}
```

Visual Basic .NET

```vbnet
Imports System
Imports System.IO
Imports System.Text.RegularExpressions
Public Class Recipe

    Private Shared _Regex As Regex = New Regex("^")

    Public Sub Run(ByVal fileName As String)
        Dim line As String
        Dim newLine As String
        Dim sr As StreamReader = File.OpenText(fileName)
        line = sr.ReadLine
        While Not line Is Nothing
            newLine = _Regex.Replace(line, "line:  ")
            Console.WriteLine("New string is: '{0}', original was: '{1}'", _
             newLine, _
             line))
            line = sr.ReadLine
        End While
        sr.Close()
    End Sub

    Public Shared Sub Main(ByVal args As String())
        Dim r As Recipe = New Recipe
        r.Run(args(0))
    End Sub

End Class
```

VBScript

```vbscript
Dim fso,s,re,line,newstr
Set fso = CreateObject("Scripting.FileSystemObject")
Set s = fso.OpenTextFile(WScript.Arguments.Item(0), 1, True)
Set re = New RegExp
re.Pattern = "^"
Do While Not s.AtEndOfStream
    line = s.ReadLine()
    newstr = re.Replace(line, "line:  ")
    WScript.Echo "New string '" & newstr & "', original '" & line & "'"
Loop
s.Close
```

JavaScript

```
<html>
<head>
<title></title>
</head>
<body>
<form name="form1">
    <input type="text" name="txtInput" />
    <div id="lblResult"></div>
    <script language="javascript">
        function replace() {
            document.getElementById('lblResult').innerHTML = ➥
document.form1.txtInput.value.replace(/^/, "line:   ");
        }
    </script>
    <input type="button" name="btnSubmit" onclick="replace()" value="Go" />
</form>
</body>
</html>
```

How It Works

This recipe uses the ^ metacharacter, which is a line anchor. This line anchor means "the beginning of the line," so the breakdown of the search recipe is simply as follows:

    ^   is the beginning of the line.

The replacement expression is anything you want to add to the beginning of the line. For this replacement, you don't need to have anything special such as back references or grouping. The line anchor ^ doesn't even need to be in the replacement expression.

Variations

As I mentioned previously, one of the variations on this expression is the combination of the two expressions to add text to the beginning and end of the line at the same time. This has many uses—consider a list you want to modify into lines of code or a set of lines you want to enclose in quotes. Here, I use back references to insert everything between the beginning and the end of the line back into the replacement expression to replace ^(.*)$ with list.add("\1"). This expression, when used on a file that contains the following:

```
apples
bananas
celery
```

will print this:

```
list.add("apples");
list.add("bananas");
list.add("celery");
```

Another variation is to use another metacharacter, such as \t, in the replacement expression. Using \t in the replacement expression will indent each line with a tab.

1-22. Replacing Smart Quotes with Straight Quotes

You can use this recipe to replace smart quotes (" and "), inserted by some word processors, with ordinary straight quotes (" and "). This recipe comes in handy when cutting and pasting from a word processor file into a code file or Hypertext Markup Language (HTML) file, where the smart quotes can sometimes cause issues.

.NET Framework

C#

```csharp
using System;
using System.IO;
using System.Text.RegularExpressions;

public class Recipe
{
    private static Regex _Regex = new Regex( @"\u201c|\u201d" );
    public void Run(string fileName)
    {
        String line;
        String newLine;
        using (StreamReader sr = new StreamReader(fileName))
        {
            while(null != (line = sr.ReadLine()))
            {
                newLine = _Regex.Replace(line, "\"");
                Console.WriteLine("New string is: '{0}', original was: '{1}'",
                    newLine,
                    line));
            }
        }
    }

    public static void Main( string[] args )
    {
        Recipe r = new Recipe();
        r.Run(args[0]);
    }
}
```

Visual Basic .NET

```vbnet
Imports System
Imports System.IO
Imports System.Text.RegularExpressions
Public Class Recipe
```

```vbnet
Private Shared _Regex As Regex = New Regex("\u201c|\u201d")

Public Sub Run(ByVal fileName As String)
    Dim line As String
    Dim newLine As String
    Dim sr As StreamReader = File.OpenText(fileName)
    line = sr.ReadLine
    While Not line Is Nothing
        newLine = _Regex.Replace(line, """")
        Console.WriteLine("New string is: '{0}', original was: '{1}'", _
         newLine, _
         line))
        line = sr.ReadLine
    End While
    sr.Close()
End Sub

Public Shared Sub Main(ByVal args As String())
    Dim r As Recipe = New Recipe
    r.Run(args(0))
End Sub

End Class
```

VBScript

```vbscript
Dim fso,s,re,line,newstr,f
Set fso = CreateObject("Scripting.FileSystemObject")
Set f = fso.GetFile(WScript.Arguments.Item(0))
Set s = f.OpenAsTextStream(1, -1)
Set re = New RegExp
re.Pattern = "\u201c|\u201d"
re.Global = True
Do While Not s.AtEndOfStream
    line = s.ReadLine()
    newstr = re.Replace(line, """")
    WScript.Echo "New string '" & newstr & "', original '" & line & "'"
Loop
s.Close
```

JavaScript

```javascript
<html>
<head>
<title></title>
</head>
<body>
```

```
<form name="form1">
    <input type="text" name="txtInput" />
    <div id="lblResult"></div>
    <script language="javascript">
        function replace() {
            document.getElementById('lblResult').innerHTML = ➡
document.form1.txtInput.value.replace(/\u201c|\u201d/g, "\"");
        }
    </script>
    <input type="button" name="btnSubmit" onclick="replace()" value="Go" />
</form>
</body>
</html>
```

How It Works

Most regular expression implementations provide the ability to specify a character by its Unicode value using the \u character class. This is the expression broken down:

\u201c	is a left double quote . . .
|	or . . .
\u201d	is a right double quote.

And the replacement expression is simply ", which is a straight double quote.

Variations

Variations on this recipe allow you to replace other special characters, such as trademark (™) and copyright (©) symbols. The Unicode values for trademark and copyright symbols are \u2122 and \u00a9, respectively. You can look up the Unicode values for various characters at http://www.unicode.org/charts.

1-23. Finding Uppercase Letters

This expression demonstrates the use of the /p{...} character class to find matches in strings. In this recipe, /p{Lu} is used to find uppercase letters.

.NET Framework

ASP.NET

```
<%@ Page Language="vb" AutoEventWireup="false" %>
<!DOCTYPE HTML PUBLIC "-//W3C//DTD HTML 4.0 Transitional//EN">
<html>
<head><title></title>
</head>
<body>
    <form Id="Form1" RunAt="server">
    <asp:TextBox id="txtInput" runat="server"></asp:TextBox>
    <asp:RegularExpressionValidator Id="revInput" RunAt="server"
        ControlToValidate="txtInput"
        ErrorMessage="Please enter a valid value"
        ValidationExpression='.*\p{Lu}.*'></asp:RegularExpressionValidator>
    <asp:Button Id="btnSubmit" RunAt="server" CausesValidation="True"
        Text="Submit"></asp:Button>
    </form>
</body>
```

C#

```
using System;
using System.IO;
using System.Text.RegularExpressions;

public class Recipe
{
    private static Regex _Regex =
        new Regex( "\p{Lu}" );

    public void Run(string fileName)
    {
        String line;
        int lineNbr = 0;
        using (StreamReader sr = new StreamReader(fileName))
        {
            while(null != (line = sr.ReadLine()))
            {
                lineNbr++;
                if (_Regex.IsMatch(line))
                {
```

```
                    Console.WriteLine("Found match '{0}' at line {1}",
                        line,
                        lineNbr);
                }
            }
        }
    }

    public static void Main( string[] args )
    {
        Recipe r = new Recipe();
        r.Run(args[0]);
    }
}
```

Visual Basic .NET

```
Imports System
Imports System.IO
Imports System.Text.RegularExpressions
Public Class Recipe

    Private Shared _Regex As Regex = _
        New Regex("\p{Lu}")

    Public Sub Run(ByVal fileName As String)
        Dim line As String
        Dim lineNbr As Integer = 0
        Dim sr As StreamReader = File.OpenText(fileName)
        line = sr.ReadLine
        While Not line Is Nothing
            lineNbr = lineNbr + 1
            If _Regex.IsMatch(line) Then
                Console.WriteLine("Found match '{0}' at line {1}", _
                    line, _
                    lineNbr)
            End If
            line = sr.ReadLine
        End While
        sr.Close()
    End Sub

    Public Shared Sub Main(ByVal args As String())
        Dim r As Recipe = New Recipe
        r.Run(args(0))
    End Sub

End Class
```

How It Works

You can break this expression down as follows:

\p{...}   is a Unicode character, where the name of the Unicode class is put inside the brackets.

In this recipe, Lu is used inside the brackets. In Unicode, Lu matches uppercase letters, so this recipe will match English letters *A–Z*. To find out what the names are for your Unicode characters, look at the Unicode properties at http://www.unicode.org/Public/UNIDATA/UCD.html#Properties.

1-24. Splitting Lines in a File

You can use this recipe to split words separated by commas onto separate lines. This can be useful to make lists more readable by placing each item of a list on a line all by itself. For example, a line such as this:

```
apples, bananas, celery
```

becomes the following:

```
apples,
bananas,
celery
```

.NET Framework

C#

```csharp
using System;
using System.IO;
using System.Text.RegularExpressions;

public class Recipe
{
    private static Regex _Regex = new Regex( @",\s*" );
    public void Run(string fileName)
    {
        String line;
        String newLine;
        using (StreamReader sr = new StreamReader(fileName))
        {
            while(null != (line = sr.ReadLine()))
            {
                newLine = _Regex.Replace(line, "," + Environment.NewLine);
                Console.WriteLine("New string is: '{0}', original was: '{1}'",
                    newLine,
                    line));
            }
        }
    }

    public static void Main( string[] args )
    {
        Recipe r = new Recipe();
        r.Run(args[0]);
    }
}
```

Visual Basic .NET

```
Imports System
Imports System.IO
Imports System.Text.RegularExpressions
Public Class Recipe

    Private Shared _Regex As Regex = New Regex(",\s*")

    Public Sub Run(ByVal fileName As String)
        Dim line As String
        Dim newLine As String
        Dim sr As StreamReader = File.OpenText(fileName)
        line = sr.ReadLine
        While Not line Is Nothing
            newLine = _Regex.Replace(line, "," + Environment.NewLine)
            Console.WriteLine("New string is: '{0}', original was: '{1}'", _
             newLine, _
             line))
            line = sr.ReadLine
        End While
        sr.Close()
    End Sub

    Public Shared Sub Main(ByVal args As String())
        Dim r As Recipe = New Recipe
        r.Run(args(0))
    End Sub

End Class
```

VBScript

```
Dim fso,s,re,line,newstr
Set fso = CreateObject("Scripting.FileSystemObject")
Set s = fso.OpenTextFile(WScript.Arguments.Item(0), 1, True)
Set re = New RegExp
re.Pattern = ",\s*"
re.Global = True
Do While Not s.AtEndOfStream
    line = s.ReadLine()
    newstr = re.Replace(line, "," + VBNewLine)
    WScript.Echo "New string '" & newstr & "', original '" & line & "'"
Loop
s.Close
```

WORDS AND TEXT

How It Works

This recipe uses a character class and a qualifier to enhance the expression to make the results a little cleaner. Here's a breakdown of the match expression:

,	is a comma followed by . . .
\s	a space . . .
*	none or many times.

The replacement expression is simply as follows:

,	is a comma followed by . . .
. . .	the appropriate constant for a newline (in other words, `Environment.NewLine` or `VBNewLine`).

The spaces after the comma go away when the replacement is made. Each line will end with a comma.

1-25. Joining Lines in a File

You can use this recipe for combining lines in a file but splitting them with another character such as a comma. For example, a file with lines such as this:

```
one
ring
to
rule
```

becomes the following:

```
one, ring, to, rule
```

.NET Framework

C#

```csharp
using System;
using System.IO;
using System.Text.RegularExpressions;

public class Recipe
{
    private static Regex _Regex = new Regex( "\r\n" );
    public void Run(string fileName)
    {
        String line;
        String newLine;
        using (StreamReader sr = new StreamReader(fileName))
        {
            if(null != (line = sr.ReadToEnd()))
            {
                newLine = _Regex.Replace(line, @", ");
                Console.WriteLine("New string is: '{0}', original was: '{1}'",
                    newLine,
                    line));
            }
        }
    }

    public static void Main( string[] args )
    {
        Recipe r = new Recipe();
        r.Run(args[0]);
    }
}
```

Visual Basic .NET

```
Imports System
Imports System.IO
Imports System.Text.RegularExpressions
Public Class Recipe

    Private Shared _Regex As Regex = New Regex("\r\n")

    Public Sub Run(ByVal fileName As String)
        Dim line As String
        Dim newLine As String
        Dim sr As StreamReader = File.OpenText(fileName)
        line = sr.ReadToEnd
        If Not line Is Nothing
            newLine = _Regex.Replace(line, ", ")
            Console.WriteLine("New string is: '{0}', original was: '{1}'", _
             newLine, _
             line))
            line = sr.ReadLine
        End If
        sr.Close()
    End Sub

    Public Shared Sub Main(ByVal args As String())
        Dim r As Recipe = New Recipe
        r.Run(args(0))
    End Sub

End Class
```

VBScript

```
Dim fso,s,re,line,newstr
Set fso = CreateObject("Scripting.FileSystemObject")
Set s = fso.OpenTextFile(WScript.Arguments.Item(0), 1, True)
Set re = New RegExp
re.Pattern = "\r\n"
re.Global = True
line = s.ReadAll()
newstr = re.Replace(line, ", ")
WScript.Echo "New string '" & newstr & "', original '" & line & "'"
s.Close
```

How It Works

This recipe breaks down into very few parts:

\r	a carriage return . . .
\n	is a newline, replaced by . . .
,	a comma followed by . . .
<space>	a space.

1-26. Removing Everything on a Line After a Certain Character

In this recipe, everything after # on a line is going to be removed, including the # sign. This can be useful for deleting line comments from scripts. For example, the recipe will turn this:

```
# This is a test line
Keep me #but remove me
```

into this:

```
Keep me
```

.NET Framework

C#

```csharp
using System;
using System.IO;
using System.Text.RegularExpressions;

public class Recipe
{
    private static Regex _Regex = new Regex( @"#.*$" );
    public void Run(string fileName)
    {
        String line;
        String newLine;
        using (StreamReader sr = new StreamReader(fileName))
        {
            while(null != (line = sr.ReadLine()))
            {
                newLine = _Regex.Replace(line, "");
                Console.WriteLine("New string is: '{0}', original was: '{1}'",
                    newLine,
                    line));
            }
        }
    }

    public static void Main( string[] args )
    {
        Recipe r = new Recipe();
        r.Run(args[0]);
    }
}
```

Visual Basic .NET

```
Imports System
Imports System.IO
Imports System.Text.RegularExpressions
Public Class Recipe

    Private Shared _Regex As Regex = New Regex("#.*$")

    Public Sub Run(ByVal fileName As String)
        Dim line As String
        Dim newLine As String
        Dim sr As StreamReader = File.OpenText(fileName)
        line = sr.ReadLine
        While Not line Is Nothing
            newLine = _Regex.Replace(line, "")
            Console.WriteLine("New string is: '{0}', original was: '{1}'", _
             newLine, _
             line))
            line = sr.ReadLine
        End While
        sr.Close()
    End Sub

    Public Shared Sub Main(ByVal args As String())
        Dim r As Recipe = New Recipe
        r.Run(args(0))
    End Sub

End Class
```

VBScript

```
Dim fso,s,re,line,newstr
Set fso = CreateObject("Scripting.FileSystemObject")
Set s = fso.OpenTextFile(WScript.Arguments.Item(0), 1, True)
Set re = New RegExp
re.Pattern = "#.*$"
Do While Not s.AtEndOfStream
    line = s.ReadLine()
    newstr = re.Replace(line, "")
    WScript.Echo "New string '" & newstr & "', original '" & line & "'"
Loop
s.Close
```

JavaScript

```
<html>
<head>
<title></title>
</head>
<body>
<form name="form1">
    <input type="text" name="txtInput" />
    <div id="lblResult"></div>
    <script language="javascript">
        function replace() {
            document.getElementById('lblResult').innerHTML = ➥
document.form1.txtInput.value.replace(/#.*$/, "");
        }
    </script>
    <input type="button" name="btnSubmit" onclick="replace()" value="Go" />
</form>
</body>
</html>
```

How It Works

You can break the recipe down like this:

followed by . . .

.   any character . . .

*   any number of times, until . . .

$ the end of the line.

The main concept in this expression is the use of the . wildcard, which matches any character. Using .* together is something you have to be careful with because it matches any character any number of times. Regular expressions are best when they're as specific as possible, even though they can be very generic.

CHAPTER 2

■■■

URLs and Paths

The recipes in this chapter focus on uniform resource locators (URLs) and file paths. These recipes can come in handy when you're trying to extract filenames, extensions, or hostnames.

Recipes 2-1 through 2-5 demonstrate how to extract and validate various parts of uniform resource identifiers (URIs) and URLs, such as the hostname (recipe 2-2) and the query string (recipe 2-5). They come together in recipe 2-6, which looks for valid URLs and adds a Hypertext Markup Language (HTML) anchor tag to the URL. URLs are subsets of URIs. RFC 2396 describes the syntax for URIs in detail. Where feasible, the regular expressions shown in this chapter enforce the rules in RFC 2396, which you can view at `http://www.ietf.org/rfc/rfc2396.txt`. It's important to note that URIs are composed of US-ASCII text characters. Hence, you'll see similar ranges in many of the examples in this chapter.

Recipes 2-7 through 2-11 demonstrate how to extract and validate various parts of file paths, including file paths with drive letters (recipe 2-7) and UNC hostnames (recipe 2-8).

While using regular expressions to extract and validate URLs and paths, keep in mind that the .NET Framework provides many ways of working with these objects. The `UriBuilder` class, for example, is excellent for extracting parts of URLs such as hostnames and paths. Similarly, the `FileInfo` class available as part of the .NET Framework is excellent for getting directory names, extension names, and other parts of file paths. You can find out more about these classes on the MSDN site at `http://msdn.microsoft.com`.

2-1. Extracting the Scheme from a URI

You can use this recipe to extract a scheme from a URI. This recipe assumes the input is a URI only.

.NET Framework

C#

```csharp
using System;
using System.IO;
using System.Text.RegularExpressions;

public class Recipe
{
    private static Regex _Regex = new Regex( @"^(?<scheme>[a-z][-a-z\d+.]+):",
        RegexOptions.IgnoreCase);

    public void Run(string fileName)
    {
        String line;
        using (StreamReader sr = new StreamReader(fileName))
        {
            while(null != (line = sr.ReadLine()))
            {
                if ( _Regex.IsMatch(line))
                {
                    Console.WriteLine("Found scheme:  '{0}'",➥
_Regex.Match(line).Result("${scheme}"));
                }
            }
        }
    }

    public static void Main( string[] args )
    {
        Recipe r = new Recipe();
        r.Run(args[0]);
    }
}
```

Visual Basic .NET

```vbnet
Imports System
Imports System.IO
Imports System.Text.RegularExpressions
Public Class Recipe
```

```
    Private Shared _Regex As Regex = New Regex("^(?<scheme>[a-z][-a-z\d+.]+):")

    Public Sub Run(ByVal fileName As String)
        Dim line As String
        Dim newLine As String
        Dim sr As StreamReader = File.OpenText(fileName)
        line = sr.ReadLine
        While Not line Is Nothing
            If _Regex.IsMatch(line) Then
                Console.WriteLine("Captured value '{0}'", ➥
_Regex.Match(line).Result("${scheme}"))
            End If
            line = sr.ReadLine
        End While
        sr.Close()
    End Sub

    Public Shared Sub Main(ByVal args As String())
        Dim r As Recipe = New Recipe
        r.Run(args(0))
    End Sub

End Class
```

VBScript

```
Dim fso,s,re,line,newstr
Set fso = CreateObject("Scripting.FileSystemObject")
Set s = fso.OpenTextFile(WScript.Arguments.Item(0), 1, True)
Set re = New RegExp
re.Pattern = "^([a-z][-a-z\d+.]+):.*$"
Do While Not s.AtEndOfStream
    line = s.ReadLine()
    newstr = re.Replace(line, "$1")
    WScript.Echo "New string '" & newstr & "', original '" & line & "'"
Loop
s.Close
```

How It Works

According to RFC 2396, the scheme is the part of the URI that describes the namespace of the URI. Many schemes are named after protocols, which is the case with Hypertext Transfer Protocol (HTTP), as you'll see later in this chapter. Other common schemes are File Transfer Protocol (FTP) and Server Message Block (SMB). The scheme must start with an alpha character from *a* to *z* (according to RFC 2396, schemes are limited to US-ASCII) but after that can include an alpha character, a digit, a plus sign (+), a period (.), or a hyphen (-). Schemes are delimited from the rest of the URI by a colon.

URLS AND PATHS

You can break the expression down as follows:

^	the beginning of a line, followed by . . .
(?<scheme>	a group named *scheme* that contains . . .
[a-z]	a character class that contains the letters from *a* to *z*, followed by . . .
[-a-z\d+.]	a character class that contains a hyphen, the letters from *a* to *z*, digits, a plus, or a period . . .
+	found one or more times . . .
)	the end of the named group, followed by . . .
:	a colon.

2-2. Extracting Domain Labels from URLs

This recipe extracts a domain label such as www.example.com from a URL such as
http://www.example.com. This recipe assumes the input is a valid URL.

.NET Framework

C#

```csharp
using System;
using System.IO;
using System.Text.RegularExpressions;

public class Recipe
{
    private static Regex _Regex = new Regex( @"://(?<host>([a-z\d][-a-z\d]*➡
[a-z\d]\.)+[a-z][-a-z\d]*[a-z])" );

    public void Run(string fileName)
    {
        String line;
        using (StreamReader sr = new StreamReader(fileName))
        {
            while(null != (line = sr.ReadLine()))
            {
                if ( _Regex.IsMatch(line))
                {
                    Console.WriteLine("Found host:  '{0}'",
                        _Regex.Match(line).Result("${host}"));
                }
            }
        }
    }

    public static void Main( string[] args )
    {
        Recipe r = new Recipe();
        r.Run(args[0]);
    }
}
```

Visual Basic .NET

```vbnet
Imports System
Imports System.IO
Imports System.Text.RegularExpressions
Public Class Recipe
```

```vbnet
        Private Shared _Regex As Regex = New Regex("://(?<host>([a-z\d][-a-z\d]➥
*[a-z\d]\.)*[a-z][-a-z\d]+[a-z])")

    Public Sub Run(ByVal fileName As String)
        Dim line As String
        Dim newLine As String
        Dim sr As StreamReader = File.OpenText(fileName)
        line = sr.ReadLine
        While Not line Is Nothing
            If _Regex.IsMatch(line) Then
                Console.WriteLine("Captured value '{0}'",➥
_Regex.Match(line).Result("${host}"))
            End If
            line = sr.ReadLine
        End While
        sr.Close()
    End Sub

    Public Shared Sub Main(ByVal args As String())
        Dim r As Recipe = New Recipe
        r.Run(args(0))
    End Sub

End Class
```

VBScript

```vbscript
Dim fso,s,re,line,newstr
Set fso = CreateObject("Scripting.FileSystemObject")
Set s = fso.OpenTextFile(WScript.Arguments.Item(0), 1, True)
Set re = New RegExp
re.Pattern = "^.*://(([a-z\d][-a-z\d]*[a-z\d]\.)+[a-z][-a-z\d]*[a-z]).*$"
Do While Not s.AtEndOfStream
    line = s.ReadLine()
    If re.Test(line) Then
        newstr = re.Replace(line, "$1")
        WScript.Echo "New string '" & newstr & "', original '" & line & "'"
    End If
Loop
s.Close
```

JavaScript

```html
<html>
<head>
<title></title>
</head>
<body>
<form name="form1">
    <input type="text" name="txtInput" />
    <div id="lblResult"></div>
    <script language="javascript">
        function replace() {
            document.getElementById('lblResult').innerHTML =
document.form1.txtInput.value.replace(/^.*:\/\/(([a-z\d][-a-z\d]*[a-z\d]\.)+➡
[a-z][-a-z\d]*[a-z])?.*$/, "$1");
        }
    </script>
    <input type="button" name="btnSubmit" onclick="replace()" value="Go" />
</form>
</body>
</html>
```

How It Works

RFC 1035, under the "Preferred Name Syntax" section, describes that domain labels should begin with a letter, end with a letter or digit, and contain a letter, digit, or hyphen. In RFC 1123, the requirement for the first character in a domain label is relaxed to also include a digit. In URLs, the domain label is delimited from the scheme by : and //.

Here's the expression broken down:

://	a colon and two slashes, which are used to assume the beginning of a domain label, followed by . . .
(?<host>	a group named *host* that contains . . .
(	another group that contains . . .
[a-z\d]	a character class that matches a letter or digit . . .
[-a-z\d]*	another character class that matches a hyphen, letter, or digit . . .
[a-z\d]	a character class that matches a letter or digit . . .
\.	a dot (period) . . .
)	the end of the first group . . .
+	found one or more times.

The domain label is followed by the top-level domain, which has similar rules; according to RFC 2396, it should start with a letter; contain a letter, hyphen, or digit; and end with a letter or digit. Here's that part of the expression broken down:

`[a-z]`	a character class that matches a letter from *a* to *z*, followed by . . .
`[-a-z\d]`	a character class that matches a hyphen, letter, or digit . . .
`*`	found any number of times . . .
`[a-z\d]`	a letter or digit . . .
`)`	the end of the group labeled *host*.

Variations

You can modify this expression to double-check for `http://` or `https://` at the beginning of the string to make sure it's an HTTP or a secure HTTP URL. I didn't do that in this recipe for brevity, but it doesn't hurt to make the expression as specific as you can.

2-3. Extracting the Port from a URL

This recipe extracts the port number for a URL, if the port is found in the URL. For example,
from the URL http://www.example.com:8080/index.html, this recipe extracts 8080. This recipe
assumes the input is a valid URL.

.NET Framework

C#

```
using System;
using System.IO;
using System.Text.RegularExpressions;

public class Recipe
{
    private static Regex _Regex = new Regex( @":(?<port>\d{1,})" );

    public void Run(string fileName)
    {
        String line;
        using (StreamReader sr = new StreamReader(fileName))
        {
            while(null != (line = sr.ReadLine()))
            {
                if ( _Regex.IsMatch(line))
                {
                    Console.WriteLine("Found protocol:  '{0}'", ➥
_Regex.Match(line).Result("${port}"));
                }
            }
        }
    }

    public static void Main( string[] args )
    {
        Recipe r = new Recipe();
        r.Run(args[0]);
    }
}
```

Visual Basic .NET

```
Imports System
Imports System.IO
Imports System.Text.RegularExpressions
Public Class Recipe
```

```vbnet
    Private Shared _Regex As Regex = New Regex(":(?<port>\d{1,})")

    Public Sub Run(ByVal fileName As String)
        Dim line As String
        Dim newLine As String
        Dim sr As StreamReader = File.OpenText(fileName)
        line = sr.ReadLine
        While Not line Is Nothing
            If (_Regex.IsMatch(line)) Then
                Console.WriteLine("Captured value '{0}'",
                    _Regex.Match(line).Result("${port}"))
            End If
            line = sr.ReadLine
        End While
        sr.Close()
    End Sub

    Public Shared Sub Main(ByVal args As String())
        Dim r As Recipe = New Recipe
        r.Run(args(0))
    End Sub

End Class
```

VBScript

```vbscript
Dim fso,s,re,line,newstr
Set fso = CreateObject("Scripting.FileSystemObject")
Set s = fso.OpenTextFile(WScript.Arguments.Item(0), 1, True)
Set re = New RegExp
re.Pattern = "^.*:(\d{1,}).*$"
Do While Not s.AtEndOfStream
    line = s.ReadLine()
    If re.Test(line) Then
        newstr = re.Replace(line, "$1")
        WScript.Echo "New string '" & newstr & "', original '" & line & "'"
    End If
Loop
s.Close
```

JavaScript

```html
<html>
<head>
<title></title>
</head>
<body>
```

```
<form name="form1">
    <input type="text" name="txtInput" />
    <div id="lblResult"></div>
    <script language="javascript">
        function replace() {
            document.getElementById('lblResult').innerHTML = ➥
document.form1.txtInput.value.replace(/^.*:(\d{1,}).*$/, "$1");
        }
    </script>
    <input type="button" name="btnSubmit" onclick="replace()" value="Go" />
</form>
</body>
</html>
```

How It Works

According to RFC 2396, a port can contain a digit and is delimited from the domain label by a colon. This makes the recipe relatively short:

:	a colon, followed by . . .
(?<port>	a group named *port* that contains . . .
\d	a digit . . .
{1,}	found one or more times (see the "Variations" section) . . .
)	the end of the group.

Variations

For brevity, this expression doesn't check the first part of the URL to make sure it's a valid one. You can add this functionality to the expression by adding the parts in the previous recipes in this chapter to check for a valid scheme and domain label.

Also, + would work fine in place of {1,} in this example, but I wanted to demonstrate how to use numeric ranges as a reminder that you have many ways to do things in regular expressions.

■**See Also** 4-1, 4-2, 4-3, 4-4, 4-5, 4-6, 4-8, 4-11, 4-12, 4-13, 4-14, 4-15, 4-17, 4-19

URLS AND PATHS

2-4. Extracting the Path from a URL

This recipe extracts the path from a URL. It assumes that the input is a valid URL.

.NET Framework

C#

```
using System;
using System.IO;
using System.Text.RegularExpressions;

public class Recipe
{
    private static Regex _Regex = new Regex( @"://[^/]+/(?<path>[^?\s<>#""]+)" );

    public void Run(string fileName)
    {
        String line;
        using (StreamReader sr = new StreamReader(fileName))
        {
            while(null != (line = sr.ReadLine()))
            {
                if (_Regex.IsMatch(line))
                {
                    Console.WriteLine("Found path:   '{0}'", ➥
_Regex.Match(line).Result("${path}"));
                }
            }
        }
    }

    public static void Main( string[] args )
    {
        Recipe r = new Recipe();
        r.Run(args[0]);
    }
}
```

Visual Basic .NET

```
Imports System
Imports System.IO
Imports System.Text.RegularExpressions
Public Class Recipe

    Private Shared _Regex As Regex = New Regex("://[^/]+/(?<path>[^?\s<>#""]+)")
```

```
    Public Sub Run(ByVal fileName As String)
        Dim line As String
        Dim newLine As String
        Dim sr As StreamReader = File.OpenText(fileName)
        line = sr.ReadLine
        While Not line Is Nothing
            If (_Regex.IsMatch(line)) Then
                Console.WriteLine("Captured value '{0}'", ➡
_Regex.Match(line).Result("${path}"))
            End If
            line = sr.ReadLine
        End While
        sr.Close()
    End Sub

    Public Shared Sub Main(ByVal args As String())
        Dim r As Recipe = New Recipe
        r.Run(args(0))
    End Sub

End Class
```

VBScript

```
Dim fso,s,re,line,newstr
Set fso = CreateObject("Scripting.FileSystemObject")
Set s = fso.OpenTextFile(WScript.Arguments.Item(0), 1, True)
Set re = New RegExp
re.Pattern = ".*://[^/]+/([^?\s<>#""]+).*"
Do While Not s.AtEndOfStream
    line = s.ReadLine()
    If re.Test(line) Then
        newstr = re.Replace(line, "$1")
        WScript.Echo "New string '" & newstr & "', original '" & line & "'"
    End If
Loop
s.Close
```

JavaScript

```
<html>
<head>
<title></title>
</head>
<body>
<form name="form1">
    <input type="text" name="txtInput" />
```

```
<div id="lblResult"></div>
<script language="javascript">
    function replace() {
        document.getElementById('lblResult').innerHTML = ➥
document.form1.txtInput.value.replace(/.*:\/\/[^\/]+\/([^?\s<>#""]+).*/, "$1");
    }
</script>
<input type="button" name="btnSubmit" onclick="replace()" value="Go" />
</form>
</body>
</html>
```

How It Works

This recipe grabs everything after the first / up to the end of the path, which can be either up to the first space or up to the first ?. It does a check for characters that aren't allowed in URIs according to RFC 2396, which are <, >, #, and ".

The part of this expression that makes sure the / that's found is actually the delimiter between the domain or domain/port combination is ://[^/]+/. It breaks down as follows:

://	a colon and two slashes, which indicate the beginning of the domain label . . .
[^/]	a character class that matches anything that isn't a slash . . .
+	found one or more times . . .
/	a slash.

The next part of the expression matches any valid URL characters, up to the first delimiter. Other than the ?, which is the delimiter that separates the query string from the rest of the URL, and a space (\s), which isn't allowed in URLs, delimiters are those characters mentioned earlier: <, >, #, and ". This is how that part breaks down:

(	a group that contains . . .
[^?\s<>#"]	a character class that doesn't match a question mark, whitespace, <, >, +, or " . . .
+	found one or more times . . .
)	the end of the group.

Variations

I left a lot out at the beginning of the expression to focus on the part of it that matches the path. If you want to be more exact about making sure the URL looks valid up to the point of the path, use the recipes found earlier in this chapter to match schemes, domain labels, and ports.

See Also 3-5, 3-6, 3-7, 3-8, 4-18, 4-19

2-5. Extracting Query Strings from URLs

This recipe extracts the query string from a URL, assuming the input is a valid URL. The query string is every valid URI character found after the first ? in the URL.

.NET Framework

C#

```
using System;
using System.IO;
using System.Text.RegularExpressions;

public class Recipe
{
    private static Regex _Regex = new Regex( "\\?(?<query>[^<>#\"]+)" );

    public void Run(string fileName)
    {
        String line;
        using (StreamReader sr = new StreamReader(fileName))
        {
            while(null != (line = sr.ReadLine()))
            {
                if (_Regex.IsMatch(line))
                {
                    Console.WriteLine("Found protocol:  '{0}'", ➥
_Regex.Match(line).Result("${query}"));
                }
            }
        }
    }

    public static void Main( string[] args )
    {
        Recipe r = new Recipe();
        r.Run(args[0]);
    }
}
```

Visual Basic .NET

```
Imports System
Imports System.IO
Imports System.Text.RegularExpressions
Public Class Recipe
```

```vbnet
    Private Shared _Regex As Regex = New Regex("\?(?<query>[^<>#""]+)")

    Public Sub Run(ByVal fileName As String)
        Dim line As String
        Dim newLine As String
        Dim sr As StreamReader = File.OpenText(fileName)
        line = sr.ReadLine
        While Not line Is Nothing
            If _Regex.IsMatch(line) Then
                Console.WriteLine("Captured value '{0}'", ➡
_Regex.Match(line).Result("${query}"))
            End If
            line = sr.ReadLine
        End While
        sr.Close()
    End Sub

    Public Shared Sub Main(ByVal args As String())
        Dim r As Recipe = New Recipe
        r.Run(args(0))
    End Sub

End Class
```

VBScript

```vbscript
Dim fso,s,re,line,newstr
Set fso = CreateObject("Scripting.FileSystemObject")
Set s = fso.OpenTextFile(WScript.Arguments.Item(0), 1, True)
Set re = New RegExp
re.Pattern = ".*\?([^<>#""]+)"
Do While Not s.AtEndOfStream
    line = s.ReadLine()
    If re.Test(line) Then
        newstr = re.Replace(line, "$1")
        WScript.Echo "New string '" & newstr & "', original '" & line & "'"
    End If
Loop
s.Close
```

JavaScript

```html
<html>
<head>
<title></title>
</head>
<body>
```

URLS AND PATHS

```
<form name="form1">
    <input type="text" name="txtInput" />
    <div id="lblResult"></div>
    <script language="javascript">
        function replace() {
            document.getElementById('lblResult').innerHTML = ➥
document.form1.txtInput.value.replace(/.*\?([^<>#"]+)/, "$1");
        }
    </script>
    <input type="button" name="btnSubmit" onclick="replace()" value="Go" />
</form>
</body>
</html>
```

How It Works

This recipe uses basically the same negated character class as the regex in recipe 2-4, with the exception of the ?:

\?	a question mark, escaped so it represents a literal question mark . . .
(	a group that contains . . .
[^<>#"]	a character class that doesn't match the URI-excluded characters <, >, #, and " . . .
+	found one or more times . . .
)	the end of the group.

RFC 2396 lists the excluded characters.

Variations

Some characters are considered "unwise" for use in URIs; however, I've seen working implementations that include characters such as curly braces. The unwise characters are {, }, |, \, ^, [,], and `. If you want to make sure these characters aren't found in your URIs, expand the negated character class to [^<>#"{}|\^\[\]`]. Remember, depending on the language you use, you may have to add some characters to escape the double quote and backward slash.

2-6. Replacing URLs with Links

This recipe combines all the regexes so far in this chapter to look for valid URLs in text and replace them with anchor tags. For instance, given the following text:

```
My homepage is http://www.example.com.
```

this recipe will print the following:

```
My homepage is <a href="http://www.example.com">http://www.example.com</a>
```

.NET Framework

C#

```csharp
using System;
using System.IO;
using System.Text.RegularExpressions;

public class Recipe
{
    private static string hostRegex = @"([a-z\d][-a-z\d]*[a-z\d]\.)*➥
[a-z][-a-z\d]*[a-z]";
    private static string portRegex = @"(:\d{1,})?";
    private static string pathRegex = @"(/[^\s?]+)?";
    private static string queryRegex = "(\\?[^<>#\"\\s]+)?";

    private static string fullRegex = @"(?:(?<=^)|(?<=\s))((ht|f)tps?://" + ➥
hostRegex + portRegex + pathRegex + queryRegex + ")" ;

    private static Regex _Regex = new Regex(fullRegex, RegexOptions.IgnoreCase);

    public void Run(string fileName)
    {
        String line;
        String newLine;
        using (StreamReader sr = new StreamReader(fileName))
        {
            while(null != (line = sr.ReadLine()))
            {
                newLine = _Regex.Replace(line, "<a href=\"$1\">$1</a>");
                Console.WriteLine(String.Format("New string is: '{0}', ➥
original was: '{1}'",
                    newLine,
                    line));
            }
        }
    }
```

```
    public static void Main( string[] args )
    {
        Recipe r = new Recipe();
        r.Run(args[0]);
    }
}
```

Visual Basic .NET

```
Imports System
Imports System.IO
Imports System.Text.RegularExpressions
Public Class Recipe

    Private Const hostRegex = "([a-z\d][-a-z\d]*[a-z\d]\.)*[a-z][-a-z\d]*[a-z]"
    Private Const portRegex = "(:\d{1,})?"
    Private Const pathRegex = "(/[^?<>#""\s]+)?"
    Private Const queryRegex = "(\?[^<>#""\s]+)?"

    Private Shared _Regex As Regex = New Regex("(?:(?<=^)|(?<=\s))((ht|f)tps?://" _
& hostRegex & portRegex & pathRegex & queryRegex & ")", RegexOptions.IgnoreCase)

    Public Sub Run(ByVal fileName As String)
        Dim line As String
        Dim newLine As String
        Dim sr As StreamReader = File.OpenText(fileName)
        line = sr.ReadLine
        While Not line Is Nothing
            newLine = _Regex.Replace(line, "cow")
            Console.WriteLine("New string is: '{0}', original was: '{1}'", _
             newLine, _
             line)
            line = sr.ReadLine
        End While
        sr.Close()
    End Sub

    Public Shared Sub Main(ByVal args As String())
        Dim r As Recipe = New Recipe
        r.Run(args(0))
    End Sub

End Class
```

VBScript

```
Dim fso,s,re,line,newstr
Private Const hostRegex = "([a-z\d][-a-z\d]*[a-z\d]\.)*[a-z][-a-z\d]*[a-z]"
```

```
Private Const portRegex = "(:\d{1,})?"
Private Const pathRegex = "(/[^?<>#""\s]+)?"
Private Const queryRegex = "(\?[^<>#""\s]+)?"
Set fso = CreateObject("Scripting.FileSystemObject")
Set s = fso.OpenTextFile(WScript.Arguments.Item(0), 1, True)
Set re = New RegExp
re.Pattern = "((ht|f)tps?://" & hostRegex & portRegex & pathRegex & queryRegex & ")"
re.IgnoreCase = True
Do While Not s.AtEndOfStream
    line = s.ReadLine()
    If re.Test(line) Then
        newstr = re.Replace(line, "<a href=""$1"">$1</a>")
        WScript.Echo "New string '" & newstr & "', original '" & line & "'"
    End If
Loop
s.Close
```

JavaScript

```
<html>
<head>
<title></title>
</head>
<body>
<form name="form1">
    <input type="text" name="txtInput" />
    <div id="lblResult"></div>
    <script language="javascript">
        function replace() {
            var hostRegex = "([a-z\\d][-a-z\\d]*[a-z\\d]\.)*[a-z][-a-z\\d]*[a-z]";
            var portRegex = "(:\\d{1,})?";
            var pathRegex = "(\/[^?<>#\"\\s]+)?";
            var queryRegex = "(\\?[^<>#\"\\s]+)?";
            var fullRegex = "((ht|f)tps?:\/\/" + hostRegex + portRegex + ➥
pathRegex + queryRegex + ")";
            alert(fullRegex);
            var re = new RegExp(fullRegex);
            re.ignoreCase = true;
            document.getElementById('lblResult').innerHTML = ➥
document.form1.txtInput.value.replace(re, "<a href=\"$1\">$1</a>");
        }
    </script>
    <input type="button" name="btnSubmit" onclick="replace()" value="Go" />
</form>
</body>
</html>
```

How It Works

This regex is simply a compilation of the previous five recipes. When it's all put together as one string, though, it becomes quite a bit more difficult to read and understand. This is why I assigned each of the regexes to a string and then concatenated the string with a regex that looks for a specific scheme. I modified the scheme expression to look for *http*, *https*, *ftp*, or *ftps* only. The following is the expression broken down; see the previous chapters for an explanation of the other parts:

(	a group that contains . . .
ht	*h, t* . . .
|	or . . .
f	*f* . . .
)	the end of the group, followed by . . .
tp	*t* and *p*, then . . .
s?	*s*, which can appear at most once . . .
:	a colon (which is the delimiter for the scheme), followed by . . .
/	a slash and . . .
/	another slash.

See Also 1-4, 4-1, 4-2, 4-5, 4-10, 4-11, 4-12, 4-15, 4-16, 4-17, 4-21, 4-22

2-7. Extracting the Drive Letter

This recipe extracts the drive letter from a path, assuming the input to the script is a valid file path.

.NET Framework

C#

```
using System;
using System.IO;
using System.Text.RegularExpressions;

public class Recipe
{
    private static Regex _Regex =
        new Regex(@"^(?<drive>[a-z]):\\?", RegexOptions.IgnoreCase);

    public void Run(string fileName)
    {
        String line;
        using (StreamReader sr = new StreamReader(fileName))
        {
            while(null != (line = sr.ReadLine()))
            {
                if (_Regex.IsMatch(line))
                {
                    Console.WriteLine("Found drive:  '{0}'", ➥
_Regex.Match(line).Result("${drive}"));
                }
            }
        }
    }

    public static void Main( string[] args )
    {
        Recipe r = new Recipe();
        r.Run(args[0]);
    }
}

Imports System
Imports System.IO
Imports System.Text.RegularExpressions
Public Class Recipe
```

```
    Private Shared _Regex As Regex = New Regex("^(?<drive>[a-z]):\\?", _
        RegexOptions.IgnoreCase)

    Public Sub Run(ByVal fileName As String)
        Dim line As String
        Dim newLine As String
        Dim sr As StreamReader = File.OpenText(fileName)
        line = sr.ReadLine
        While Not line Is Nothing
            If _Regex.IsMatch(line) Then
                Console.WriteLine("Captured value '{0}'", _
                    _Regex.Match(line).Result("${drive}"))
            End If
            line = sr.ReadLine
        End While
        sr.Close()
    End Sub

    Public Shared Sub Main(ByVal args As String())
        Dim r As Recipe = New Recipe
        r.Run(args(0))
    End Sub

End Class
```

VBScript

```
Dim fso,s,re,line,newstr
Set fso = CreateObject("Scripting.FileSystemObject")
Set s = fso.OpenTextFile(WScript.Arguments.Item(0), 1, True)
Set re = New RegExp
re.Pattern = "^([a-z]):\\?.*"
re.IgnoreCase = True
Do While Not s.AtEndOfStream
    line = s.ReadLine()
    If re.Test(line) Then
        newstr = re.Replace(line, "$1")
        WScript.Echo "New string '" & newstr & "', original '" & line & "'"
    End If
Loop
s.Close
```

JavaScript

```
<html>
<head>
<title></title>
</head>
<body>
<form name="form1">
    <input type="text" name="txtInput" />
    <div id="lblResult"></div>
    <script language="javascript">
        function replace() {
            document.getElementById('lblResult').innerHTML = ➡
document.form1.txtInput.value.replace(/^([a-z]):\\?.*/i, "$1");
        }
    </script>
    <input type="button" name="btnSubmit" onclick="replace()" value="Go" />
</form>
</body>
</html>
```

How It Works

This recipe works under the assumption that the drive letter is a single letter from *a* to *z* (which can be uppercase as well) delimited from the rest of the path by a colon or a colon and slash combination (: or :\). The .NET example, shown here, uses named groups for easy extraction with the Replace method:

^	the beginning of the line, followed by . . .
(?<drive>	a group named *drive* that contains . . .
[a-z]	a letter, from *a* to *z*, followed by . . .
)	the end of the named group and . . .
:	a colon and . . .
\	a slash (that may be escaped) . . .
?	found at most one time.

■**See Also** 1-1, 1-9, 1-12, 1-17, 1-21, 3-5, 3-6, 3-7, 3-8, 4-1, 4-2, 4-5, 4-7, 4-9, 4-10, 4-13, 4-14, 4-15, 4-16, 4-17, 4-18, 4-19, 4-20, 4-21, 4-22

2-8. Extracting UNC Hostnames

This recipe extracts the hostname from a valid UNC path. Given the path *myserver**files*, the recipe extracts *myserver*.

.NET Framework

C#

```
using System;
using System.IO;
using System.Text.RegularExpressions;

public class Recipe
{
    private static Regex _Regex = new Regex( ➥
@"\\(?<unc>[^~!@#$^&()=+\[\]{}\\|;:',<>/?]+)" );

    public void Run(string fileName)
    {
        String line;
        using (StreamReader sr = new StreamReader(fileName))
        {
            while(null != (line = sr.ReadLine()))
            {
                if (_Regex.IsMatch(line))
                {
                    Console.WriteLine("Found UNC hostname:  '{0}'", ➥
_Regex.Match(line).Result("${unc}"));
                }
            }
        }
    }

    public static void Main( string[] args )
    {
        Recipe r = new Recipe();
        r.Run(args[0]);
    }
}
```

Visual Basic .NET

```
Imports System
Imports System.IO
Imports System.Text.RegularExpressions
Public Class Recipe
```

```
        Private Shared _Regex As Regex = New ➡
Regex("\\\\(?<unc>[^~!@#$^&()=+\[\]{}\\|;:',<>/?]+)")

    Public Sub Run(ByVal fileName As String)
        Dim line As String
        Dim newLine As String
        Dim sr As StreamReader = File.OpenText(fileName)
        line = sr.ReadLine
        While Not line Is Nothing
            If (_Regex.IsMatch(line)) Then
                Console.WriteLine("Captured value '{0}'", _
                    _Regex.Match(line).Result("${unc}"))
            End If
            line = sr.ReadLine
        End While
        sr.Close()
    End Sub

    Public Shared Sub Main(ByVal args As String())
        Dim r As Recipe = New Recipe
        r.Run(args(0))
    End Sub

End Class
```

VBScript

```
Dim fso,s,re,line,newstr
Set fso = CreateObject("Scripting.FileSystemObject")
Set s = fso.OpenTextFile(WScript.Arguments.Item(0), 1, True)
Set re = New RegExp
re.Pattern = "\\\\([^~!@#$^&()=+\[\]{}\\|;:',<>/?]+).*"
Do While Not s.AtEndOfStream
    line = s.ReadLine()
    If re.Test(line) Then
        newstr = re.Replace(line, "$1")
        WScript.Echo "New string '" & newstr & "', original '" & line & "'"
    End If
Loop
s.Close
```

JavaScript

```
<html>
<head>
<title></title>
</head>
```

```
<body>
<form name="form1">
    <input type="text" name="txtInput" />
    <div id="lblResult"></div>
    <script language="javascript">
        function replace() {
            document.getElementById('lblResult').innerHTML = ➡
document.form1.txtInput.value.replace(➡
/\\\\([^~!@#$^&()=+\[\]{}\\|;:',<>\/?]+).*/, "$1");
        }
    </script>
    <input type="button" name="btnSubmit" onclick="replace()" value="Go" />
</form>
</body>
</html>
```

How It Works

This recipe works by simply matching characters that aren't invalid characters for hostnames. In Windows, hostnames can't contain the following characters: ~, !, @, #, $, ^, &, (,), =, +, [,], {, }, \, |, ;, :, ', ", <, >, /, and ?. The bulk of this expression, and the main source of its ugliness, is the negated character class that matches anything but these characters. This expression is as follows:

\\	two slashes that start the UNC path, followed by . . .
(	a group that contains . . .
[^~!@#$^&()=+\[\]{}\\|;:',<>\/?]	a character class that doesn't match the characters listed previously . . .
+	found one or more times . . .
)	the end of the group.

The regex doesn't have to check for a slash at the end of the path because that's one of the characters listed in the negated character class, so the regex will stop matching as soon as it finds it.

■ **See Also** 1-3, 1-10, 1-11, 1-14, 1-15, 3-1, 3-2, 3-5, 3-6, 4-4, 4-5, 4-7, 4-11, 4-18, 4-19, 4-20

2-9. Extracting Filenames from Paths

This recipe extracts text that could be a filename from a file path. It assumes the input is a valid path only.

.NET Framework

C#

```
using System;
using System.IO;
using System.Text.RegularExpressions;

public class Recipe
{
    private static Regex _Regex = new Regex( ➥
"(?<path>(\\\\(?<file>[^\\\\/:*?\"<>|.][^\\\\/:*?\"<>|]*))+)" );

    public void Run(string fileName)
    {
        String line;
        using (StreamReader sr = new StreamReader(fileName))
        {
            while(null != (line = sr.ReadLine()))
            {
                if (_Regex.IsMatch(line))
                {
                    Console.WriteLine("Found file '{0}' in path '{1}'",
                        _Regex.Match(line).Result("${file}"),
                        _Regex.Match(line).Result("${path}"));
                }
            }
        }
    }

    public static void Main( string[] args )
    {
        Recipe r = new Recipe();
        r.Run(args[0]);
    }
}
```

Visual Basic .NET

```
Imports System
Imports System.IO
Imports System.Text.RegularExpressions
Public Class Recipe

    Private Shared _Regex As Regex = New ➡
Regex("(?<path>(\\(?<file>[^\\/:*?""<>|.][^\\/:*?""<>|]*))+)")

    Public Sub Run(ByVal fileName As String)
        Dim line As String
        Dim newLine As String
        Dim sr As StreamReader = File.OpenText(fileName)
        line = sr.ReadLine
        While Not line Is Nothing
            If _Regex.IsMatch(line) Then
                Console.WriteLine("Found file '{0}' in path '{1}'", _
                    _Regex.Match(line).Result("${file}"), _
                    _Regex.Match(line).Result("${path}"))
            End If
            line = sr.ReadLine
        End While
        sr.Close()
    End Sub

    Public Shared Sub Main(ByVal args As String())
        Dim r As Recipe = New Recipe
        r.Run(args(0))
    End Sub

End Class
```

VBScript

```
Dim fso,s,re,line,newstr
Set fso = CreateObject("Scripting.FileSystemObject")
Set s = fso.OpenTextFile(WScript.Arguments.Item(0), 1, True)
Set re = New RegExp
re.Pattern = "^[^\\]+((\\([^\\/:*?""<>|.][^\\/:*?""<>|]*))+)"
Do While Not s.AtEndOfStream
    line = s.ReadLine()
    If re.Test(line) Then
        newstr = re.Replace(line, "$1")
        WScript.Echo "New string '" & newstr & "', original '" & line & "'"
    End If
Loop
s.Close
```

JavaScript

```
<html>
<head>
<title></title>
</head>
<body>
<form name="form1">
    <input type="text" name="txtInput" />
    <div id="lblResult"></div>
    <script language="javascript">
        function replace() {
            document.getElementById('lblResult').innerHTML = ➡
document.form1.txtInput.value.replace(➡
/^[^\\]+((\\([^\\\/:*?\"<>|.][^\\\/:*?\"<>|]*))+)/, "$1");
        }
    </script>
    <input type="button" name="btnSubmit" onclick="replace()" value="Go" />
</form>
</body>
</html>
```

How It Works

This recipe works by looking first for a \, which delimits either a server name or a drive letter from a file or path. The rest of the recipe is mostly a negated character class that matches anything except the invalid filename characters in Windows, which are \, /, :, *, ?, ", <, >, and |. Also, a rule is that Windows files and directories can't begin with a period (.), so what looks like repetition in this recipe is actually two character classes that differ only by a period. The expression breaks down as follows:

(?<path>	a group named *path* that contains . . .
(	another group that includes . . .
\\	a slash (escaped here) . . .
(?<file>	a group named *file* . . .
[^\\\/:*?""<>|.]	a character class that matches anything except the invalid filename characters, plus a dot . . .
[^\\\/:*?""<>|]	a character class that doesn't match invalid characters . . .
*	found zero or more times . . .
)	the end of the file group . . .
)	the end of the group . . .
+	that will appear one or more times . . .
)	the end of the path group.

This is where, depending on the purpose, it might be better to use a class that's provided by the language you're using if you need to determine whether the name represents a file or directory. For instance, given the text *C:\MyFile*, it's impossible to tell by looking at the text alone whether it's a file or a directory. If you need to know these details in .NET for instance, it's probably better for you to use the `FileInfo` class to get more information about the file.

2-10. Extracting Extensions from Filenames

This recipe extracts a file extension from a valid file path, if the extension exists.

.NET Framework

C#

```csharp
using System;
using System.IO;
using System.Text.RegularExpressions;

public class Recipe
{
    private static Regex _Regex = new Regex( ➥
"\\\\[^\\\\/:*?\"<>|]+\\.(?<ext>[^.\\\\/:*?\"<>|]+)" );

    public void Run(string fileName)
    {
        String line;
        using (StreamReader sr = new StreamReader(fileName))
        {
            while(null != (line = sr.ReadLine()))
            {
                if (_Regex.IsMatch(line))
                {
                    Console.WriteLine("Found protocol: '{0}'",
                        _Regex.Match(line).Result("${ext}"));
                }
            }
        }
    }

    public static void Main( string[] args )
    {
        Recipe r = new Recipe();
        r.Run(args[0]);
    }
}
```

```vbnet
Imports System
Imports System.IO
Imports System.Text.RegularExpressions
Public Class Recipe

    Private Shared _Regex As Regex = New ➥
Regex("\\[^\\/:*?""<>|]+\.(?<ext>[^.\\/:*?""<>|]+)")
```

```vbnet
    Public Sub Run(ByVal fileName As String)
        Dim line As String
        Dim newLine As String
        Dim sr As StreamReader = File.OpenText(fileName)
        line = sr.ReadLine
        While Not line Is Nothing
            If (_Regex.IsMatch(line)) Then
                Console.WriteLine("Captured value '{0}'", _
                    _Regex.Match(line).Result("${ext}"))
            End If
            line = sr.ReadLine
        End While
        sr.Close()
    End Sub

    Public Shared Sub Main(ByVal args As String())
        Dim r As Recipe = New Recipe
        r.Run(args(0))
    End Sub

End Class
```

VBScript

```vbscript
Dim fso,s,re,line,newstr
Set fso = CreateObject("Scripting.FileSystemObject")
Set s = fso.OpenTextFile(WScript.Arguments.Item(0), 1, True)
Set re = New RegExp
re.Pattern = "[^\\]+\\[^\\/:*?""<>|]+\.([^.\\/:*?""<>|]+)"
Do While Not s.AtEndOfStream
    line = s.ReadLine()
    If re.Test(line) Then
        newstr = re.Replace(line, "$1")
        WScript.Echo "New string '" & newstr & "', original '" & line & "'"
    End If
Loop
s.Close
```

JavaScript

```html
<html>
<head>
<title></title>
</head>
<body>
<form name="form1">
    <input type="text" name="txtInput" />
```

```
        <div id="lblResult"></div>
        <script language="javascript">
            function replace() {
                document.getElementById('lblResult').innerHTML = ➡
document.form1.txtInput.value.replace(➡
/[^\\]+\\[^\\\/:*?\"<>|]+\.([^.\\\/:*?\"<>|]+)/, "$1");
            }
        </script>
        <input type="button" name="btnSubmit" onclick="replace()" value="Go" />
    </form>
</body>
</html>
```

How It Works

This recipe looks for an extension in a file path. The first part of the expression will match everything up to the last dot in the path, making sure each character is valid along the way:

\\	a slash, followed by . . .
[^\\/:*?"<>|]	a character class that doesn't match invalid filename characters . . .
+	found one or more times.

The second part of the regex matches the extension, which starts at the last dot found in the file path and goes until the end of the path:

\.	a dot (.), escaped so it has literal meaning . . .
(?<ext>	a group named *ext* that contains . . .
[^.\\/:*?"<>|]	a character class that doesn't match an invalid filename character or another dot (.) . . .
+	found one or more times . . .
)	the end of the group.

CHAPTER 3

■■■

CSV and Tab-Delimited Files

The recipes in this chapter focus on working with tab-delimited and comma-separated-value (CSV) files. These handy recipes allow you to find lines with a specific number of fields and even give you the ability to transform tab-delimited files to CSV, and vice versa.

Before getting into the recipes, it's worth mentioning how tab-delimited and CSV files are put together and why a simple text replacement often doesn't cut it. It might be tempting to replace all commas in a CSV file with tabs and be done with it. However, this breaks fields that have commas embedded in them.

When a comma is included in a field in a CSV file, the field is wrapped with double quotes. Since double quotes have special meaning as text qualifiers, they're escaped in a CSV file by doubling them up. You can find more on the makeup of a properly formed CSV file at http://en.wikipedia.org/wiki/Comma-separated_values. I've also included some CSV files, made by exporting values from Microsoft Excel, as samples in the downloadable code available in the Downloads section at http://www.apress.com.

Tab-delimited files exported from Microsoft Excel actually follow a similar format, as they also show fields with commas (or tabs) enclosed in double quotes. Double quotes are also doubled up to denote literal double quotes that aren't acting as text qualifiers. Tab-delimited files that aren't exported from Microsoft Excel can't be expected to follow the same format, so the recipes here will make a couple extra passes to escape characters before making the conversion. Just remember, when working strictly with Microsoft Excel files, those extra steps are unnecessary.

Finally, the last few recipes in this chapter address fixed-width files and their conversion to CSV and tab-delimited formats. A handy variation in recipe 3-3 shows you how to remove whitespace from these files, which is bound to happen when working with conversions from fixed-width format.

3-1. Finding Valid CSV Records

You can use this recipe to isolate records in a CSV file that don't have the correct number of fields, which can sometimes be caused by commas appearing in fields, and so on.

.NET Framework

C#

```csharp
using System;
using System.IO;
using System.Text.RegularExpressions;

public class Recipe
{
    // Alternatively "([^,\"]+|\"([^\"]|\"\")*\")";
    private static string csvFieldRegex = @"([^,""]+|""([^""]|"""")*"")";
    private static Regex _Regex = new Regex(csvFieldRegex);

    public void Run(string fileName)
    {
        String line;
        int lineNbr = 0;
        using (StreamReader sr = new StreamReader(fileName))
        {
            while(null != (line = sr.ReadLine()))
            {
                lineNbr++;
                if (_Regex.Matches(line).Count == 3)
                {
                    Console.WriteLine("Found match '{0}' at line {1}",
                        line,
                        lineNbr);
                }
            }
        }
    }

    public static void Main( string[] args )
    {
        Recipe r = new Recipe();
        r.Run(args[0]);
    }
}
```

Visual Basic .NET

```
Imports System
Imports System.IO
Imports System.Text.RegularExpressions
Public Class Recipe

    Private Shared _Regex As Regex = New Regex("([^,""]+|""([^""]|"""")*"")")

    Public Sub Run(ByVal fileName As String)
        Dim line As String
        Dim sr As StreamReader = File.OpenText(fileName)
        line = sr.ReadLine
        While Not line Is Nothing
            If (_Regex.Matches(line).Count = 3) Then
                Console.WriteLine("Found match '{0}' at line {1}", _
                    line, _
                    lineNbr)
            End If
            line = sr.ReadLine
        End While
        sr.Close()
    End Sub

    Public Shared Sub Main(ByVal args As String())
        Dim r As Recipe = New Recipe
        r.Run(args(0))
    End Sub

End Class
```

VBScript

```
Dim fso,s,re,line,lineNbr
Set fso = CreateObject("Scripting.FileSystemObject")
Set s = fso.OpenTextFile(WScript.Arguments.Item(0), 1, True)
Set re = New RegExp
Const csvFieldRegex = "([^,""]+|""([^""]|"""")*"")"
re.Pattern = "^" + csvFieldRegex + "," + csvFieldRegex + "," + csvFieldRegex + "$"
lineNbr = 0
Do While Not s.AtEndOfStream
    line = s.ReadLine()
    lineNbr = lineNbr + 1
    If re.Test(line) Then
        WScript.Echo "Found match: '" & line & "' at line " & lineNbr
    End If
Loop
s.Close
```

CSV AND TAB-DELIMITED FILES

How It Works

This recipe works by searching for a certain number of valid CSV fields per line. The regex in this recipe represents a single field, and the features of each language manufacture an entire regex. This might be "cheating" a little, but it yields code that's a little easier to read. You'll be happier doing it this way if you're maintaining the code.

Take a look at the next line, which is a record from one of the sample files included in the downloadable code I used to write this book:

```
"Smith, ""Maddog"" Bob",123 Any St.,Anytown
```

Two types of fields are possible in this or any other valid CSV record: a field that isn't wrapped in quotes, such as Anytown in the previous line, and a field that's wrapped in quotes, such as "Smith, ""Maddog"" Bob".

To match these two types of fields, the regex ([^,"]+|"([^"]|"")*") looks for the two conditions: a field that isn't wrapped in quotes or a field that is wrapped in quotes. The part of the regex that looks for normal CSV fields is as follows:

[^,"]   a character class that matches anything that isn't a comma or a double quote . . .

*   found any number of times.

The two parts of the regex are separated by a pipe (|), which simply means "or." It allows the regex to match either condition. The second part of the expression looks for a field that's enclosed in double quotes. It's presumably enclosed in quotes in order to escape a comma, so it's not used as a field delimiter. The regex doesn't care particularly about the contents of the field—it's just making sure that if the field contains a double quote, the double quote is escaped with another one. The second part of the regex is as follows:

"   a double quote, followed by . . .

(a group that contains . . .

[^"]   any character that isn't a double quote . . .

| or . . .

""   an escaped double quote, followed by . . .

)   the end of the group . . .

*   where the group is found any number of times, ending in . . .

"   a double quote.

Variations

To improve performance with this particular recipe, you can use noncapturing parentheses. I didn't use them in the initial recipe because they make the expressions difficult to read. Using noncapturing parentheses, the expression (`[^",]+|"([^"]|"")*"`) becomes (`?:[^",]+|"(?:[^"]|"")*"`).

Also, for the sake of brevity, the initial recipe doesn't handle empty fields very well. Since an empty field is `,,`, just add it as another "or" condition in the expression. The expression used to handle empty fields is (`[^",]+|"([^"]|"")*"|,,`).

See Also 1-3, 1-8, 1-11, 1-16, 1-22, 2-6, 2-8, 2-9, 2-10, 4-2, 4-3, 4-6, 4-10, 4-11, 4-12, 4-13, 4-14, 4-15, 4-16, 4-22

3-2. Finding Valid Tab-Delimited Records

You can use this recipe to find records in a tab-delimited file that have three fields in them.

.NET Framework

C#

```
using System;
using System.IO;
using System.Text.RegularExpressions;

public class Recipe
{
    private static Regex _Regex = new Regex(@"[^\t]+");

    public void Run(string fileName)
    {
        String line;
        int lineNbr = 0;
        using (StreamReader sr = new StreamReader(fileName))
        {
            while(null != (line = sr.ReadLine()))
            {
                lineNbr++;
                if (_Regex.Matches(line).Count == 3)
                {
                    Console.WriteLine("Found match '{0}' at line {1}",
                        line,
                        lineNbr);
                }
            }
        }
    }

    public static void Main( string[] args )
    {
        Recipe r = new Recipe();
        r.Run(args[0]);
    }
}
```

Visual Basic .NET

```
Imports System
Imports System.IO
Imports System.Text.RegularExpressions
Public Class Recipe

    Private Shared _Regex As Regex = New Regex("[^\t]+")

    Public Sub Run(ByVal fileName As String)
        Dim line As String
        Dim lineNbr As Integer = 0
        Dim sr As StreamReader = File.OpenText(fileName)
        line = sr.ReadLine
        While Not line Is Nothing
            lineNbr = lineNbr + 1
            If (_Regex.Matches(line).Count = 3) Then
                Console.WriteLine("Found match '{0}' at line {1}", _
                    line, _
                    lineNbr)
            End If
            line = sr.ReadLine
        End While
        sr.Close()
    End Sub

    Public Shared Sub Main(ByVal args As String())
        Dim r As Recipe = New Recipe
        r.Run(args(0))
    End Sub

End Class
```

VBScript

```
Dim fso,s,re,line,lineNbr
Set fso = CreateObject("Scripting.FileSystemObject")
Set s = fso.OpenTextFile(WScript.Arguments.Item(0), 1, True)
Set re = New RegExp
re.Pattern = "^[^\t]+(\t[^\t]+){2}$"
lineNbr = 0
Do While Not s.AtEndOfStream
    line = s.ReadLine()
    lineNbr = lineNbr + 1
    If re.Test(line) Then
        WScript.Echo "Found match: '" & line & "' at line " & lineNbr
    End If
Loop
s.Close
```

How It Works

The .NET Framework uses the Matches property of the Regex class to find out how many matches were found in the string.

The expression is as follows:

[^\t]   any character that isn't a tab . . .

*   found any number of times.

3-3. Changing CSV Files to Tab-Delimited Files

This recipe shows you how to change CSV files to tab-delimited files, taking care to not replace commas that are inside quotes.

.NET Framework

C#

```csharp
using System;
using System.IO;
using System.Text.RegularExpressions;

public class Recipe
{
    private static Regex _Regex = new Regex( ➡
",(?=(?:[^\"]*$)|(?:[^\"]*\"[^\"]*\"[^\"]*)*$)" );
    public void Run(string fileName)
    {
        String line;
        String newLine;
        using (StreamReader sr = new StreamReader(fileName))
        {
            while(null != (line = sr.ReadLine()))
            {
                newLine = _Regex.Replace(line, "\t");
                Console.WriteLine("New string is: '{0}', ➡
original was: '{1}'",
                    newLine,
                    line);
            }
        }
    }

    public static void Main( string[] args )
    {
        Recipe r = new Recipe();
        r.Run(args[0]);
    }
}
```

Visual Basic .NET

```vbnet
Imports System
Imports System.IO
Imports System.Text.RegularExpressions
Public Class Recipe
```

```
        Private Shared _Regex As Regex = New _
Regex(",(?=(?:[^""]*$)|(?:[^""]*""[^""]*""[^""]*)*$)")

    Public Sub Run(ByVal fileName As String)
        Dim line As String
        Dim newLine As String
        Dim sr As StreamReader = File.OpenText(fileName)
        line = sr.ReadLine
        While Not line Is Nothing
            newLine = _Regex.Replace(line, ControlChars.Tab)
            Console.WriteLine("New string is: '{0}', original was: '{1}'", _
             newLine, _
             line)
            line = sr.ReadLine
        End While
        sr.Close()
    End Sub

    Public Shared Sub Main(ByVal args As String())
        Dim r As Recipe = New Recipe
        r.Run(args(0))
    End Sub

End Class
```

VBScript

```
Dim fso,s,re,line,newstr
Set fso = CreateObject("Scripting.FileSystemObject")
Set s = fso.OpenTextFile(WScript.Arguments.Item(0), 1, True)
Set re = New RegExp
re.Pattern = ",(?=(?:[^""]*$)|(?:[^""]*""[^""]*""[^""]*)*$)"
Do While Not s.AtEndOfStream
    line = s.ReadLine()
    newstr = re.Replace(line, vbTab)
    WScript.Echo "New string '" & newstr & "', original '" & line & "'"
Loop
s.Close
```

How It Works

This expression will work only on valid CSV files. It works by assuming that only commas outside quotes should be replaced with tabs, and it accomplishes that task by making sure an even number of quotes appear *after* each comma or making sure no quotes appear after the comma at all.

This works even with escaped quotes in CSV files, because in CSV files the double quote is escaped by doubling it: "". This makes the expression for checking the even number of quotes a lot easier.

You may wonder why I didn't check to see if the number of quotes *before* each comma is even. This is because of a limitation in the regular expression interpreters used by .NET and scripting languages in this book—variable-length expressions aren't allowed in look-behinds. Therefore, you have to use a look-ahead that in the end accomplishes the same result. After all, quotes appear in even numbers. If an odd number before a comma suggests it's in quotes, then an odd number after the comma also suggests it's in quotes.

Here's the expression, broken down at a high level:

`,`	a comma . . .
`(?=`	a positive look-ahead that contains . . .
`(?:...)`	a noncapturing group that contains the first expression . . .
`|`	or . . .
`(?:...)`	a noncapturing group that contains the second expression.

The first expression makes sure no quotes appear between the comma and the end of the line:

`[^"]`	a character class that matches anything that isn't a double quote . . .
`*`	found zero or more times . . .
`$`	the end of the line.

The second noncapturing group contains an expression that makes sure if a quote appears between the comma and the end of the line, then the comma isn't preceded by a quote and is followed by another one. This method ensures an even number of quotes appears between the comma and the end of the line. This part of the expression is as follows:

`[^"]`	a character class that matches anything that isn't a double quote . . .
`*`	found zero or more times . . .
`"`	a quote, followed by . . .
`[^"]`	a character class that matches anything that isn't a double quote . . .
`*`	found zero or more times . . .
`"`	a double quote . . .
`[^"]`	a character class that matches anything that isn't a double quote . . .
`*`	found zero or more times . . .
`)`	the end of the group . . .
`*`	found zero or more times . . .
`$`	the end of the line.

Variations

By making slight variations, you can use this regular expression to strip whitespace around commas in CSV files. The expression is already looking for commas that aren't inside quotes, which is good because the regex shouldn't strip whitespace that's inside quotes. Simply add variable whitespace (\s*) around the comma, and you'll have this expression:

`\s*,\s*(?=(?:[^""]*$)|(?:[^""]*""[^""]*""[^""]*)*$)`

Then, instead of using \t as the replacement, use a comma (,). This will strip out all the whitespace around the commas in a CSV file.

■**See Also** 1-7, 1-9, 4-4, 4-6

3-4. Changing Tab-Delimited Files to CSV Files

This recipe allows you to change a tab-delimited file into a CSV file. Commas and quotes in the fields are escaped already; however, if they aren't escaped yet, expressions in the "Variations" section of this recipe will show you how to escape the quotes and wrap fields that contain commas.

.NET Framework

C#

```
using System;
using System.IO;
using System.Text.RegularExpressions;

public class Recipe
{
    private static Regex _Regex = new Regex( ➥
"\\t(?=(?:[^\"]*$)|(?:[^\"]*\"[^\"]*\")*$)" );
    public void Run(string fileName)
    {
        String line;
        String newLine;
        using (StreamReader sr = new StreamReader(fileName))
        {
            while(null != (line = sr.ReadLine()))
            {
                newLine = _Regex.Replace(line, @",");
                Console.WriteLine("New string is: '{0}', original was: '{1}'",
                    newLine,
                    line);
            }
        }
    }

    public static void Main( string[] args )
    {
        Recipe r = new Recipe();
        r.Run(args[0]);
    }
}
```

Visual Basic .NET

```
Imports System
Imports System.IO
Imports System.Text.RegularExpressions
Public Class Recipe
```

```vbnet
    Private Shared _Regex As Regex = New _
Regex("\t(?=(?:[^""]*$)|(?:[^""]*""[^""]*"")*$)")

    Public Sub Run(ByVal fileName As String)
        Dim line As String
        Dim newLine As String
        Dim sr As StreamReader = File.OpenText(fileName)
        line = sr.ReadLine
        While Not line Is Nothing
            newLine = _Regex.Replace(line, ",")
            Console.WriteLine("New string is: '{0}', original was: '{1}'", _
             newLine, _
             line)
            line = sr.ReadLine
        End While
        sr.Close()
    End Sub

    Public Shared Sub Main(ByVal args As String())
        Dim r As Recipe = New Recipe
        r.Run(args(0))
    End Sub

End Class
```

VBScript

```vbscript
Dim fso,s,re,line,newstr
Set fso = CreateObject("Scripting.FileSystemObject")
Set s = fso.OpenTextFile(WScript.Arguments.Item(0), 1, True)
Set re = New RegExp
re.Pattern = "\t(?=(?:[^""]*$)|(?:[^""]*""[^""]*"")*$)"
re.Global = True
Do While Not s.AtEndOfStream
    line = s.ReadLine()
    newstr = re.Replace(line, ",")
    WScript.Echo "New string '" & newstr & "', original '" & line & "'"
Loop
s.Close
```

How It Works

Here's the expression broken down:

\t	a tab ...
(?=	a positive look-ahead that contains ...
(?:	a nonmatching group that contains ...
[^"]	a character class that isn't a double quote ...
*	found zero or more times ...
$	the end of the line ...
)	the end of the group ...
|	or ...
(?:	a noncapturing group that contains ...
[^"]	a character class that isn't a double quote ...
*	found zero or more times ...
"	a quote, followed by ...
[^"]	a character class that isn't a double quote ...
*	found zero or more times ...
"	a double quote ...
)	the end of the group ...
*	found zero or more times ...
$	the end of the line ...
)	the end of the group.

Variations

In case the tab-delimited file was created by a program that doesn't escape fields with commas and quotes in them, you might end up with a mess if you run this recipe on them without escaping quotes and commas first. The expressions to do this are straightforward.

First, with each iteration, replace every occurrence of a double quote with two double quotes. Second, wrap each field that contains a comma in quotes. The expression to find a field that contains a quote is ([^\t]*,[^\t]*), and the replacement expression is "$1". You might recognize the negated character class [^\t] as a method of finding tab-delimited fields—this expression is just looking for a comma somewhere in the middle of the field.

The loop, when finished, will look a lot like this in C#:

```
while(null != (line = sr.ReadLine()))
{
    newLine = Regex.Replace(line, "\"", "\"\"");
    newLine = Regex.Replace(newLine, @"([^\t]*,[^\t]*)", "\"$1\"");
    newLine = _Regex.Replace(newLine, @",");
    Console.WriteLine("New string is: '{0}', original was: '{1}'",
        newLine,
        line);
}
```

For brevity, I used the static `Replace` method on the `Regex` class, which means I don't have to instantiate an instance of the class. It takes an extra parameter, which is the search expression.

3-5. Extracting CSV Fields

This recipe shows you how to extract a particular field from a correctly formatted CSV file. In this recipe, let's assume you want to extract the second field in each line.

.NET Framework

C#

```csharp
using System;
using System.IO;
using System.Text.RegularExpressions;

public class Recipe
{
    private static Regex _Regex = new Regex( ➥
"^(?:[^\",]+|\"(?:[^\"]|\\\")*\"),(?<field>[^\",]+|\"(?:[^\"]|\\\")*\")" );

    public void Run(string fileName)
    {
        String line;
        using (StreamReader sr = new StreamReader(fileName))
        {
            while(null != (line = sr.ReadLine()))
            {
                Console.WriteLine("Found field:  '{0}'", ➥
_Regex.Match(line).Result("${field}"));
            }
        }
    }

    public static void Main( string[] args )
    {
        Recipe r = new Recipe();
        r.Run(args[0]);
    }
}
```

Visual Basic .NET

```vbnet
Imports System
Imports System.IO
Imports System.Text.RegularExpressions
Public Class Recipe

    Private Shared _Regex As Regex = New _
        Regex("^(?:[^"",]+|""(?:[^""]|\"")*""),(?<field>[^"",]+➥
        |""(?:[^""]|\"")*"")")
```

```vbnet
    Public Sub Run(ByVal fileName As String)
        Dim line As String
        Dim newLine As String
        Dim sr As StreamReader = File.OpenText(fileName)
        line = sr.ReadLine
        While Not line Is Nothing
            Console.WriteLine("Captured value '{0}'", ➥
_Regex.Match(line).Result("${field}"))
            line = sr.ReadLine
        End While
        sr.Close()
    End Sub

    Public Shared Sub Main(ByVal args As String())
        Dim r As Recipe = New Recipe
        r.Run(args(0))
    End Sub

End Class
```

VBScript

```vbscript
Dim fso,s,re,line,newstr
Set fso = CreateObject("Scripting.FileSystemObject")
Set s = fso.OpenTextFile(WScript.Arguments.Item(0), 1, True)
Set re = New RegExp
re.Pattern = ➥
"^(?:[^"",]+|""(?:[^""]|\\"")*""),([^"",]+|""(?:[^""]|\\"")*"")"
Do While Not s.AtEndOfStream
    line = s.ReadLine()
    newstr = re.Replace(line, "$1")
    WScript.Echo "New string '" & newstr & "', original '" & line & "'"
Loop
s.Close
```

How It Works

This expression uses noncapturing parentheses, which are set off by (?:, to ignore parts of the CSV record that aren't important to the replacement. Since recipe 3-1 explains the expression for a single CSV field, the following is a high-level overview of the expression:

^	the beginning of the line . . .
(?: . . .)	a single CSV field, followed by . . .
,	a comma, then . . .
(?< . . .> . . .)	a named capturing CSV field.

The CSV field expression is `(?:[^",]+|"(?:[^"]|\")*")`, which doesn't actually capture any text. The second expression is nearly the same but is `(?<field>[^",]+|"(?:[^"]|\")*")`. These two expressions have two differences: one is that the first is a noncapturing group, and the second is that the latter group is a named group.

3-6. Extracting Tab-Delimited Fields

You can use this recipe to print a single field from a correctly formatted tab-delimited record. For the sake of this example, the second field will be extracted from each record in a file or set of lines.

.NET Framework

C#

```csharp
using System;
using System.IO;
using System.Text.RegularExpressions;

public class Recipe
{
    private static Regex _Regex = new Regex( @"^(?:[^\t]+\t)(?<field>[^\t]+)" );

    public void Run(string fileName)
    {
        String line;
        using (StreamReader sr = new StreamReader(fileName))
        {
            while(null != (line = sr.ReadLine()))
            {
                Console.WriteLine("Found field:  '{0}'", ➥
_Regex.Match(line).Result("${field}"));
            }
        }
    }

    public static void Main( string[] args )
    {
        Recipe r = new Recipe();
        r.Run(args[0]);
    }
}
```

Visual Basic .NET

```vbnet
Imports System
Imports System.IO
Imports System.Text.RegularExpressions
Public Class Recipe

    Private Shared _Regex As Regex = New Regex("^(?:[^\t]+\t)(?<field>[^\t]+)")
```

```
    Public Sub Run(ByVal fileName As String)
        Dim line As String
        Dim newLine As String
        Dim sr As StreamReader = File.OpenText(fileName)
        line = sr.ReadLine
        While Not line Is Nothing
            Console.WriteLine("Captured value '{0}'", ➥
_Regex.Match(line).Result("${field}"))
            line = sr.ReadLine
        End While
        sr.Close()
    End Sub

    Public Shared Sub Main(ByVal args As String())
        Dim r As Recipe = New Recipe
        r.Run(args(0))
    End Sub

End Class
```

VBScript

```
Dim fso,s,re,line,newstr
Set fso = CreateObject("Scripting.FileSystemObject")
Set s = fso.OpenTextFile(WScript.Arguments.Item(0), 1, True)
Set re = New RegExp
re.Pattern = "^(?:[^\t]+\t)([^\t]+)"
re.Global = True
Do While Not s.AtEndOfStream
    line = s.ReadLine()
    newstr = re.Replace(line, "$1")
    WScript.Echo "New string '" & newstr & "', original '" & line & "'"
Loop
s.Close
```

How It Works

This expression uses a negated character class, [^\t], to say, "anything that isn't a tab," which this expression will assume defines a tab-delimited field. Some changes are modifying the groups with (?: to make them noncapturing groups so there's no confusion about what will be included in the back reference.

The expression breaks down as follows:

^	the beginning of the line, followed by a . . .
(?:	a noncapturing group that includes . . .
[^\t]	a character class that isn't a tab . . .

+	found one or more times, up to . . .
\t	a tab, then . . .
)	the end of the group . . .
(?<. . .>	a named capturing group that includes . . .
[^\t]	a character class that isn't a tab . . .
+	one or more times, followed by . . .
)	the end of the group . . .
(?:	a noncapturing group . . .
\t	a tab . . .
.	any character . . .
*	zero, one, or many times, up to . . .
)	the end of the group . . .
$	the end of the line.

The capturing group here is named `field` and is evaluated with the `Result` method on the `Match` object. One addition is that the `Result` method will throw an exception if a match hasn't been made.

3-7. Extracting Fields from Fixed-Width Files

This recipe shows how to extract fixed-width fields from a file. As an example, this recipe takes
a three-field file; the lengths of the three fields are 10, 30, and 15 characters.

.NET Framework

C#

```csharp
using System;
using System.IO;
using System.Text.RegularExpressions;

public class Recipe
{
    private static Regex _Regex = new ➥
Regex("^(?<f1>.{10})(?<f2>.{30})(?<f3>.{15})");

    public void Run(string fileName)
    {
        String line;
        int lineNbr = 0;
        using (StreamReader sr = new StreamReader(fileName))
        {
            while(null != (line = sr.ReadLine()))
            {
                lineNbr++;
                if (_Regex.IsMatch(line)
                {
                    Console.WriteLine(_Regex.Match(line).Result("${f2}"));
                }
            }
        }
    }

    public static void Main( string[] args )
    {
        Recipe r = new Recipe();
        r.Run(args[0]);
    }
}
```

Visual Basic .NET

```
Imports System
Imports System.IO
Imports System.Text.RegularExpressions
Public Class Recipe

    Private Shared _Regex As Regex =
        New Regex("^(?<f1>.{10})(?<f2>.{30})(?<f3>.{15})")

    Public Sub Run(ByVal fileName As String)
        Dim line As String
        Dim sr As StreamReader = File.OpenText(fileName)
        line = sr.ReadLine
        While Not line Is Nothing
            If _Regex.IsMatch(line) Then
                Console.WriteLine(_Regex.Match(line).Result("${f2}"))
            End If
            line = sr.ReadLine
        End While
        sr.Close()
    End Sub

    Public Shared Sub Main(ByVal args As String())
        Dim r As Recipe = New Recipe
        r.Run(args(0))
    End Sub

End Class
```

VBScript

```
Dim fso,s,re,line,newstr
Set fso = CreateObject("Scripting.FileSystemObject")
Set s = fso.OpenTextFile(WScript.Arguments.Item(0), 1, True)
Set re = New RegExp
re.Pattern = ""^(.{10})(.{30})(.{15})""
re.Global = True
Do While Not s.AtEndOfStream
    line = s.ReadLine()
    newstr = re.Replace(line, "$2")
    WScript.Echo "New string '" & newstr & "', original '" & line & "'"
Loop
s.Close
```

How It Works

This recipe works simply by counting the number of characters using the range qualifier and a wildcard, as shown here:

.   any character . . .

$\{n\}$ found exactly *n* times.

It uses named groups to easily refer to the field that was captured, so a named group that captures a field looks like (?<f2>{20}). This is only slightly easier than using the SubString method to capture slices of the string—the only benefit is that with the regular expression you can capture it all in one line.

3-8. Converting Fixed-Width Files to CSV Files

This recipe builds on many of the recipes in this chapter to demonstrate how to convert a fixed-width file to a valid CSV file. This recipe also uses a three-field record, with the lengths of 10, 20, and 15.

.NET Framework

C#

```csharp
using System;
using System.IO;
using System.Text.RegularExpressions;

public class Recipe
{
    private static Regex _Regex = new ➡
Regex(@"^(?<f1>.{10})(?<f2>.{20})(?<f3>.{15})");

    public void Run(string fileName)
    {
        String line;
        using (StreamReader sr = new StreamReader(fileName))
        {
            while(null != (line = sr.ReadLine()))
            {
                if (_Regex.IsMatch(line))
                {
                    Console.WriteLine("{0},{1},{2}",
                        EscapeField(_Regex.Match(line).Result("${f1}")),
                        EscapeField(_Regex.Match(line).Result("${f2}")),
                        EscapeField(_Regex.Match(line).Result("${f3}")));
                }
            }
        }
    }

    private string EscapeField(string s)
    {
        string tmpStr = Regex.Replace(s.Trim(),"\"", "\"\"");
        return Regex.Replace(tmpStr, @"([^\t]*,[^\t]*)", "\"$1\"");
    }
}
```

```csharp
public static void Main( string[] args )
{
    Recipe r = new Recipe();
    r.Run(args[0]);
}
}
```

Visual Basic .NET

```vbnet
Imports System
Imports System.IO
Imports System.Text.RegularExpressions

Public Class Recipe
    Private Shared _Regex As Regex = New ➥
Regex("^(?<f1>.{10})(?<f2>.{20})(?<f3>.{15})")

    Public Sub Run(ByVal fileName As String)
        Dim line As String
        Dim sr As StreamReader = File.OpenText(fileName)
        line = sr.ReadLine
        While Not line Is Nothing
            If _Regex.IsMatch(line) Then
                Console.WriteLine("{0},{1},{2}", _
                    EscapeField(_Regex.Match(line).Result("${f1}")), _
                    EscapeField(_Regex.Match(line).Result("${f2}")), _
                    EscapeField(_Regex.Match(line).Result("${f3}")))
            End If
            line = sr.ReadLine
        End While
        sr.Close()
    End Sub

    Private Function EscapeField(ByVal s As String) As String
        Dim tmpStr As String = Regex.Replace(s.Trim, """", """""")
        Return Regex.Replace(tmpStr, "([^\t]*,[^\t]*)", """$1""")
    End Function

    Public Shared Sub Main(ByVal args As String())
        Dim r As Recipe = New Recipe
        r.Run(args(0))
    End Sub
End Class
```

VBScript

```vbscript
Public Function EscapeField(s)
    Dim tmpStr,myRe
    Set myRe = New RegExp
    myRe.Pattern = """"
    myRe.Global = True
    tmpStr = myRe.Replace(Trim(s),"""""")
    myRe.Pattern = "([^\t]*,[^\t]*)"
    EscapeField = myRe.Replace(tmpStr, """$1""")
End Function

Dim fso,s,re,line
Set fso = CreateObject("Scripting.FileSystemObject")
Set s = fso.OpenTextFile(WScript.Arguments.Item(0), 1, True)
Set re = New RegExp
re.Pattern = "^(.{10})(.{20})(.{15})"
Do While Not s.AtEndOfStream
    line = s.ReadLine()
    WScript.Echo EscapeField(re.Replace(line,"$1")) & _
        "," & EscapeField(re.Replace(line,"$2")) & _
        "," & EscapeField(re.Replace(line,"$3"))
Loop
s.Close
```

How It Works

This recipe is a compilation of some of the other concepts shown in this chapter. The search expression, explained in recipe 3-7, searches for the fields by using ranges to specify lengths and named groups for easy access later.

The code in the EscapeField method in the samples should look similar to the regexes in the "Variations" section in recipe 3-4. The only real difference is that I'm using the Trim() method of the string to eliminate whitespace in the first replacement. Even though I really like using regular expressions, sometimes using existing methods is just shorter and easier.

CHAPTER 4

■■■

Formatting and Validating

The recipes in this chapter focus on formatting and validating text. They're particularly useful in validation routines in applications, where user input can vary but must conform to basic rules. U.S. postal codes are an example of this—some applications may require all nine digits, and some may allow all nine but just require five, as in the case of 55555-0000 or 55555, respectively.

Certain classes in .NET provide some of the functionality in this chapter, such as date parsing and number formatting. Depending on your requirements, you might find these objects better to use than regular expressions. Where classes are available as alternatives, I'll point them out to you. For more details about the classes, see the MSDN documentation at http://msdn.microsoft.com/netframework.

4-1. Formatting U.S. Phone Numbers

You can use this recipe to format a string of numbers, such as changing 3334445555 into (333) 444-5555. The regular expressions will allow you to do the work without using substrings and without finding positions of characters within the string. The recipe will also format the phone number into the new format if it looks like 333.444.5555 or 333-444-5555.

.NET Framework

C#

```
using System;
using System.IO;
using System.Text.RegularExpressions;

public class Recipe
{
    private static Regex _Regex = new Regex( @"^\(?(\d{3})\)?[- .]?➥
(\d{3})[- .]?(\d{4})$" );
    public void Run(string fileName)
    {
        String line;
        String newLine;
        using (StreamReader sr = new StreamReader(fileName))
        {
            while(null != (line = sr.ReadLine()))
            {
                newLine = _Regex.Replace(line, @"($1) $2-$3");
                Console.WriteLine("New string is: '{0}', original was: '{1}'",
                    newLine,
                    line);
            }
        }
    }

    public static void Main( string[] args )
    {
        Recipe r = new Recipe();
        r.Run(args[0]);
    }
}
```

Visual Basic .NET

```
Imports System
Imports System.IO
Imports System.Text.RegularExpressions
Public Class Recipe

    Private Shared _Regex As Regex = _
        New Regex("^\(?(\d{3})\)?[- .]?(\d{3})[- .]?(\d{4})$")

    Public Sub Run(ByVal fileName As String)
        Dim line As String
        Dim newLine As String
        Dim sr As StreamReader = File.OpenText(fileName)
        line = sr.ReadLine
        While Not line Is Nothing
            newLine = _Regex.Replace(line, "($1) $2-$3")
            Console.WriteLine("New string is: '{0}', ➡
original was: '{1}'", _
                newLine, _
                line)
            line = sr.ReadLine
        End While
        sr.Close()
    End Sub

    Public Shared Sub Main(ByVal args As String())
        Dim r As Recipe = New Recipe
        r.Run(args(0))
    End Sub

End Class
```

VBScript

```
Dim fso,s,re,line,newstr
Set fso = CreateObject("Scripting.FileSystemObject")
Set s = fso.OpenTextFile(WScript.Arguments.Item(0), 1, True)
Set re = New RegExp
re.Pattern = "^\(?(\d{3})\)?[- .]?(\d{3})[- .]?(\d{4})$"
Do While Not s.AtEndOfStream
    line = s.ReadLine()
    newstr = re.Replace(line, "($1) $2-$3")
    WScript.Echo "New string '" & newstr & "', original '" & line & "'"
Loop
s.Close
```

FORMATTING AND VALIDATING

JavaScript

```
<html>
<head>
<title>4-1. Formatting U.S. Phone Numbers</title>
</head>
<body>
<form name="form1">
    <input type="text" name="txtInput" />
    <div id="lblResult"></div>
    <script language="javascript">
        function replace() {
            document.getElementById('lblResult').innerHTML = ➥
document.form1.txtInput.value.replace(/^\(?(\d{3})\)?[- .]?(\d{3})➥
[- .]?(\d{4})$/, "($1) $2-$3");
        }
    </script>
    <input type="button" name="btnSubmit" onclick="replace()" value="Go" />
</form>
</body>
</html>
```

How It Works

This recipe captures three groups of digits and uses them in the replacement expression. The character class \d is used instead of [0-9], which makes it a little more concise. The following is the expression broken down into parts:

^	the beginning of the line . . .
\(	a literal parenthesis . . .
?	found zero or one time . . .
(	a capturing group containing . . .
\d	a digit . . .
{3}	found three times . . .
)	the end of the group . . .
\)	up to a literal parenthesis . . .
[- .]	a character class that matches a hyphen (-), a space ( ), or a dot (.) . . .
?	found at most once . . .
. . .	the rest of the expression.

The rest of the expression is essentially a repeat of the previous one, with a few modifications. A literal (and) may appear around the first group of three digits.

The character class [- .] matches a hyphen, space, or dot (period). The ? after the class makes it optional, which is why the expression also matches numbers that run together. Note the hyphen (-) is first in the character class—this is important if the hyphen is to be taken literally and not used to define a range within the character class.

See Also 2-1, 2-2, 2-3, 4-1, 4-2, 4-3, 4-4, 4-5, 4-6, 4-8, 4-11, 4-12, 4-13, 4-14, 4-15, 4-17, 4-19

4-2. Formatting U.S. Dates

This recipe demonstrates changing different date formats into one format. This recipe will change 3/1/2004 or 3.1.2004 into 3-1-2004.

.NET Framework

C#

```csharp
using System;
using System.IO;
using System.Text.RegularExpressions;

public class Recipe
{
    private static Regex _Regex = new Regex( @"^(\d{1,2})[-\/.]?(\d{1,2})➡
[-\/.]?((?:\d{2}|\d{4}))$" );
    public void Run(string fileName)
    {
        String line;
        String newLine;
        using (StreamReader sr = new StreamReader(fileName))
        {
            while(null != (line = sr.ReadLine()))
            {
                newLine = _Regex.Replace(line, @"$1-$2-$3");
                Console.WriteLine("New string is: '{0}', original was: '{1}'",
                    newLine,
                    line);
            }
        }
    }

    public static void Main( string[] args )
    {
        Recipe r = new Recipe();
        r.Run(args[0]);
    }
}
```

Visual Basic .NET

```vbnet
Imports System
Imports System.IO
Imports System.Text.RegularExpressions
Public Class Recipe
```

```vb
    Private Shared _Regex As Regex = New Regex("^(\d{1,2})[-\/.]?(\d{1,2})➡
[-\/.]?((?:\d{2}|\d{4}))$")

    Public Sub Run(ByVal fileName As String)
        Dim line As String
        Dim newLine As String
        Dim sr As StreamReader = File.OpenText(fileName)
        line = sr.ReadLine
        While Not line Is Nothing
            newLine = _Regex.Replace(line, "$1-$2-$3")
            Console.WriteLine("New string is: '{0}', original was: '{1}'", _
             newLine, _
             line)
            line = sr.ReadLine
        End While
        sr.Close()
    End Sub

    Public Shared Sub Main(ByVal args As String())
        Dim r As Recipe = New Recipe
        r.Run(args(0))
    End Sub

End Class
```

VBScript

```vbscript
Dim fso,s,re,line,newstr
Set fso = CreateObject("Scripting.FileSystemObject")
Set s = fso.OpenTextFile(WScript.Arguments.Item(0), 1, True)
Set re = New RegExp
re.Pattern = "^(\d{1,2})[-\/.]?(\d{1,2})[-\/.]?((?:\d{2}|\d{4}))$"
Do While Not s.AtEndOfStream
    line = s.ReadLine()
    newstr = re.Replace(line, "$1-$2-$3")
    WScript.Echo "New string '" & newstr & "', original '" & line & "'"
Loop
s.Close
```

JavaScript

```html
<html>
<head>
<title>4-2. Formatting U.S. Dates</title>
</head>
<body>
<form name="form1">
```

```
<input type="text" name="txtInput" />
<div id="lblResult"></div>
<script language="javascript">
    function replace() {
        document.getElementById('lblResult').innerHTML = ➡
document.form1.txtInput.value.replace(/^(\d{1,2})[-\/.](\d{1,2})➡
[-\/.](\d{2}|\d{4})$/, "$1-$2-$3");
    }
</script>
<input type="button" name="btnSubmit" onclick="replace()" value="Go" />
</form>
</body>
</html>
```

How It Works

This recipe uses the \d character class as a shortcut to refer to [0-9]. It groups the numbers in the original string and uses back references to replace the string with a reformatted version. The following is the expression broken down into parts:

^	the beginning of the line . . .
(	a capturing group . . .
\d	a digit . . .
{1,2}	found one to two times . . .
)	the end of the group . . .
[-\/.]	a character class that can include a dash, a slash, or a dot . . .
. . .	this group repeats for the DD part of the date . . .
(	a group that contains . . .
\d	a digit . . .
{2}	found two times . . .
|	for . . .
\d	a digit . . .
{4}	found four times . . .
)	the end of the group . . .
$	the end of the line.

■**See Also** 4-5, 4-8

4-3. Validating Alternate Dates

This expression validates dates in a different format than the ones in recipe 4-2. Matches for this are as follows:

```
20-Jul-2004
1-Oct-1999
```

It's even smart enough to match months with the correct number of days, but it won't check to see if the leap year is correct.

.NET Framework

ASP.NET

```
<%@ Page Language="vb" AutoEventWireup="false" Debug="true"%>
<!DOCTYPE HTML PUBLIC "-//W3C//DTD HTML 4.0 Transitional//EN">
<html>
<head><title></title>
</head>
<body>
    <form Id="Form1" RunAt="server">
    <asp:TextBox id="txtInput" runat="server"></asp:TextBox>
    <asp:RegularExpressionValidator Id="revInput" RunAt="server"
        ControlToValidate="txtInput"
        ErrorMessage="Please enter a valid value"
        ValidationExpression="((0[1-9]|[12][0-9]|30)-(Sep|Apr|Jun|Nov)|➡
(0[1-9]|[12][0-9])-Feb|(0[1-9]|[12][0-9]|3[01])-➡
(Jan|Mar|May|Jul|Aug|Oct|Dec))-\d{4}">
        </asp:RegularExpressionValidator>
    <asp:Button Id="btnSubmit" RunAt="server" CausesValidation="True"
        Text="Submit"></asp:Button>
    </form>
</body>
```

C#

```
using System;
using System.IO;
using System.Text.RegularExpressions;

public class Recipe
{

    private static string month29 = "(0[1-9]|[12][0-9])-Feb";
    private static string month30 = "(0[1-9]|[12][0-9]|30)-(Sep|Apr|Jun|Nov)";
    private static string month31 = "(0[1-9]|[12][0-9]|3[01])-➡
-(Jan|Mar|May|Jul|Aug|Oct|Dec)";
```

```
    private static Regex _Regex =
        new Regex(String.Format("({0}|{1}|{2})",
            month29,
            month30,
            month31
            ) + @"-\d{4}");

    public void Run(string fileName)
    {
        Console.WriteLine("Full regex is:  '{0}'", _Regex.ToString());
        String line;
        int lineNbr = 0;
        using (StreamReader sr = new StreamReader(fileName))
        {
            while(null != (line = sr.ReadLine()))
            {
                lineNbr++;
                if (_Regex.IsMatch(line))
                {
                    Console.WriteLine("Found match '{0}' at line {1}",
                        line,
                        lineNbr);
                }
            }
        }
    }

    public static void Main( string[] args )
    {
        Recipe r = new Recipe();
        r.Run(args[0]);
    }
}
```

Visual Basic .NET

```
Imports System
Imports System.IO
Imports System.Text.RegularExpressions
Public Class Recipe

    Private Const month29 = "(0[1-9]|[12][0-9])-Feb"
    Private Const month30 = "(0[1-9]|[12][0-9]|30)-(Sep|Apr|Jun|Nov)"
    Private Const month31 = "(0[1-9]|[12][0-9]|3[01])-(Jan|Mar|May|Jul|Aug|Oct|Dec)"

    Private Shared _Regex As Regex = New Regex(String.Format("({0}|{1}|{2})", _
                                        month29, _
```

```
                                        month30, _
                                        month31 _
                                        ) + "-\d{4}")

    Public Sub Run(ByVal fileName As String)
        Dim line As String
        Dim lineNbr As Integer = 0
        Dim sr As StreamReader = File.OpenText(fileName)
        line = sr.ReadLine
        While Not line Is Nothing
            lineNbr = lineNbr + 1
            If _Regex.IsMatch(line) Then
                Console.WriteLine("Found match '{0}' at line {1}", _
                    line, _
                    lineNbr)
            End If
            line = sr.ReadLine
        End While
        sr.Close()
    End Sub

    Public Shared Sub Main(ByVal args As String())
        Dim r As Recipe = New Recipe
        r.Run(args(0))
    End Sub

End Class
```

VBScript

```
Dim fso,s,re,line,lineNbr
Set fso = CreateObject("Scripting.FileSystemObject")
Set s = fso.OpenTextFile(WScript.Arguments.Item(0), 1, True)
Set re = New RegExp
Private Const month29 = "(0[1-9]|[12][0-9])-Feb"
Private Const month30 = "(0[1-9]|[12][0-9]|30)-(Sep|Apr|Jun|Nov)"
Private Const month31 = "(0[1-9]|[12][0-9]|3[01])-(Jan|Mar|May|Jul|Aug|Oct|Dec)"
re.Pattern = "(" + month29 + "|" + month30 + "|" + month31 + ")-\d{4}"
lineNbr = 0
Do While Not s.AtEndOfStream
    line = s.ReadLine()
    lineNbr = lineNbr + 1
    If re.Test(line) Then
        WScript.Echo "Found match: '" & line & "' at line " & lineNbr
    End If
Loop
s.Close
```

JavaScript

```
<html>
<head>
<title>4-3. Validating Alternate Dates</title>
</head>
<body>
<form name="form1">
    <input type="textbox" name="txtInput" />
    <script type="text/javascript">
    function validate() {
        var month29 = "(0[1-9]|[12][0-9])-Feb";
        var month30 = "(0[1-9]|[12][0-9]|30)-(Sep|Apr|Jun|Nov)";
        var month31 = "(0[1-9]|[12][0-9]|3[01])-(Jan|Mar|May|Jul|Aug|Oct|Dec)";
        var re = new RegExp('(' + month29 + '|' + month30 + '|' + ➥
month31 + ')-\\d{4}', 'i')
        if (! document.form1.txtInput.value.match(re)) {
            alert("Please enter valid value!")
        } else {
            alert("Success!")
        }
    }
    </script>
    <input type="button" name="btnSubmit" onclick="validate()" value="Go" />
</form>
</body>
</html>
```

How It Works

To make this regex more readable, I've broken it up into parts. Each part combines an expression that uses ranges to match the maximum number of days with a different expression that matches month abbreviations.

The part of the expression that matches 30 days with September, April, June, or November is as follows:

(	a group that contains . . .
0[1-9]	a zero, followed by one through nine (which catches 01–09) . . .
|	or . . .
[12][0-9]	a one or a two followed by zero through nine (this catches 10–29) . . .
|	or . . .
30	a three followed by a zero, then . . .
)	the end of the first group, followed by . . .
-	a hyphen . . .

(	the beginning of another group that contains . . .
Sep	*S, e, p* . . .
|	or . . .
Apr	*A, p, r* . . .
|	or . . .
Jun	*J, u, n* . . .
|	or . . .
Nov	*N, o, v,* followed by . . .
)	the end of the second group.

Variations

This regex is fairly particular, but to make it a little more lenient, you can pass the `RegexOptions.IgnoreCase` option in the .NET Framework or use `IgnoreCase = True` in VBScript or the `i` option in JavaScript.

Also, you can make the leading zero optional in the numbers less than ten by adding `?` in front of the zero, like this: `0?[0-9]`.

■**See Also** 1-3, 1-11, 1-16, 1-22, 2-6, 2-8, 2-9, 2-10, 3-1, 3-3, 3-4, 3-5, 4-2, 4-3, 4-6, 4-10, 4-11, 4-12, 4-13, 4-14, 4-15, 4-16, 4-22

4-4. Formatting Large Numbers

This recipe adds commas to large numbers to make them more readable. A number such as 383894012 becomes 383,894,012. This recipe operates on whole numbers and assumes no decimal point appears in the number.

■**Note** This regex requires using negative back references, which aren't supported in VBScript and JavaScript.

.NET Framework

C#

```
using System;
using System.IO;
using System.Text.RegularExpressions;

public class Recipe
{
    private static Regex _Regex = new Regex( @"(?<=\d)(?=(\d{3})+(?!\d))" );
    public void Run(string fileName)
    {
        String line;
        String newLine;
        using (StreamReader sr = new StreamReader(fileName))
        {
            while(null != (line = sr.ReadLine()))
            {
                newLine = _Regex.Replace(line, ",");
                Console.WriteLine("New string is: '{0}', original was: '{1}'",
                    newLine,
                    line);
            }
        }
    }

    public static void Main( string[] args )
    {
        Recipe r = new Recipe();
        r.Run(args[0]);
    }
}
```

Visual Basic .NET

```
Imports System
Imports System.IO
Imports System.Text.RegularExpressions
Public Class Recipe

    Private Shared _Regex As Regex = New Regex("(?<=\d)(?=(\d{3})+(?!\d))")

    Public Sub Run(ByVal fileName As String)
        Dim line As String
        Dim newLine As String
        Dim sr As StreamReader = File.OpenText(fileName)
        line = sr.ReadLine
        While Not line Is Nothing
            newLine = _Regex.Replace(line, ",")
            Console.WriteLine("New string is: '{0}', original was: '{1}'", _
             newLine, _
             line)
            line = sr.ReadLine
        End While
        sr.Close()
    End Sub

    Public Shared Sub Main(ByVal args As String())
        Dim r As Recipe = New Recipe
        r.Run(args(0))
    End Sub

End Class
```

How It Works

This recipe consists entirely of look-aheads and look-behinds. The following is the expression broken down into parts:

(?<=	a positive look-behind including . . .
\d	a number . . .
)	the end of the positive look-behind . . .
(?=	a positive look-ahead including . . .
(	a group that contains . . .
\d	a number . . .
{3}	found three times . . .
)	the end of the group . . .

+	found one or more times . . .
(?!	a negative look-ahead that contains . . .
\d	a number . . .
)	the end of the negative look-ahead . . .
)	the end of the positive look-ahead.

The position where the comma is inserted is between the look-behind and look-ahead. The look-ahead groups numbers in threes where a number doesn't appear afterward (that could be the end of the line, a decimal point, or a label such as Kb).

■**See Also** 1-7, 1-20, 2-6, 4-6

4-5. Formatting Negative Numbers

This recipe identifies negative numbers, such as -34.44, and wraps them in parentheses to get (34.44).

.NET Framework

C#

```csharp
using System;
using System.IO;
using System.Text.RegularExpressions;

public class Recipe
{
    private static Regex _Regex = new Regex( @"^-(\d{1,3}(,\d{3})*(\.\d+)?)$" );
    public void Run(string fileName)
    {
        String line;
        String newLine;
        using (StreamReader sr = new StreamReader(fileName))
        {
            while(null != (line = sr.ReadLine()))
            {
                newLine = _Regex.Replace(line, @"($1)");
                Console.WriteLine("New string is: '{0}', original was: '{1}'",
                    newLine,
                    line);
            }
        }
    }

    public static void Main( string[] args )
    {
        Recipe r = new Recipe();
        r.Run(args[0]);
    }
}
```

Visual Basic .NET

```vbnet
Imports System
Imports System.IO
Imports System.Text.RegularExpressions
Public Class Recipe

    Private Shared _Regex As Regex = New Regex("^-(\d{1,3}(,\d{3})*(\.\d+)?)$")
```

```vbnet
    Public Sub Run(ByVal fileName As String)
        Dim line As String
        Dim newLine As String
        Dim sr As StreamReader = File.OpenText(fileName)
        line = sr.ReadLine
        While Not line Is Nothing
            newLine = _Regex.Replace(line, "($1)")
            Console.WriteLine("New string is: '{0}', original was: '{1}'", _
             newLine, _
             line)
            line = sr.ReadLine
        End While
        sr.Close()
    End Sub

    Public Shared Sub Main(ByVal args As String())
        Dim r As Recipe = New Recipe
        r.Run(args(0))
    End Sub

End Class
```

VBScript

```vbscript
Dim fso,s,re,line,newstr
Set fso = CreateObject("Scripting.FileSystemObject")
Set s = fso.OpenTextFile(WScript.Arguments.Item(0), 1, True)
Set re = New RegExp
re.Pattern = "^-(\d{1,3}(,\d{3})*(\.\d+)?)$"
Do While Not s.AtEndOfStream
    line = s.ReadLine()
    newstr = re.Replace(line, "($1)")
    WScript.Echo "New string '" & newstr & "', original '" & line & "'"
Loop
s.Close
```

JavaScript

```html
<html>
<head>
<title>4-5. Formatting Negative Numbers</title>
</head>
<body>
<form name="form1">
    <input type="text" name="txtInput" />
    <div id="lblResult"></div>
    <script language="javascript">
```

```
    function replace() {
        document.getElementById('lblResult').innerHTML = ➡
document.form1.txtInput.value.replace(/^-(\d{1,3}(,\d{3})*(\.\d+)?)$/, "($1)");
    }
    </script>
    <input type="button" name="btnSubmit" onclick="replace()" value="Go" />
</form>
</body>
</html>
```

How It Works

This recipe works by finding groups of three numbers that are separated from the rest of the number by commas. But first, the regex attempts to match a minus sign or hyphen that signifies the negative number, as shown here:

^	the beginning of a line, followed by . . .
-	a minus sign (hyphen), then . . .
(	a group that contains . . .
\d	a digit . . .
{1,3}	found between one and three times, followed by . . .
(	another group that contains . . .
,	a comma, followed by . . .
\d	a digit . . .
{3}	found exactly three times, followed by . . .
)	the end of the group . . .
*	where the group can be found any number of times, followed by . . .
(	another group . . .
\.	containing a literal dot and . . .
\d	a digit . . .
+	found one or more times . . .
)	the end of the group . . .
?	where the group can be found zero or one time . . .
)	the end of the outer group, then . . .
$	the end of the line.

FORMATTING AND VALIDATING

The first digit and range in the regex, \d{1,3}, captures a digit one to three times. This will match numbers such as 3, 25, and 111 but will also match the numbers to the left of a comma such as 1,333,333 or 23,234.

The group (,\d{3}) matches groups of three numbers (digits) that have a comma in front of them, so in 1,233 this bit matches ,233 (1 is matched by \d{1,3}).

Finally, (\.\d+)? matches an optional set of numbers after a decimal point. There must be at least one number to the right of the decimal if the decimal point is present.

4-6. Formatting Single Digits

This recipe adds a zero to the beginning of a number that's a single digit, such as a number less than ten. An example is 3/4/2004, which will be reprinted as 03/04/2004.

Note This expression uses look-behinds, which aren't supported in VBScript or JavaScript.

.NET Framework

C#

```
using System;
using System.IO;
using System.Text.RegularExpressions;

public class Recipe
{
    private static Regex _Regex =
        new Regex( @"(?:(?<=^)|(?<=[^\d]))(\d)(?=[^\d])" );
    public void Run(string fileName)
    {
        String line;
        String newLine;
        using (StreamReader sr = new StreamReader(fileName))
        {
            while(null != (line = sr.ReadLine()))
            {
                newLine = _Regex.Replace(line, @"0$1");
                Console.WriteLine("New string is: '{0}', original was: '{1}'",
                    newLine,
                    line);
            }
        }
    }

    public static void Main( string[] args )
    {
        Recipe r = new Recipe();
        r.Run(args[0]);
    }
}
```

Visual Basic .NET

```vbnet
Imports System
Imports System.IO
Imports System.Text.RegularExpressions
Public Class Recipe

    Private Shared _Regex As Regex = New Regex("(?:(?<=^)|(?<=[^\d]))(\d)(?=[^\d])")

    Public Sub Run(ByVal fileName As String)
        Dim line As String
        Dim newLine As String
        Dim sr As StreamReader = File.OpenText(fileName)
        line = sr.ReadLine
        While Not line Is Nothing
            newLine = _Regex.Replace(line, "0$1")
            Console.WriteLine("New string is: '{0}',➡
 original was: '{1}'", _
                newLine, _
                line)
            line = sr.ReadLine
        End While
        sr.Close()
    End Sub

    Public Shared Sub Main(ByVal args As String())
        Dim r As Recipe = New Recipe
        r.Run(args(0))
    End Sub

End Class
```

How It Works

This expression uses look-behinds and look-aheads to take notice of what's located around the single digit. It then uses a back reference to add a zero to the beginning of the digit. The following is a breakdown of the group that looks behind the digit:

(?:	a noncapturing group that contains . . .
(?<=	a positive look-behind that contains . . .
^	the beginning of the line . . .
)	the end of the positive look-behind . . .
|	or . . .
(?<=	another positive look-behind that contains . . .

[^\d]   a character class that isn't a digit . . .

)   the end of the positive look-behind . . .

)   the end of the noncapturing group.

The digit is captured by (\d), which is then followed by a look-ahead group that simply looks for a nondigit matched by the character class [^\d].

See Also 1-7, 1-20, 2-6, 4-4

4-7. Limiting User Input to Alpha Characters

This simple recipe allows you to make sure user input is limited to characters in the alphabet.

.NET Framework

ASP.NET

```
<%@ Page Language="vb" AutoEventWireup="false" %>
<!DOCTYPE HTML PUBLIC "-//W3C//DTD HTML 4.0 Transitional//EN">
<html>
<head><title></title>
</head>
<body>
    <form Id="Form1" RunAt="server">
    <asp:TextBox id="txtInput" runat="server"></asp:TextBox>
    <asp:RegularExpressionValidator Id="revInput" RunAt="server"
        ControlToValidate="txtInput"
        ErrorMessage="Please enter a valid value"
        ValidationExpression="[\p{Lu}\p{Ll}]+">
    </asp:RegularExpressionValidator>
    <asp:Button Id="btnSubmit" RunAt="server" CausesValidation="True"
        Text="Submit"></asp:Button>
    </form>
</body>
```

C#

```csharp
using System;
using System.IO;
using System.Text.RegularExpressions;

public class Recipe
{
    private static Regex _Regex = new Regex( @"^[\p{Lu}\p{Ll}]+$" );

    public void Run(string fileName)
    {
        String line;
        int lineNbr = 0;
        using (StreamReader sr = new StreamReader(fileName))
        {
            while(null != (line = sr.ReadLine()))
            {
                lineNbr++;
                if (_Regex.IsMatch(line))
                {
                    Console.WriteLine("Found match '{0}' at line {1}",
```

```
                    line,
                    lineNbr);
            }
        }
    }
}

    public static void Main( string[] args )
    {
        Recipe r = new Recipe();
        r.Run(args[0]);
    }
}
```

Visual Basic .NET

```
Imports System
Imports System.IO
Imports System.Text.RegularExpressions
Public Class Recipe

    Private Shared _Regex As Regex = New Regex("^[\p{Lu}\p{Ll}]+$")

    Public Sub Run(ByVal fileName As String)
        Dim line As String
        Dim lineNbr As Integer = 0
        Dim sr As StreamReader = File.OpenText(fileName)
        line = sr.ReadLine
        While Not line Is Nothing
            lineNbr = lineNbr + 1
            If _Regex.IsMatch(line) Then
                Console.WriteLine("Found match '{0}' at line {1}", _
                    line, _
                    lineNbr)
            End If
            line = sr.ReadLine
        End While
        sr.Close()
    End Sub

    Public Shared Sub Main(ByVal args As String())
        Dim r As Recipe = New Recipe
        r.Run(args(0))
    End Sub

End Class
```

VBScript

```vbscript
Dim fso,s,re,line,lineNbr
Set fso = CreateObject("Scripting.FileSystemObject")
Set s = fso.OpenTextFile(WScript.Arguments.Item(0), 1, True)
Set re = New RegExp
re.Pattern = "^[a-z]+$"
re.IgnoreCase = True
lineNbr = 0
Do While Not s.AtEndOfStream
    line = s.ReadLine()
    lineNbr = lineNbr + 1
    If re.Test(line) Then
        WScript.Echo "Found match: '" & line & "' at line " & lineNbr
    End If
Loop
s.Close
```

JavaScript

```html
<html>
<head>
<title>4-7. Limiting User Input to Alpha Characters</title>
</head>
<body>
<form name="form1">
    <input type="textbox" name="txtInput" />
    <script type="text/javascript">
    function validate() {
        if (! document.form1.txtInput.value.match(/^[a-z]+$/i)) {
            alert("Please enter valid value!")
        } else {
            alert("Success!")
        }
    }
    </script>
    <input type="button" name="btnSubmit" onclick="validate()" value="Go" />
</form>
</body>
</html>
```

How It Works

The .NET Framework regex shown here uses \p to make matches using Unicode classes:

^	the beginning of the line, followed by . . .
[	a character class that contains . . .
\p{Lu}	a lowercase Unicode letter, or . . .
\p{Ll}	an uppercase Unicode letter . . .
]	the end of the character class . . .
+	that's found one or more times, followed by . . .
$	the end of the line.

The scripting languages VBScript and JavaScript demonstrate a much simpler example that takes into account letters in the English character set only. The recipe is as follows:

^	the beginning of the line, followed by . . .
[a-z]	a character class that matches the letters *a* to *z* . . .
+	found one or more times, then . . .
$	the end of the line.

To ignore case in VBScript and JavaScript, use the IgnoreCase property and i option, respectively. For more information about using these options, see the "Syntax Overview" section at the beginning of this book.

■ See Also 1-23

4-8. Validating U.S. Currency

This simple recipe validates U.S. currency. It checks for the existence of a dollar sign at the beginning, allows any number of digits, and requires a decimal point with two numbers after it. Valid matches are $1,000.00, $34.83, and $343.33.

.NET Framework

ASP.NET

```
<%@ Page Language="vb" AutoEventWireup="false" %>
<!DOCTYPE HTML PUBLIC "-//W3C//DTD HTML 4.0 Transitional//EN">
<html>
<head><title></title>
</head>
<body>
    <form Id="Form1" RunAt="server">
    <asp:TextBox id="txtInput" runat="server"></asp:TextBox>
    <asp:RegularExpressionValidator Id="revInput" RunAt="server"
        ControlToValidate="txtInput"
        ErrorMessage="Please enter a valid value"
        ValidationExpression="\$\d{1,3}(,\d{3})*\.\d\d">
    </asp:RegularExpressionValidator>
    <asp:Button Id="btnSubmit" RunAt="server" CausesValidation="True"
        Text="Submit"></asp:Button>
    </form>
</body>
```

C#

```
using System;
using System.IO;
using System.Text.RegularExpressions;

public class Recipe
{
    private static Regex _Regex = new Regex( @"^\$\d{1,3}(,\d{3})*\.\d\d$" );

    public void Run(string fileName)
    {
        String line;
        int lineNbr = 0;
        using (StreamReader sr = new StreamReader(fileName))
        {
            while(null != (line = sr.ReadLine()))
            {
                lineNbr++;
                if (_Regex.IsMatch(line))
```

```
            {
                Console.WriteLine("Found match '{0}' at line {1}",
                    line,
                    lineNbr);
            }
        }
    }
}

public static void Main( string[] args )
{
    Recipe r = new Recipe();
    r.Run(args[0]);
}
}
```

Visual Basic .NET

```
Imports System
Imports System.IO
Imports System.Text.RegularExpressions
Public Class Recipe

    Private Shared _Regex As Regex = New Regex("^\$\d{1,3}(,\d{3})*\.\d\d$")

    Public Sub Run(ByVal fileName As String)
        Dim line As String
        Dim lineNbr As Integer = 0
        Dim sr As StreamReader = File.OpenText(fileName)
        line = sr.ReadLine
        While Not line Is Nothing
            lineNbr = lineNbr + 1
            If _Regex.IsMatch(line) Then
                Console.WriteLine("Found match '{0}' at line {1}", _
                    line, _
                    lineNbr)
            End If
            line = sr.ReadLine
        End While
        sr.Close()
    End Sub

    Public Shared Sub Main(ByVal args As String())
        Dim r As Recipe = New Recipe
        r.Run(args(0))
    End Sub

End Class
```

VBScript

```
Dim fso,s,re,line,lineNbr
Set fso = CreateObject("Scripting.FileSystemObject")
Set s = fso.OpenTextFile(WScript.Arguments.Item(0), 1, True)
Set re = New RegExp
re.Pattern = "^\$\d{0,3}(,\d{3})*\.\d\d$"
lineNbr = 0
Do While Not s.AtEndOfStream
    line = s.ReadLine()
    lineNbr = lineNbr + 1
    If re.Test(line) Then
        WScript.Echo "Found match: '" & line & "' at line " & lineNbr
    End If
Loop
s.Close
```

JavaScript

```
<html>
<head>
<title>4-8. Validating U.S. Currency</title>
</head>
<body>
<form name="form1">
    <input type="textbox" name="txtInput" />
    <script type="text/javascript">
    function validate() {
        if (! document.form1.txtInput.value.match(/^\$\d{0,3}(,\d{3})*\.\d\d$/)) {
            alert("Please enter valid value!")
        } else {
            alert("Success!")
        }
    }
    </script>
    <input type="button" name="btnSubmit" onclick="validate()" value="Go" />
</form>
</body>
</html>
```

How It Works

The expression, broken down, is as follows:

^	the beginning of the line . . .
\$	a literal dollar sign ($) . . .
\d	a number, zero through nine . . .
{1,3}	found between one and three times . . .
(	the beginning of a group that contains . . .
,	a comma . . .
\d	a number . . .
{3}	found three times . . .
)	the end of the group . . .
*	where the group may be found any number of times . . .
\.	a literal period (.) . . .
\d	a number . . .
\d	another number . . .
$	the end of the line.

The group (,\d{3})* matches occurrences of three numbers preceded by a comma, such as ,999 and ,000. Since the expression before that, \d{1,3}, captures between one and three digits, matches such as 1,999 and 22,000 are valid. Since the group of three numbers preceded by a comma is completely optional, numbers such as 1 and 12 are also valid. This expression requires at least one leading number before the decimal point, which is still valid if the number is less than $1, such as $0.34.

See Also 2-1, 2-2, 2-3

4-9. Limiting User Input to 15 Characters

This expression highlights the technique of using ranges in qualifiers to limit user input to 15 characters. You can modify the expression to allow any minimum or maximum string length.

.NET Framework

ASP.NET

```
<%@ Page Language="vb" AutoEventWireup="false" %>
<!DOCTYPE HTML PUBLIC "-//W3C//DTD HTML 4.0 Transitional//EN">
<html>
<head><title></title>
</head>
<body>
    <form Id="Form1" RunAt="server">
    <asp:TextBox id="txtInput" runat="server"></asp:TextBox>
    <asp:RegularExpressionValidator Id="revInput" RunAt="server"
        ControlToValidate="txtInput"
        ErrorMessage="Please enter a valid value"
        ValidationExpression=".{0,15}">
    </asp:RegularExpressionValidator>
    <asp:Button Id="btnSubmit" RunAt="server" CausesValidation="True"
        Text="Submit"></asp:Button>
    </form>
</body>
```

C#

```
using System;
using System.IO;
using System.Text.RegularExpressions;

public class Recipe
{
    private static Regex _Regex = new Regex( @"^.{0,15}$" );

    public void Run(string fileName)
    {
        String line;
        int lineNbr = 0;
        using (StreamReader sr = new StreamReader(fileName))
        {
            while(null != (line = sr.ReadLine()))
            {
                lineNbr++;
                if (_Regex.IsMatch(line))
                {
```

```
                    Console.WriteLine("Found match '{0}' at line {1}",
                        line,
                        lineNbr);
                }
            }
        }
    }

    public static void Main( string[] args )
    {
        Recipe r = new Recipe();
        r.Run(args[0]);
    }
}
```

Visual Basic .NET

```
Imports System
Imports System.IO
Imports System.Text.RegularExpressions
Public Class Recipe

    Private Shared _Regex As Regex = New Regex("^.{0,15}$")

    Public Sub Run(ByVal fileName As String)
        Dim line As String
        Dim lineNbr As Integer = 0
        Dim sr As StreamReader = File.OpenText(fileName)
        line = sr.ReadLine
        While Not line Is Nothing
            lineNbr = lineNbr + 1
            If _Regex.IsMatch(line) Then
                Console.WriteLine("Found match '{0}' at line {1}", _
                    line, _
                    lineNbr)
            End If
            line = sr.ReadLine
        End While
        sr.Close()
    End Sub

    Public Shared Sub Main(ByVal args As String())
        Dim r As Recipe = New Recipe
        r.Run(args(0))
    End Sub

End Class
```

VBScript

```
Dim fso,s,re,line,lineNbr
Set fso = CreateObject("Scripting.FileSystemObject")
Set s = fso.OpenTextFile(WScript.Arguments.Item(0), 1, True)
Set re = New RegExp
re.Pattern = "^.{0,15}$"
lineNbr = 0
Do While Not s.AtEndOfStream
    line = s.ReadLine()
    lineNbr = lineNbr + 1
    If re.Test(line) Then
        WScript.Echo "Found match: '" & line & "' at line " & lineNbr
    End If
Loop
s.Close
```

JavaScript

```
<html>
<head>
<title>4-9. Limiting User Input to 15 Characters</title>
</head>
<body>
<form name="form1">
    <input type="textbox" name="txtInput" />
    <script type="text/javascript">
    function validate() {
        if (! document.form1.txtInput.value.match(/^.{0,15}$/)) {
            alert("Please enter valid value!")
        } else {
            alert("Success!")
        }
    }
    </script>
    <input type="button" name="btnSubmit" onclick="validate()" value="Go" />
</form>
</body>
</html>
```

How It Works

The expression says quite simply the following:

^	the beginning of the line . . .
.	any character . . .
{0,15}	found zero through fifteen times . . .
$	the end of the line.

See Also 1-9, 2-3, 3-7, 3-8, 4-1, 4-2, 4-3, 4-4, 4-5, 4-8, 4-10, 4-12, 4-13, 4-14, 4-15, 4-17

4-10. Validating IP Addresses

You can use this recipe to validate an IP address as four groups of numbers between 0 and 255 separated by periods. The address 192.168.0.1 is valid, but 256.0.1.2 isn't.

.NET Framework

ASP.NET

```
<%@ Page Language="vb" AutoEventWireup="false" %>
<!DOCTYPE HTML PUBLIC "-//W3C//DTD HTML 4.0 Transitional//EN">
<html>
<head><title></title>
</head>
<body>
    <form Id="Form1" RunAt="server">
    <asp:TextBox id="txtInput" runat="server"></asp:TextBox>
    <asp:RegularExpressionValidator Id="revInput" RunAt="server"
        ControlToValidate="txtInput"
        ErrorMessage="Please enter a valid value"
        ValidationExpression="^ (([1-9]?[0-9]|1[0-9]{2}|2[0-4][0-9]|25[0-5]).)➥
{3}([1-9]?[0-9]|1[0-9]{2}|2[0-4][0-9]|25[0-5])$">
    </asp:RegularExpressionValidator>
    <asp:Button Id="btnSubmit" RunAt="server" CausesValidation="True"
        Text="Submit"></asp:Button>
    </form>
</body>
```

C#

```
using System;
using System.IO;
using System.Text.RegularExpressions;

public class Recipe
{
    private static string octetRegex =
        "([1-9]?[0-9]|1[0-9]{2}|2[0-4][0-9]|25[0-5])";
    private static Regex _Regex =
        new Regex(String.Format(@"^{0}\.{0}\.{0}\.{0}$", octetRegex));

    public void Run(string fileName)
    {
        String line;
        int lineNbr = 0;
        using (StreamReader sr = new StreamReader(fileName))
        {
            while(null != (line = sr.ReadLine()))
```

```
        {
            lineNbr++;
            if (_Regex.IsMatch(line))
            {
                Console.WriteLine("Found match '{0}' at line {1}",
                    line,
                    lineNbr);
            }
        }
    }
}

public static void Main( string[] args )
{
    Recipe r = new Recipe();
    r.Run(args[0]);
}
}
```

Visual Basic .NET

```
Imports System
Imports System.IO
Imports System.Text.RegularExpressions
Public Class Recipe

    Private Const octetRegex = "([1-9]?[0-9]|1[0-9]{2}|2[0-4][0-9]|25[0-5])"
    Private Shared _Regex As Regex = _
        New Regex(String.Format("^{0}\.{0}\.{0}\.{0}$", octetRegex))

    Public Sub Run(ByVal fileName As String)
        Dim line As String
        Dim lineNbr As Integer = 0
        Dim sr As StreamReader = File.OpenText(fileName)
        line = sr.ReadLine
        While Not line Is Nothing
            lineNbr = lineNbr + 1
            If _Regex.IsMatch(line) Then
                Console.WriteLine("Found match '{0}' at line {1}", _
                    line, _
                    lineNbr)
            End If
            line = sr.ReadLine
        End While
        sr.Close()
    End Sub
```

```
        Public Shared Sub Main(ByVal args As String())
            Dim r As Recipe = New Recipe
            r.Run(args(0))
        End Sub

End Class
```

VBScript

```
Dim fso,s,re,line,lineNbr
Set fso = CreateObject("Scripting.FileSystemObject")
Set s = fso.OpenTextFile(WScript.Arguments.Item(0), 1, True)
Set re = New RegExp
Const octetRegex = "([1-9]?[0-9]|1[0-9]{2}|2[0-4][0-9]|25[0-5])"
re.Pattern = "^(" + octetRegex + "\.){3}" + octetRegex + "$"
lineNbr = 0
Do While Not s.AtEndOfStream
    line = s.ReadLine()
    lineNbr = lineNbr + 1
    If re.Test(line) Then
        WScript.Echo "Found match: '" & line & "' at line " & lineNbr
    End If
Loop
s.Close
```

JavaScript

```
<html>
<head>
<title>4-10. Validating IP Addresses</title>
</head>
<body>
<form name="form1">
    <input type="textbox" name="txtInput" />
    <script type="text/javascript">
    function validate() {
        if (! document.form1.txtInput.value.match(/^(([1-9]?[0-9]|1[0-9]{2}|➡
2[0-4][0-9]|25[0-5]).){3}([1-9]?[0-9]|1[0-9]{2}|2[0-4][0-9]|25[0-5])$/)) {
            alert("Please enter valid value!")
        } else {
            alert("Success!")
        }
    }
    </script>
    <input type="button" name="btnSubmit" onclick="validate()" value="Go" />
</form>
</body>
</html>
```

How It Works

The bulk of this expression is a group that breaks down the numbers that range from 0 to 255. The expression would be a lot shorter if 002 or 015 were valid instead of 2 and 15, respectively, but for this expression you want to specify the IP address without the leading zeros.

The range from 0 to 255 breaks down into other ranges: 0–99, 100–199, 200–249, and 250–255. The expression to match this is ([1-9]?[0-9]|1[0-9]{2}|2[0-4][0-9]|25[0-5]), which can be broken down into [1-9]?[0-9], which will match 0–99; 1[0-9]{2}, which will match 100–199; 2[0-4][0-9], which will match 200–249; and 25[0-5], which will match 250–255.

After taking out the IP address validation expression, the rest of it breaks down like this:

^	the beginning of the line . . .
(	the beginning of a group that contains . . .
(. . .)	the IP address expression explained previously . . .
\.	a literal dot . . .
)	the end of the group . . .
{3}	occurring exactly three times . . .
(. . .)	another occurrence of the IP address . . .
$	the end of the line.

See Also 1-9, 4-3, 4-13, 4-15, 4-16

4-11. Validating E-mail Addresses

This recipe checks to make sure an e-mail address looks like a valid address, containing a username, at sign (@), and valid hostname. For example, null@example.com is valid, but NOSPAM@spam isn't valid. For information about what makes an address look like a valid one, see RFC 2822.

.NET Framework

ASP.NET

```
<%@ Page Language="vb" AutoEventWireup="false" %>
<!DOCTYPE HTML PUBLIC "-//W3C//DTD HTML 4.0 Transitional//EN">
<html>
<head><title></title>
</head>
<body>
    <form Id="Form1" RunAt="server">
    <asp:TextBox id="txtInput" runat="server"></asp:TextBox>
    <asp:RegularExpressionValidator Id="revInput" RunAt="server"
        ControlToValidate="txtInput"
        ErrorMessage="Please enter a valid zipcode"
        ValidationExpression="[\w\d!#$%&'*+-/=?^`{|}~]+(\.[\w\d!#$%&➥
'*+-/=?^`{|}~]+)*@([a-z\d][-a-z\d]*[a-z\d]\.)*[a-z][-a-z\d]*[a-z]">
    </asp:RegularExpressionValidator>
    <asp:Button Id="btnSubmit" RunAt="server" CausesValidation="True"
        Text="Submit"></asp:Button>
    </form>
</body>
</html>
```

C#

```
using System;
using System.IO;
using System.Text.RegularExpressions;

public class Recipe
{
    // Any ASCII character except CTRL chars, space, and ()<>@,;:\".[]
    private static string localRegex =
        @"[\w\d!#$%&'*+-/=?^`{|}~]+(\.[\w\d!#$%&'*+-/=?^`{|}~]+)*";
    private static string hostNameRegex =
        @"([a-z\d][-a-z\d]*[a-z\d]\.)*[a-z][-a-z\d]*[a-z]";
    private static Regex _Regex = new Regex("^" + localRegex + "@" + hostNameRegex +
        "$", RegexOptions.IgnoreCase);
```

```csharp
public void Run(string fileName)
{
    String line;
    int lineNbr = 0;
    using (StreamReader sr = new StreamReader(fileName))
    {
        while(null != (line = sr.ReadLine()))
        {
            lineNbr++;
            if (_Regex.IsMatch(line))
            {
                Console.WriteLine("Found match '{0}' at line {1}",
                    line,
                    lineNbr);
            }
        }
    }
}

public static void Main( string[] args )
{
    Recipe r = new Recipe();
    r.Run(args[0]);
}
}
```

Visual Basic .NET

```vbnet
Imports System
Imports System.IO
Imports System.Text.RegularExpressions
Public Class Recipe


    Private Const localRegex = _
        "[\w\d!#$%&'*+-/=?^`{|}~]+(\.[\w\d!#$%&'*+-/=?^`{|}~]+)*"
    Private Const hostNameRegex = _
        "([a-z\d][-a-z\d]*[a-z\d]\.)*[a-z][-a-z\d]*[a-z]"
    Private Shared _Regex As Regex = New Regex("^" & localRegex & "@" & _
        hostNameRegex & "$", RegexOptions.IgnoreCase)

    Public Sub Run(ByVal fileName As String)
        Dim line As String
        Dim lineNbr As Integer = 0
        Dim sr As StreamReader = File.OpenText(fileName)
```

```
        line = sr.ReadLine
        While Not line Is Nothing
            lineNbr = lineNbr + 1
            If _Regex.IsMatch(line) Then
                Console.WriteLine("Found match '{0}' at line {1}", _
                    line, _
                    lineNbr)
            End If
            line = sr.ReadLine
        End While
        sr.Close()
    End Sub

    Public Shared Sub Main(ByVal args As String())
        Dim r As Recipe = New Recipe
        r.Run(args(0))
    End Sub

End Class
```

VBScript

```
Dim fso,s,re,line,lineNbr
Set fso = CreateObject("Scripting.FileSystemObject")
Set s = fso.OpenTextFile(WScript.Arguments.Item(0), 1, True)
Set re = New RegExp
Private Const localRegex = "[\w\d!#$%&'*+-/=?^`{|}~]+(\.[\w\d!#$%&'*+-/=?^`{|}~]+)*"
Private Const hostNameRegex = "([a-z\d][-a-z\d]*[a-z\d]\.)*[a-z][-a-z\d]*[a-z]"
re.Pattern = "^" & localRegex & "@" & hostNameRegex & "$"
re.IgnoreCase = True
lineNbr = 0
Do While Not s.AtEndOfStream
    line = s.ReadLine()
    lineNbr = lineNbr + 1
    If re.Test(line) Then
        WScript.Echo "Found match: '" & line & "' at line " & lineNbr
    End If
Loop
s.Close
```

JavaScript

```
<html>
<head>
<title>Validating E-mail Addresses</title>
</head>
<body>
<form name="form1">
    <input type="textbox" name="txtInput" />
    <script type="text/javascript">
    function validate() {
        if (! document.form1.txtInput.value.match(/^[\w\d!#$%&'*+-➡
\/=?^`{|}~]+(\.[\w\d!#$%&'*+-\/=?^`{|}~]+)*@➡
([a-z\d][-a-z\d]*[a-z\d]\.)*[a-z][-a-z\d]*[a-z]$/)) {
            alert("Please enter valid value!")
        } else {
            alert("Success!")
        }
    }
    </script>
    <input type="button" name="btnSubmit" onclick="validate()" value="Go" />
</form>
</body>
</html>
```

How It Works

The @ in the expression separates two different parts that match a username and a hostname. The expression to match the username is [\w\d!#$%&'*+-/=?^`{|}~]+(\.[\w\d!#$%&'*+-/=?^`{|}~]+)*, which is a lot more straightforward than it actually looks. It just matches any US-ASCII character that isn't a control character, a space, or one of the special characters (see RFC 2882 for more information). After it matches one or more of those characters, it then matches more of the same separated by a period:

(\.[\w\d!#$%&'*+-/=?^`{|}~]+)*

The second expression, which matches the hostname, comes from recipe 2-2.

See Also 1-5, 1-9, 2-1, 2-2, 2-7, 4-20

4-12. Validating U.S. Phone Numbers

You can use this recipe to validate a U.S. phone number, with flexibility. It allows a phone number to have no formatting, to start with a 1 for long distance, and to have spaces, periods, or hyphens separating the parts. These are valid numbers: 1-800-555-4444, 555-333-444, 5556663333, (555) 333-4444, and 555.333.4444. These aren't valid numbers: 555-4444, 1-800-555-OINK, 800#555#3333, and 555-555.

.NET Framework

ASP.NET

```
<%@ Page Language="vb" AutoEventWireup="false" %>
<!DOCTYPE HTML PUBLIC "-//W3C//DTD HTML 4.0 Transitional//EN">
<html>
<head><title></title>
</head>
<body>
    <form Id="Form1" RunAt="server">
    <asp:TextBox id="txtInput" runat="server"></asp:TextBox>
    <asp:RegularExpressionValidator Id="revInput" RunAt="server"
        ControlToValidate="txtInput"
        ErrorMessage="Please enter a valid value"
        ValidationExpression="((1 )?\(\d{3}\) \d{3}-\d{4})|(1-)?➥
(\d{3}-){2}\d{4}|(1\.)?(\d{3}\.){2}\d{4}|1?\d{10}">
    </asp:RegularExpressionValidator>
    <asp:Button Id="btnSubmit" RunAt="server" CausesValidation="True"
        Text="Submit"></asp:Button>
    </form>
</body>
```

C#

```
using System;
using System.IO;
using System.Text.RegularExpressions;

public class Recipe
{
    private static Regex _Regex = new Regex( @"^((1 )?\(\d{3}\) \d{3}-\d{4})➥
|(1-)?(\d{3}-){2}\d{4}|(1\.)?(\d{3}\.){2}\d{4}|1?\d{10}$" );

    public void Run(string fileName)
    {
        String line;
        int lineNbr = 0;
        using (StreamReader sr = new StreamReader(fileName))
        {
```

```
            while(null != (line = sr.ReadLine()))
            {
                lineNbr++;
                if (_Regex.IsMatch(line))
                {
                    Console.WriteLine("Found match '{0}' at line {1}",
                        line,
                        lineNbr);
                }
            }
        }
    }
}

    public static void Main( string[] args )
    {
        Recipe r = new Recipe();
        r.Run(args[0]);
    }
}
```

Visual Basic .NET

```
Imports System
Imports System.IO
Imports System.Text.RegularExpressions
Public Class Recipe

    Private Shared _Regex As Regex = New Regex("^((1 )?\(\d{3}\) \d{3}-\d{4})➡
|(1-)?(\d{3}-){2}\d{4}|(1\.)?(\d{3}\.){2}\d{4}|1?\d{10}$")

    Public Sub Run(ByVal fileName As String)
        Dim line As String
        Dim lineNbr As Integer = 0
        Dim sr As StreamReader = File.OpenText(fileName)
        line = sr.ReadLine
        While Not line Is Nothing
            lineNbr = lineNbr + 1
            If _Regex.IsMatch(line) Then
                Console.WriteLine("Found match '{0}' at line {1}", _
                    line, _
                    lineNbr)
            End If
            line = sr.ReadLine
        End While
        sr.Close()
    End Sub
```

```
    Public Shared Sub Main(ByVal args As String())
        Dim r As Recipe = New Recipe
        r.Run(args(0))
    End Sub

End Class
```

VBScript

```
Dim fso,s,re,line,lineNbr
Set fso = CreateObject("Scripting.FileSystemObject")
Set s = fso.OpenTextFile(WScript.Arguments.Item(0), 1, True)
Set re = New RegExp
re.Pattern = "^((1 )?\(\d{3}\) \d{3}-\d{4})|(1-)?(\d{3}-➥
){2}\d{4}|(1\.)?(\d{3}\.){2}\d{4}|1?\d{10}$"
lineNbr = 0
Do While Not s.AtEndOfStream
    line = s.ReadLine()
    lineNbr = lineNbr + 1
    If re.Test(line) Then
        WScript.Echo "Found match: '" & line & "' at line " & lineNbr
    End If
Loop
s.Close
```

JavaScript

```
<html>
<head>
<title>4-13. Validating U.S. Phone Numbers</title>
</head>
<body>
<form name="form1">
    <input type="textbox" name="txtInput" />
    <script type="text/javascript">
    function validate() {
        if (! document.form1.txtInput.value.match(/^((1 )?\(\d{3}\) \d{3}-\d{4})➥
|(1-)?(\d{3}-){2}\d{4}|(1\.)?(\d{3}\.){2}\d{4}|1?\d{10}$/)) {
            alert("Please enter valid value!")
        } else {
            alert("Success!")
        }
    }
    </script>
    <input type="button" name="btnSubmit" onclick="validate()" value="Go" />
</form>
</body>
</html>
```

How It Works

This recipe looks for groups of numbers or digits, identified here by the \d character class, with certain optional delimiters such as spaces, dots, or dashes. It also allows the parentheses that sometimes occur around the area code to be optional.

This regex has three nearly identical groups, differing mostly by the character used to separate the parts of the phone number. I'll break down the first part of the regex here:

(	the beginning of a group that contains . . .
(1)	a one, followed by a space . . .
?	found zero or one time . . .
\(	a literal opening parenthesis, followed by . . .
\d{3}	a digit, found three times, then . . .
\)	the literal closing parenthesis, followed by . . .
<space>	a space . . .
\d{3}	a digit, found three times, and . . .
-	a hyphen, then . . .
\d{4}	a digit, found four times . . .
)	the end of the group.

This regex will match 1 (800) 555-5555 or (555) 555-5555. The other groups are extremely similar, only dropping the pair of literal parentheses around the area code and swapping out a space with either a dot or a hyphen.

See Also 2-1, 2-2, 2-3, 4-1, 4-2, 4-3, 4-4, 4-5, 4-6, 4-8, 4-11, 4-13, 4-14, 4-15, 4-17, 4-19

4-13. Validating U.S. Social Security Numbers

This recipe validates U.S. Social Security numbers. The number format itself is fairly straightforward—it consists of a three-digit area code, followed by a two-digit group code, and finally followed by a four-digit serial number. This recipe takes it a step further and makes sure the area number is somewhat accurate. According to http://www.ssa.gov/employer/highgroup.txt, the highest current area number is 772, 000 is invalid, and several ranges exist between 000–772 in which numbers are currently unassigned. As of the time of this writing, the valid numbers for the area number are 001–665, 667–690, 700–733, 750, and 764–772.

.NET Framework

ASP.NET

```
<%@ Page Language="vb" AutoEventWireup="false" %>
<!DOCTYPE HTML PUBLIC "-//W3C//DTD HTML 4.0 Transitional//EN">
<html>
<head><title></title>
</head>
<body>
    <form Id="Form1" RunAt="server">
    <asp:TextBox id="txtInput" runat="server"></asp:TextBox>
    <asp:RegularExpressionValidator Id="revInput" RunAt="server"
        ControlToValidate="txtInput"
        ErrorMessage="Please enter a valid value"
        ValidationExpression="^(00[1-9]|0[1-9]\d|[1-5]\d{2}|6[0-5]\d|66[0-5]➡
|66[7-9]|6[7-8]\d|690|7[0-2]\d|73[0-3]|750|76[4-9]|77[0-2])-(?!00)\d{2}-➡
(?!0000)\d{4}$">
    </asp:RegularExpressionValidator>
    <asp:Button Id="btnSubmit" RunAt="server" CausesValidation="True"
        Text="Submit"></asp:Button>
    </form>
</body>
```

C#

```
using System;
using System.IO;
using System.Text.RegularExpressions;

public class Recipe
{
    private static Regex _Regex = new Regex( @"^(00[1-9]|0[1-9]\d|[1-5]\d{2}➡
|6[0-5]\d|66[0-5]|66[7-9]|6[7-8]\d|690|7[0-2]\d|73[0-3]|750|76[4-9]|77[0-2])-➡
(?!00)\d{2}-(?!0000)\d{4}$" );
```

```csharp
    public void Run(string fileName)
    {
        String line;
        int lineNbr = 0;
        using (StreamReader sr = new StreamReader(fileName))
        {
            while(null != (line = sr.ReadLine()))
            {
                lineNbr++;
                if (_Regex.IsMatch(line))
                {
                    Console.WriteLine("Found match '{0}' at line {1}",
                        line,
                        lineNbr);
                }
            }
        }
    }

    public static void Main( string[] args )
    {
        Recipe r = new Recipe();
        r.Run(args[0]);
    }
}
```

Visual Basic .NET

```vbnet
Imports System
Imports System.IO
Imports System.Text.RegularExpressions
Public Class Recipe

    Private Shared _Regex As Regex = New Regex("^(00[1-9]|0[1-9]\d|[1-5]\d{2}➡
|6[0-5]\d|66[0-5]|66[7-9]|6[7-8]\d|690|7[0-2]\d|73[0-3]|750|76[4-9]|➡
77[0-2])-(?!00)\d{2}-(?!0000)\d{4}$")

    Public Sub Run(ByVal fileName As String)
        Dim line As String
        Dim lineNbr As Integer = 0
        Dim sr As StreamReader = File.OpenText(fileName)
        line = sr.ReadLine
        While Not line Is Nothing
            lineNbr = lineNbr + 1
            If _Regex.IsMatch(line) Then
```

```vb
                Console.WriteLine("Found match '{0}' at line {1}", _
                    line, _
                    lineNbr)
            End If
            line = sr.ReadLine
        End While
        sr.Close()
    End Sub

    Public Shared Sub Main(ByVal args As String())
        Dim r As Recipe = New Recipe
        r.Run(args(0))
    End Sub

End Class
```

VBScript

```vbscript
Dim fso,s,re,line,lineNbr
Set fso = CreateObject("Scripting.FileSystemObject")
Set s = fso.OpenTextFile(WScript.Arguments.Item(0), 1, True)
Set re = New RegExp
re.Pattern = "^(00[1-9]|0[1-9]\d|[1-5]\d{2}|6[0-5]\d|66[0-5]|66[7-9]|➡
6[7-8]\d|690|7[0-2]\d|73[0-3]|750|76[4-9]|77[0-2])-(?!00)\d{2}-➡
(?!0000)\d{4}$"
lineNbr = 0
Do While Not s.AtEndOfStream
    line = s.ReadLine()
    lineNbr = lineNbr + 1
    If re.Test(line) Then
        WScript.Echo "Found match: '" & line & "' at line " & lineNbr
    End If
Loop
s.Close
```

JavaScript

```javascript
<html>
<head>
<title>4-13. Validating U.S. Social Security Numbers</title>
</head>
<body>
<form name="form1">
    <input type="textbox" name="txtInput" />
    <script type="text/javascript">
    function validate() {
        if (! document.form1.txtInput.value.match(/^(00[1-9]|0[1-9]\d|➡
```

```
[1-5]\d{2}|6[0-5]\d|66[0-5]|66[7-9]|6[7-8]\d|690|7[0-2]\d|73[0-3]|750|➥
76[4-9]|77[0-2])-(?!00)\d{2}-(?!0000)\d{4}$/)) {
            alert("Please enter valid value!")
        } else {
            alert("Success!")
        }
    }
    </script>
    <input type="button" name="btnSubmit" onclick="validate()" value="Go" />
</form>
</body>
</html>
```

How It Works

This recipe is the longest and most difficult to read example in this book that deals with ranges. Since they're explained in greater detail elsewhere, I'll point out what makes this recipe different from most of the others—the (?! operator you see in the second and third groups previously.

The operator excludes the groups 00 and 0000 from the second and third groups of numbers, respectively. The expression breaks down as follows:

(?!   a group that doesn't contain . . .

00   a zero followed by a zero . . .

)   the end of the group . . .

\d   a digit . . .

{2}   found exactly two times.

See Also 1-9, 4-3, 4-10, 4-15, 4-16

4-14. Validating Credit Card Numbers

You can use this recipe to validate credit card numbers entered by a user. It validates the number in groups, such as 4444-4444-4444-4444, with or without the dashes or with spaces instead.

.NET Framework

ASP.NET

```
<%@ Page Language="vb" AutoEventWireup="false" %>
<!DOCTYPE HTML PUBLIC "-//W3C//DTD HTML 4.0 Transitional//EN">
<html>
<head><title></title>
</head>
<body>
    <form Id="Form1" RunAt="server">
    <asp:TextBox id="txtInput" runat="server"></asp:TextBox>
    <asp:RegularExpressionValidator Id="revInput" RunAt="server"
        ControlToValidate="txtInput"
        ErrorMessage="Please enter a valid value"
        ValidationExpression="^(\d{4}-){3}|(\d{4} ){3}\d{4}|\d{15,16}|➥
\d{4} \d{2} \d{4} \d{5}|\d{4}-\d{2}-\d{4}-\d{5}$">
    </asp:RegularExpressionValidator>
    <asp:Button Id="btnSubmit" RunAt="server" CausesValidation="True"
        Text="Submit"></asp:Button>
    </form>
</body>
```

C#

```csharp
using System;
using System.IO;
using System.Text.RegularExpressions;

public class Recipe
{
    private static Regex _Regex = new Regex( @"^(\d{4}-){3}|➥
(\d{4} ){3}\d{4}|\d{15,16}|\d{4} \d{2} \d{4} \d{5}|➥
\d{4}-\d{2}-\d{4}-\d{5}$" );

    public void Run(string fileName)
    {
        String line;
        int lineNbr = 0;
        using (StreamReader sr = new StreamReader(fileName))
        {
            while(null != (line = sr.ReadLine()))
```

```csharp
        {
            lineNbr++;
            if (_Regex.IsMatch(line))
            {
                Console.WriteLine("Found match '{0}' at line {1}",
                    line,
                    lineNbr);
            }
        }
    }
}

public static void Main( string[] args )
{
    Recipe r = new Recipe();
    r.Run(args[0]);
}
}
```

Visual Basic .NET

```vbnet
Imports System
Imports System.IO
Imports System.Text.RegularExpressions
Public Class Recipe

    Private Shared _Regex As Regex = New Regex("^(\d{4}-){3}|➡
(\d{4} ){3}\d{4}|\d{15,16}|\d{4} \d{2} \d{4} \d{5}|➡
\d{4}-\d{2}-\d{4}-\d{5}$")

    Public Sub Run(ByVal fileName As String)
        Dim line As String
        Dim lineNbr As Integer = 0
        Dim sr As StreamReader = File.OpenText(fileName)
        line = sr.ReadLine
        While Not line Is Nothing
            lineNbr = lineNbr + 1
            If _Regex.IsMatch(line) Then
                Console.WriteLine("Found match '{0}' at line {1}", _
                    line, _
                    lineNbr)
            End If
            line = sr.ReadLine
        End While
        sr.Close()
    End Sub
```

```
Public Shared Sub Main(ByVal args As String())
    Dim r As Recipe = New Recipe
    r.Run(args(0))
End Sub

End Class
```

VBScript

```
Dim fso,s,re,line,lineNbr
Set fso = CreateObject("Scripting.FileSystemObject")
Set s = fso.OpenTextFile(WScript.Arguments.Item(0), 1, True)
Set re = New RegExp
re.Pattern = " ^(\d{4}-){3}|(\d{4} ){3}\d{4}|\d{15,16}|➥
\d{4} \d{2} \d{4} \d{5}|\d{4}-\d{2}-\d{4}-\d{5}$"
lineNbr = 0
Do While Not s.AtEndOfStream
    line = s.ReadLine()
    lineNbr = lineNbr + 1
    If re.Test(line) Then
        WScript.Echo "Found match: '" & line & "' at line " & lineNbr
    End If
Loop
s.Close
```

JavaScript

```
<html>
<head>
<title>4-14. Validating Credit Card Numbers</title>
</head>
<body>
<form name="form1">
    <input type="textbox" name="txtInput" />
    <script type="text/javascript">
    function validate() {
        if (! document.form1.txtInput.value.match(/^(\d{4}-){3}|➥
(\d{4} ){3}\d{4}|\d{15,16}|\d{4} \d{2} \d{4} \d{5}|➥
\d{4}-\d{2}-\d{4}-\d{5}$/)) {
            alert("Please enter valid value!")
        } else {
            alert("Success!")
        }
    }
```

```
    </script>
    <input type="button" name="btnSubmit" onclick="validate()" value="Go" />
</form>
</body>
</html>
```

How It Works

This expression will not necessarily validate the credit card number itself but will make sure only that what was entered appears to be a complete credit card number. More accurate methods of checking the number out exist, such as the Luhn algorithm described at http:// en.wikipedia.org/wiki/Luhn_algorithm. Whether or not you use a regex depends on what the uses are—this might be a perfectly adequate test to catch simple user input errors before making a call to a vendor for verification.

This regex consists of four different groups that check to make sure the number entered is formatted like a major credit card. The first group, `(\d{4}-){3}|(\d{4} ){3}\d{4}`, looks for four groups or four numbers (16 in all) where the groups are separated by either a dash or a space, as shown here:

(	the beginning of a group that contains . . .
\d{4}	a digit, found exactly four times, followed by . . .
-	a hyphen . . .
){3}	where this group is found three times . . .
|	or . . .
(	a different group that contains . . .
\d{4}	a digit found exactly four times, followed by . . .
<space>	a space . . .
){3}	where this group is found exactly three times, followed by . . .
\d{4}	any four digits.

This regex will match 5555-5555-5555-5555 or 5555 5555 5555 5555. The second regex, separated from this one by an "or" operator (|), is \d{15,16}. It's straightforward: it will find any string of digits between 15 and 16 digits long. This will match sequences such as 5555555555555555 or 555555555555555.

Finally, the last two groups match American Express–style numbers that are in NNNN NN NNNN NNNNN format. The two groups differ only by the spaces and hyphens.

4-15. Validating Dates in MM/DD/YYYY Format

This expression validates dates in MM/DD/YYYY format. It goes a little further than just looking for digits—it will validate 1–12 for the MM, 1–31 for the date, and any four-digit number for the year.

■**Note** If you're using the .NET Framework, you might consider using the methods on the Date class instead of using regular expressions.

.NET Framework

ASP.NET

```
<%@ Page Language="vb" AutoEventWireup="false" %>
<!DOCTYPE HTML PUBLIC "-//W3C//DTD HTML 4.0 Transitional//EN">
<html>
<head><title></title>
</head>
<body>
    <form Id="Form1" RunAt="server">
    <asp:TextBox id="txtInput" runat="server"></asp:TextBox>
    <asp:RegularExpressionValidator Id="revInput" RunAt="server"
        ControlToValidate="txtInput"
        ErrorMessage="Please enter a valid value"
        ValidationExpression="^(0?2/(0?[1-9]|[12][0-9])|➥
(0?[469]|11)/(0?[1-9]|[12][0-9]|30)|➥
(0?[13578]|1[02])/(0?[1-9]|[12][0-9]|3[01]))/\d{4}$">
    </asp:RegularExpressionValidator>
    <asp:Button Id="btnSubmit" RunAt="server" CausesValidation="True"
        Text="Submit"></asp:Button>
    </form>
</body>
</html>
```

C#

```
using System;
using System.IO;
using System.Text.RegularExpressions;

public class Recipe
{
    private static string month29 = "0?2/(0?[1-9]|[12][0-9])";
    private static string month30 = "(0?[469]|11)/(0?[1-9]|[12][0-9]|30)";
    private static string month31 = "(0?[13578]|1[02])/(0?[1-9]|[12][0-9]|3[01])";
    private static Regex _Regex = new Regex(String.Format("^({0}|{1}|{2})",
```

```
                                            month29,
                                            month30,
                                            month31
                                            ) + @"/\d{4}$");

    public void Run(string fileName)
    {
        String line;
        int lineNbr = 0;
        using (StreamReader sr = new StreamReader(fileName))
        {
            while(null != (line = sr.ReadLine()))
            {
                lineNbr++;
                if (_Regex.IsMatch(line))
                {
                    Console.WriteLine("Found match '{0}' at line {1}",
                        line,
                        lineNbr);
                }
            }
        }
    }

    public static void Main( string[] args )
    {
        Recipe r = new Recipe();
        r.Run(args[0]);
    }
}
```

Visual Basic .NET

```
Imports System
Imports System.IO
Imports System.Text.RegularExpressions
Public Class Recipe

    Private Const month29 = "0?2/(0?[1-9]|[12][0-9])"
    Private Const month30 = "(0?[469]|11)/(0?[1-9]|[12][0-9]|30)"
    Private Const month31 = "(0?[13578]|1[02])/(0?[1-9]|[12][0-9]|3[01])"
    Private Shared _Regex As Regex = New Regex(String.Format("^({0}|{1}|{2})", _
                                            month29, _
                                            month30, _
                                            month31 _
                                            ) & "/\d{4}$")
```

```vbnet
    Public Sub Run(ByVal fileName As String)
        Dim line As String
        Dim lineNbr As Integer = 0
        Dim sr As StreamReader = File.OpenText(fileName)
        line = sr.ReadLine
        While Not line Is Nothing
            lineNbr = lineNbr + 1
            If _Regex.IsMatch(line) Then
                Console.WriteLine("Found match '{0}' at line {1}", _
                    line, _
                    lineNbr)
            End If
            line = sr.ReadLine
        End While
        sr.Close()
    End Sub

    Public Shared Sub Main(ByVal args As String())
        Dim r As Recipe = New Recipe
        r.Run(args(0))
    End Sub

End Class
```

VBScript

```vbscript
Dim fso,s,re,line,lineNbr
Set fso = CreateObject("Scripting.FileSystemObject")
Set s = fso.OpenTextFile(WScript.Arguments.Item(0), 1, True)
Set re = New RegExp
re.Pattern = "^(0?2/(0?[1-9]|[12][0-9])|➡
(0?[469]|11)/(0?[1-9]|[12][0-9]|30)|➡
(0?[13578]|1[02])/(0?[1-9]|[12][0-9]|3[01]))/\d{4}$"
lineNbr = 0
Do While Not s.AtEndOfStream
    line = s.ReadLine()
    lineNbr = lineNbr + 1
    If re.Test(line) Then
        WScript.Echo "Found match: '" & line & "' at line " & lineNbr
    End If
Loop
s.Close
```

JavaScript

```
<html>
<head>
<title>4-15. Validating Dates in MM/DD/YYYY</title>
</head>
<body>
<form name="form1">
    <input type="textbox" name="txtInput" />
    <script type="text/javascript">
    function validate() {
        if (! document.form1.txtInput.value.match(/^(0?2/(0?[1-9]|[12][0-9])|➡
(0?[469]|11)/(0?[1-9]|[12][0-9]|30)|➡
(0?[13578]|1[02])/(0?[1-9]|[12][0-9]|3[01]))/\d{4}$/)) {
            alert("Please enter valid value!")
        } else {
            alert("Success!")
        }
    }
    </script>
    <input type="button" name="btnSubmit" onclick="validate()" value="Go" />
</form>
</body>
</html>
```

How It Works

This recipe is based a little on recipe 4-3 as far as the day ranges are concerned. Instead of looking for month names, it looks for month numbers that match with the number of maximum days. The first group, which matches 02/01–02/29 or 2/1–2/29, is as follows:

0	A zero . . .
?	found zero or one time, followed by . . .
2	a two, then . . .
/	a slash . . .
(	a second group that contains . . .
0	a zero . . .
?	which is optional (it can be found zero or one time), followed by . . .
[1-9]	a range of one through nine . . .

| or . . .

[12]   a one or a two, followed by . . .

[0-9]   a digit, zero through nine . . .

)   the end of the group.

See Also 2-1, 2-2, 2-3, 4-1, 4-2, 4-3, 4-4, 4-5, 4-6, 4-8, 4-11, 4-12, 4-13, 4-14, 4-17, 4-19

4-16. Validating Times

This recipe validates times on a 12-hour clock. The times *12:00 PM*, *12:21 P.M.*, and *1:38 A.M.* are valid; *13:00 PM* and *12:67 A.M.* aren't valid. Seconds are allowed (*12:32:12 P.M.* is valid). This expression is case-sensitive, so *12:00 PM* will match, but *12:00 p.m.* won't. See the "Variations" section of this recipe for tips on how to match 24-hour clocks.

.NET Framework

ASP.NET

```
<%@ Page Language="vb" AutoEventWireup="false" %>
<!DOCTYPE HTML PUBLIC "-//W3C//DTD HTML 4.0 Transitional//EN">
<html>
<head><title></title>
</head>
<body>
    <form Id="Form1" RunAt="server">
    <asp:TextBox id="txtInput" runat="server"></asp:TextBox>
    <asp:RegularExpressionValidator Id="revInput" RunAt="server"
        ControlToValidate="txtInput"
        ErrorMessage="Please enter a valid value"
        ValidationExpression="^(?:0?[1-9]|1[0-2]):(?:[0-5][0-9])➥
(?::[0-5][0-9])? ?(?:[PA]\.M\.|[PA]M)$">
    </asp:RegularExpressionValidator>
    <asp:Button Id="btnSubmit" RunAt="server" CausesValidation="True"
        Text="Submit"></asp:Button>
    </form>
</body>
```

C#

```
using System;
using System.IO;
using System.Text.RegularExpressions;

public class Recipe
{
    private static Regex _Regex = new Regex( @"^(?:0?[1-9]|1[0-2]):➥
(?:[0-5][0-9])(?::[0-5][0-9])? ?(?:[PA]\.M\.|[PA]M)$" );

    public void Run(string fileName)
    {
        String line;
        int lineNbr = 0;
        using (StreamReader sr = new StreamReader(fileName))
        {
            while(null != (line = sr.ReadLine()))
```

```
            {
                lineNbr++;
                if (_Regex.IsMatch(line))
                {
                    Console.WriteLine("Found match '{0}' at line {1}",
                        line,
                        lineNbr);
                }
            }
        }
    }

    public static void Main( string[] args )
    {
        Recipe r = new Recipe();
        r.Run(args[0]);
    }
}
```

Visual Basic .NET

```
Imports System
Imports System.IO
Imports System.Text.RegularExpressions
Public Class Recipe

    Private Shared _Regex As Regex = New Regex("^(?:0?[1-9]|1[0-2]):➡
(?:[0-5][0-9])(?::[0-5][0-9])? ?(?:[PA]\.M\.|[PA]M)$")

    Public Sub Run(ByVal fileName As String)
        Dim line As String
        Dim lineNbr As Integer = 0
        Dim sr As StreamReader = File.OpenText(fileName)
        line = sr.ReadLine
        While Not line Is Nothing
            lineNbr = lineNbr + 1
            If _Regex.IsMatch(line) Then
                Console.WriteLine("Found match '{0}' at line {1}", _
                    line, _
                    lineNbr)
            End If
            line = sr.ReadLine
        End While
        sr.Close()
    End Sub
```

```
Public Shared Sub Main(ByVal args As String())
    Dim r As Recipe = New Recipe
    r.Run(args(0))
End Sub

End Class
```

VBScript

```
Dim fso,s,re,line,lineNbr
Set fso = CreateObject("Scripting.FileSystemObject")
Set s = fso.OpenTextFile(WScript.Arguments.Item(0), 1, True)
Set re = New RegExp
re.Pattern = "^(?:0?[1-9]|1[0-2]):(?:[0-5][0-9])➡
(?::[0-5][0-9])? ?(?:[PA]\.M\.|[PA]M)$"
re.IgnoreCase = True
lineNbr = 0
Do While Not s.AtEndOfStream
    line = s.ReadLine()
    lineNbr = lineNbr + 1
    If re.Test(line) Then
        WScript.Echo "Found match: '" & line & "' at line " & lineNbr
    End If
Loop
s.Close
```

JavaScript

```
<html>
<head>
<title>4-16. Validating Times</title>
</head>
<body>
<form name="form1">
    <input type="textbox" name="txtInput" />
    <script type="text/javascript">
    function validate() {
        if (! document.form1.txtInput.value.match(/^(?:0?[1-9]|1[0-2]):➡
(?:[0-5][0-9])(?::[0-5][0-9])? ?(?:[PA]\.M\.|[PA]M)$/)) {
            alert("Please enter valid value!")
        } else {
            alert("Success!")
        }
    }
    </script>
```

```
      <input type="button" name="btnSubmit" onclick="validate()" value="Go" />
</form>
</body>
</html>
```

How It Works

The crux of this expression, and also what makes it so verbose, is the splitting up of numbers to make sure the time given is within the appropriate ranges. To make this expression easier to digest, I'll break it down into four parts: the hour portion, the minutes expression, the optional seconds expression, and the p.m./a.m. expression. The following is a breakdown of the hour portion of the expression:

(?:	a noncapturing group containing . . .
0	a zero . . .
?	that's optional, followed by . . .
[1-9]	any number one through nine . . .
|	or . . .
1	a one followed by . . .
[0-2]	anything from zero to two.

That will catch anything from 1–12. The next group, as follows, will match numbers 00–59:

(?:	a noncapturing group containing . . .
[0-5]	any number zero through five, followed by . . .
[0-9]	any number zero through nine . . .
)	the end of the noncapturing group.

This group is repeated with a ? at the end of it for the seconds expression to make it optional, and a colon is added in the group to separate minutes from seconds. The last group, which matches either *A.M.* or *P.M.*, is as follows:

(?:	a noncapturing group containing . . .
[PA]	a *P* or *A*, then . . .
\.	a literal period (.) . . .
M	an *M*, followed by . . .
\.	a literal period . . .
|	or . . .

[PA]   a *P* or *A*, then . . .

M   an *M* . . .

)   the end of the noncapturing group.

This expression allows *PM*, *P.M.*, *AM*, and *A.M.*; setting `IgnoreCase` to `True` tells the interpreter to ignore the case in the string, so lowercase versions of the abbreviations will also match.

Variations

You may be in a situation where you need to validate a 24-hour time instead of the 12-hour time shown in this recipe. If that's the case, you can easily modify this recipe to validate for 24-hour times. You won't need the a.m. or p.m. checks anymore, and you'll need to modify the ranges to allow for any number 00–24, like so:

```
^(?:0[1-9]|1[0-9]|2[0-3]):(?:[0-5][0-9])(?::[0-5][0-9])?
```

If you'd like to match both 12-hour and 24-hour times, just join the two expressions with an |, like this (I took out the noncapturing group notation for brevity):

```
^(0?[1-9]|1[0-2]):([0-5][0-9])(:[0-5][0-9])? ?([PA](\.M\.|M))|➡
(0?[1-9]|1[0-9]|2[0-3]):([0-5][0-9])(:[0-5][0-9])$
```

See Also 1-9, 4-3, 4-10, 4-13, 4-15

4-17. Validating U.S. Postal Codes

You can use this recipe to validate U.S. postal codes. It accepts ZIP+4 codes as an option. The numbers 55555-5555 and 55555 are valid, but 444 and 444-4444 aren't.

.NET Framework

ASP.NET

```
<%@ Page Language="vb" AutoEventWireup="false" %>
<!DOCTYPE HTML PUBLIC "-//W3C//DTD HTML 4.0 Transitional//EN">
<html>
<head><title></title>
</head>
<body>
    <form Id="Form1" RunAt="server">
    <asp:TextBox id="txtInput" runat="server"></asp:TextBox>
    <asp:RegularExpressionValidator Id="revInput" RunAt="server"
        ControlToValidate="txtInput"
        ErrorMessage="Please enter a valid value"
        ValidationExpression="^\d{5}(?:-\d{4})?$">
    </asp:RegularExpressionValidator>
    <asp:Button Id="btnSubmit" RunAt="server" CausesValidation="True"
        Text="Submit"></asp:Button>
    </form>
</body>
```

C#

```
using System;
using System.IO;
using System.Text.RegularExpressions;

public class Recipe
{
    private static Regex _Regex = new Regex( @"^\d{5}(?:-\d{4})?$" );

    public void Run(string fileName)
    {
        String line;
        int lineNbr = 0;
        using (StreamReader sr = new StreamReader(fileName))
        {
            while(null != (line = sr.ReadLine()))
            {
                lineNbr++;
                if (_Regex.IsMatch(line))
                {
```

```csharp
                    Console.WriteLine("Found match '{0}' at line {1}",
                        line,
                        lineNbr);
                }
            }
        }
    }

    public static void Main( string[] args )
    {
        Recipe r = new Recipe();
        r.Run(args[0]);
    }
}
```

Visual Basic .NET

```vbnet
Imports System
Imports System.IO
Imports System.Text.RegularExpressions
Public Class Recipe

    Private Shared _Regex As Regex = New Regex("^\d{5}(?:-\d{4})?$")

    Public Sub Run(ByVal fileName As String)
        Dim line As String
        Dim lineNbr As Integer = 0
        Dim sr As StreamReader = File.OpenText(fileName)
        line = sr.ReadLine
        While Not line Is Nothing
            lineNbr = lineNbr + 1
            If _Regex.IsMatch(line) Then
                Console.WriteLine("Found match '{0}' at line {1}", _
                    line, _
                    lineNbr)
            End If
            line = sr.ReadLine
        End While
        sr.Close()
    End Sub

    Public Shared Sub Main(ByVal args As String())
        Dim r As Recipe = New Recipe
        r.Run(args(0))
    End Sub

End Class
```

VBScript

```vbscript
Dim fso,s,re,line,lineNbr
Set fso = CreateObject("Scripting.FileSystemObject")
Set s = fso.OpenTextFile(WScript.Arguments.Item(0), 1, True)
Set re = New RegExp
re.Pattern = "^\d{5}(?:-\d{4})?$"
lineNbr = 0
Do While Not s.AtEndOfStream
    line = s.ReadLine()
    lineNbr = lineNbr + 1
    If re.Test(line) Then
        WScript.Echo "Found match: '" & line & "' at line " & lineNbr
    End If
Loop
s.Close
```

JavaScript

```html
<html>
<head>
<title>4-17. Validating U.S. Postal Codes</title>
</head>
<body>
<form name="form1">
    <input type="textbox" name="txtInput" />
    <script type="text/javascript">
    function validate() {
        if (! document.form1.txtInput.value.match(/^\d{5}(?:-\d{4})?$/)) {
            alert("Please enter valid value!")
        } else {
            alert("Success!")
        }
    }
    </script>
    <input type="button" name="btnSubmit" onclick="validate()" value="Go" />
</form>
</body>
</html>
```

How It Works

This expression looks for five digits, which make up U.S. postal codes. It also allows the +4 portion of the postal code to be added with a dash separating the two. The details are as follows:

^	the beginning of the line . . .
\d	a number . . .
{5}	found five times, followed by . . .
(?:	a noncapturing group containing . . .
-	a dash . . .
\d	a number . . .
{4}	found four times . . .
)	the end of the noncapturing group . . .
?	which is optional, then . . .
$	the end of the line.

4-18. Extracting Usernames from E-mail Addresses

You can use this recipe to grab the username from an e-mail address. Given *myname@example.com*, the result will be *myname*.

.NET Framework

C#

```csharp
using System;
using System.IO;
using System.Text.RegularExpressions;

public class Recipe
{
    private static Regex _Regex = new Regex( @"^(?<user>[^@]+)" );

    public void Run(string fileName)
    {
        String line;
        using (StreamReader sr = new StreamReader(fileName))
        {
            while(null != (line = sr.ReadLine()) && _Regex.IsMatch(line))
            {
                Console.WriteLine("Found user name:  '{0}'",
                    _Regex.Match(line).Result("${user}"));
            }
        }
    }

    public static void Main( string[] args )
    {
        Recipe r = new Recipe();
        r.Run(args[0]);
    }
}
```

Visual Basic .NET

```vbnet
Imports System
Imports System.IO
Imports System.Text.RegularExpressions
Public Class Recipe

    Private Shared _Regex As Regex = New Regex("^(?<user>[^@]+)")
```

```
    Public Sub Run(ByVal fileName As String)
        Dim line As String
        Dim newLine As String
        Dim sr As StreamReader = File.OpenText(fileName)
        line = sr.ReadLine
        While Not line Is Nothing
            If _Regex.IsMatch(line) Then
                Console.WriteLine("Captured value '{0}'", _
                    _Regex.Match(line).Result("${user}"))
            End If
            line = sr.ReadLine
        End While
        sr.Close()
    End Sub

    Public Shared Sub Main(ByVal args As String())
        Dim r As Recipe = New Recipe
        r.Run(args(0))
    End Sub

End Class
```

VBScript

```
Dim fso,s,re,line,newstr
Set fso = CreateObject("Scripting.FileSystemObject")
Set s = fso.OpenTextFile(WScript.Arguments.Item(0), 1, True)
Set re = New RegExp
re.Pattern = "^([^@]+)"
Do While Not s.AtEndOfStream
    line = s.ReadLine()
    newstr = re.Replace(line, "$1")
    WScript.Echo "New string '" & newstr & "', original '" & line & "'"
Loop
s.Close
```

JavaScript

```
<html>
<head>
<title>4-18. Extracting Usernames from E-mail Addresses</title>
</head>
<body>
<form name="form1">
    <input type="text" name="txtInput" />
    <div id="lblResult"></div>
    <script language="javascript">
```

```
        function replace() {
            document.getElementById('lblResult').innerHTML = ➥
document.form1.txtInput.value.replace(/^([^@]+)/, "$1");
        }
    </script>
    <input type="button" name="btnSubmit" onclick="replace()" value="Go" />
</form>
</body>
</html>
```

How It Works

This expression works to extract a username from an e-mail address because it grabs everything up to the at (@) sign in one group.

Note This expression doesn't validate the address. For more about e-mail address validation, see recipe 4-11.

The following is the expression, broken down into parts:

^   the beginning of the line . . .

(?< . . . >   a capturing group containing . . .

[^@]   everything that isn't an at (@) sign . . .

+   found one or more times.

See Also 1-7, 1-17, 1-20, 2-4, 2-5, 2-8, 2-9, 2-10, 3-1, 3-2, 3-3, 3-4, 3-5, 3-6, 4-6

4-19. Extracting Country Codes from International Phone Numbers

You can use this expression to extract the country code from an international phone number. It assumes the country code starts after the plus (+) sign and goes up to the first space or hyphen for a maximum of three characters. Given +1 1-555-333-4444, it will extract the 1.

.NET Framework

C#

```csharp
using System;
using System.IO;
using System.Text.RegularExpressions;

public class Recipe
{
    private static Regex _Regex = new Regex( @"^\+(?<dc>[-\d]+)" );

    public void Run(string fileName)
    {
        String line;
        using (StreamReader sr = new StreamReader(fileName))
        {
            while(null != (line = sr.ReadLine()) && _Regex.IsMatch(line))
            {
                Console.WriteLine("Found protocol:  '{0}'",
                    _Regex.Match(line).Result("${dc}"));
            }
        }
    }

    public static void Main( string[] args )
    {
        Recipe r = new Recipe();
        r.Run(args[0]);
    }
}
```

Visual Basic .NET

```
Imports System
Imports System.IO
Imports System.Text.RegularExpressions
Public Class Recipe

    Private Shared _Regex As Regex = New Regex("^\+(?<dc>[-\d]+)")

    Public Sub Run(ByVal fileName As String)
        Dim line As String
        Dim newLine As String
        Dim sr As StreamReader = File.OpenText(fileName)
        line = sr.ReadLine
        While Not line Is Nothing
            If _Regex.IsMatch(line) Then
                Console.WriteLine("Captured value '{0}'", _
                    _Regex.Match(line).Result("${dc}"))
            End If
            line = sr.ReadLine
        End While
        sr.Close()
    End Sub

    Public Shared Sub Main(ByVal args As String())
        Dim r As Recipe = New Recipe
        r.Run(args(0))
    End Sub

End Class
```

VBScript

```
Dim fso,s,re,line,newstr
Set fso = CreateObject("Scripting.FileSystemObject")
Set s = fso.OpenTextFile(WScript.Arguments.Item(0), 1, True)
Set re = New RegExp
re.Pattern = "^\+([-\d]+)"
Do While Not s.AtEndOfStream
    line = s.ReadLine()
    newstr = re.Replace(line, "$1")
    WScript.Echo "New string '" & newstr & "', original '" & line & "'"
Loop
s.Close
```

JavaScript

```
<html>
<head>
<title>4-19. Extracting Dialing Codes from International Phone Numbers</title>
</head>
<body>
<form name="form1">
    <input type="text" name="txtInput" />
    <div id="lblResult"></div>
    <script language="javascript">
        function replace() {
            document.getElementById('lblResult').innerHTML = ➨
document.form1.txtInput.value.replace(/^\+([-\d]+)/, "$1");
        }
    </script>
    <input type="button" name="btnSubmit" onclick="replace()" value="Go" />
</form>
</body>
</html>
```

How It Works

By capturing everything after the dialing code but not putting it back in the replacement, this expression drops all but what was found as the dialing code. The following is the search expression, broken down:

^	the beginning of the line . . .
\+	a literal plus (+) . . .
(?< . . . >	a named group that captures . . .
[-\d]	a character class that matches a hyphen or a digit . . .
+	one or more times, up to . . .
)	the end of the group.

4-20. Reformatting People's Names (*First Name, Last Name*)

This expression will look at a string and try to parse it as a proper name given in *firstname, lastname* format. If it finds a suitable match, it will rewrite the name as *lastname, firstname*.

.NET Framework

C#

```csharp
using System;
using System.IO;
using System.Text.RegularExpressions;

public class Recipe
{
    private static Regex _Regex = new Regex( @"^(.*)\s([a-z][-a-z'] +[a-z])$",
        RegexOptions.IgnoreCase );
    public void Run(string fileName)
    {
        String line;
        String newLine;
        using (StreamReader sr = new StreamReader(fileName))
        {
            while(null != (line = sr.ReadLine()))
            {
                newLine = _Regex.Replace(line, @"$2, $1");
                Console.WriteLine("New string is: '{0}', ➥
original was: '{1}'",
                    newLine,
                    line);
            }
        }
    }

    public static void Main( string[] args )
    {
        Recipe r = new Recipe();
        r.Run(args[0]);
    }
}
```

Visual Basic .NET

```
Imports System
Imports System.IO
Imports System.Text.RegularExpressions
Public Class Recipe

    Private Shared _Regex As Regex = New Regex("^(.*)\s([a-z][-a-z'] +[a-z])$", _
        RegexOptions.IgnoreCase)

    Public Sub Run(ByVal fileName As String)
        Dim line As String
        Dim newLine As String
        Dim sr As StreamReader = File.OpenText(fileName)
        line = sr.ReadLine
        While Not line Is Nothing
            newLine = _Regex.Replace(line, "$2, $1")
            Console.WriteLine("New string is: '{0}', ➡
original was: '{1}'", _
              newLine, _
              line)
            line = sr.ReadLine
        End While
        sr.Close()
    End Sub

    Public Shared Sub Main(ByVal args As String())
        Dim r As Recipe = New Recipe
        r.Run(args(0))
    End Sub

End Class
```

VBScript

```
Dim fso,s,re,line,newstr
Set fso = CreateObject("Scripting.FileSystemObject")
Set s = fso.OpenTextFile(WScript.Arguments.Item(0), 1, True)
Set re = New RegExp
re.Pattern = "^(.*)\s([a-z][-a-z'] +[a-z])$"
re.IgnoreCase = True
Do While Not s.AtEndOfStream
    line = s.ReadLine()
    newstr = re.Replace(line, "$2, $1")
    WScript.Echo "New string '" & newstr & "', original '" & line & "'"
Loop
s.Close
```

JavaScript

```
<html>
<head>
<title>Reformatting People's Names (First Name, Last Name)</title>
</head>
<body>
<form name="form1">
    <input type="text" name="txtInput" />
    <div id="lblResult"></div>
    <script language="javascript">
        function replace() {
            document.getElementById('lblResult').innerHTML = ➡
document.form1.txtInput.value.replace(/^(.*)\s([a-z][-a-z'] +[a-z])$/i, "$2, $1");
        }
    </script>
    <input type="button" name="btnSubmit" onclick="replace()" value="Go" />
</form>
</body>
</html>
```

How It Works

This expression breaks down like this:

^	the beginning of the line . . .
(.*)	a group that captures anything up to . . .
\s	a space, followed by . . .
(	a group that contains . . .
[a-z]	a character class that matches letters from *a* to *z* . . .
[-a-z'] +	a character class that matches letters from *a* to *z*, a hyphen (-), or a single quote (') . . .
[a-z]	a character class that matches letters from *a* to *z* . . .
)	the end of the group . . .
$	the end of the line.

The combination [a-z][-a-z'][a-z] looks for letters, hyphens, and single quotes sandwiched between letters at the beginning and end of the word. This is a guess for what a name should look like, taking into account names such as *Smith* and *O'Brian* and *Doe-Ray* but figuring names such as -*Smith*- and '*Doe* are wrong.

Variations

Depending on the text or data you're working with, it's probable that you might need to match characters outside the English ASCII set. An easy way to modify this expression is to just use [\p{Lu}\p{Ll}] in place of [a-z].

■**See Also** 1-5, 1-9, 2-1, 2-2, 2-7, 4-11

4-21. Finding Addresses with Post Office Boxes

Some input may require a street address, especially when shipping information is required. This recipe catches *PO*, *P.O.*, and *Box* to catch addresses, so an application can warn users if there appears to be a post office box address instead of a street address.

.NET Framework

ASP.NET

```
<%@ Page Language="vb" AutoEventWireup="false" %>
<!DOCTYPE HTML PUBLIC "-//W3C//DTD HTML 4.0 Transitional//EN">
<html>
<head><title></title>
</head>
<body>
    <form Id="Form1" RunAt="server">
    <asp:TextBox id="txtInput" runat="server"></asp:TextBox>
    <asp:RegularExpressionValidator Id="revInput" RunAt="server"
        ControlToValidate="txtInput"
        ErrorMessage="Please enter a valid value"
        ValidationExpression="^(?:P\.?O\.?\s)?(?:BOX)\b">
    </asp:RegularExpressionValidator>
    <asp:Button Id="btnSubmit" RunAt="server" CausesValidation="True"
        Text="Submit"></asp:Button>
    </form>
</body>
```

C#

```csharp
using System;
using System.IO;
using System.Text.RegularExpressions;

public class Recipe
{
    private static Regex _Regex = new Regex( @"^(?:P\.?O\.?\s)?(?:BOX)\b",
        RegexOptions.IgnoreCase );

    public void Run(string fileName)
    {
        String line;
        int lineNbr = 0;
        using (StreamReader sr = new StreamReader(fileName))
        {
            while(null != (line = sr.ReadLine()))
            {
                lineNbr++;
                if (_Regex.IsMatch(line))
```

```csharp
                    {
                        Console.WriteLine("Found match '{0}' at line {1}",
                            line,
                            lineNbr);
                    }
                }
            }
        }

    public static void Main( string[] args )
    {
        Recipe r = new Recipe();
        r.Run(args[0]);
    }
}
```

Visual Basic .NET

```vbnet
Imports System
Imports System.IO
Imports System.Text.RegularExpressions
Public Class Recipe

    Private Shared _Regex As Regex = New Regex("^(?:P\.?0\.?\s)?(?:BOX)\b")

    Public Sub Run(ByVal fileName As String)
        Dim line As String
        Dim lineNbr As Integer = 0
        Dim sr As StreamReader = File.OpenText(fileName)
        line = sr.ReadLine
        While Not line Is Nothing
            lineNbr = lineNbr + 1
            If _Regex.IsMatch(line) Then
                Console.WriteLine("Found match '{0}' at line {1}", _
                    line, _
                    lineNbr)
            End If
            line = sr.ReadLine
        End While
        sr.Close()
    End Sub

    Public Shared Sub Main(ByVal args As String())
        Dim r As Recipe = New Recipe
        r.Run(args(0))
    End Sub

End Class
```

VBScript

```
Dim fso,s,re,line,lineNbr
Set fso = CreateObject("Scripting.FileSystemObject")
Set s = fso.OpenTextFile(WScript.Arguments.Item(0), 1, True)
Set re = New RegExp
re.Pattern = "^(?:P\.?O\.?\s)?(?:BOX)\b"
re.IgnoreCase = True
lineNbr = 0
Do While Not s.AtEndOfStream
    line = s.ReadLine()
    lineNbr = lineNbr + 1
    If re.Test(line) Then
        WScript.Echo "Found match: '" & line & "' at line " & lineNbr
    End If
Loop
s.Close
```

JavaScript

```
<html>
<head>
<title>4-21. Finding Addresses with Post Office Boxes</title>
</head>
<body>
<form name="form1">
    <input type="textbox" name="txtInput" />
    <script type="text/javascript">
    function validate() {
        if (! document.form1.txtInput.value.match(/^(?:P\.?O\.?\s)?(?:BOX)\b/i)) {
            alert("Please enter valid value!")
        } else {
            alert("Success!")
        }
    }
    </script>
    <input type="button" name="btnSubmit" onclick="validate()" value="Go" />
</form>
</body>
</html>
```

How It Works

This expression operates on the assumption that an address that starts with *Box, PO Box*, or *P.O. Box* isn't a street address. If the match succeeds, the previous script spits out a message to the screen. Otherwise, it tells you it's happily shipping to the address you've provided.

The expression breaks down like this:

^	the beginning of the line . . .
(?:	a noncapturing group containing . . .
P	a *P* . . .
\.	a period . . .
?	that's optional . . .
O	an *O* . . .
\.	a period . . .
?	that's optional . . .
)	the end of the noncapturing group . . .
?	where the previous group is optional . . .
(?:	a noncapturing group that contains . . .
BOX	*B, O*, and then *X* . . .
)	the end of the noncapturing group . . .
\b	a word boundary.

4-22. Validating Affirmative Responses

You can use this recipe as a user-friendly method of detecting positive configuration values. With this recipe, code for checking for *True*, *true*, *Y*, or *Yes* is unnecessary.

.NET Framework

C#

```csharp
using System;
using System.IO;
using System.Text.RegularExpressions;

public class Recipe
{
    private static Regex _Regex = new Regex( @"^(t(rue)?|y(es)?)$",
        RegexOptions.IgnoreCase );

    public void Run(string fileName)
    {
        String line;
        int lineNbr = 0;
        using (StreamReader sr = new StreamReader(fileName))
        {
            while(null != (line = sr.ReadLine()))
            {
                lineNbr++;
                if (_Regex.IsMatch(line))
                {
                    Console.WriteLine("Found match '{0}' at line {1}",
                        line,
                        lineNbr);
                }
            }
        }
    }

    public static void Main( string[] args )
    {
        Recipe r = new Recipe();
        r.Run(args[0]);
    }
}
```

Visual Basic .NET

```
Imports System
Imports System.IO
Imports System.Text.RegularExpressions
Public Class Recipe

    Private Shared _Regex As Regex = New Regex("^(t(rue)?|y(es)?)$", _
        RegexOptions.IgnoreCase)

    Public Sub Run(ByVal fileName As String)
        Dim line As String
        Dim lineNbr As Integer = 0
        Dim sr As StreamReader = File.OpenText(fileName)
        line = sr.ReadLine
        While Not line Is Nothing
            lineNbr = lineNbr + 1
            If _Regex.IsMatch(line) Then
                Console.WriteLine("Found match '{0}' at line {1}", _
                    line, _
                    lineNbr)
            End If
            line = sr.ReadLine
        End While
        sr.Close()
    End Sub

    Public Shared Sub Main(ByVal args As String())
        Dim r As Recipe = New Recipe
        r.Run(args(0))
    End Sub

End Class
```

VBScript

```
Dim fso,s,re,line,lineNbr
Set fso = CreateObject("Scripting.FileSystemObject")
Set s = fso.OpenTextFile(WScript.Arguments.Item(0), 1, True)
Set re = New RegExp
re.Pattern = "^(t(rue)?|y(es)?)$"
re.IgnoreCase = True
lineNbr = 0
Do While Not s.AtEndOfStream
```

```
    line = s.ReadLine()
    lineNbr = lineNbr + 1
    If re.Test(line) Then
        WScript.Echo "Found match: '" & line & "' at line " & lineNbr
    End If
Loop
s.Close
```

JavaScript

```
<html>
<head>
<title>4-22. Validating Affirmative Responses</title>
</head>
<body>
<form name="form1">
    <input type="textbox" name="txtInput" />
    <script type="text/javascript">
    function validate() {
        if (! document.form1.txtInput.value.match(/^(t(rue)?|y(es)?)$/i)) {
            alert("Please enter valid value!")
        } else {
            alert("Success!")
        }
    }
    </script>
    <input type="button" name="btnSubmit" onclick="validate()" value="Go" />
</form>
</body>
</html>
```

How It Works

This expression checks for *true*, *t*, *yes*, and *y* with case insensitivity. It can be handy when checking for positive values without putting a bunch of if...else statements in your code.
The following is the expression, broken down into parts:

^	the beginning of the line . . .
(	a group that contains . . .
t	a *t* . . .
(	a group that has . . .
rue	*r, u, e* . . .
)	the end of the group . . .
?	found zero or one times . . .

|	or . . .
y	a *y* . . .
(	a group contains . . .
e	an *e* . . .
s	an *s* . . .
)	the end of the group . . .
?	found zero or one time . . .
)	the end of the outermost group.

The `RegexOptions.IgnoreCase` option makes the search case insensitive, so the expression doesn't have to include the uppercase and lowercase letters.

See Also 1-3, 1-11, 1-16, 1-22, 2-6, 2-8, 2-9, 2-10, 3-1, 3-3, 3-4, 3-5, 4-2, 4-3, 4-6, 4-10, 4-11, 4-12, 4-13, 4-14, 4-15, 4-16

CHAPTER 5

■ ■ ■

HTML and XML

This chapter contains recipes that work with Hypertext Markup Language (HTML), Cascading Style Sheets (CSS), and Extensible Markup Language (XML) files.

For many of the tasks in this chapter, you should probably use already existing APIs instead of regular expressions. However, the recipes in this chapter show some useful techniques that you can modify and use to perform other processing tasks.

5-1. Finding an XML Tag

This recipe allows you to find an XML tag. You can modify the regex with groups to extract the names of the tags, attributes, and values.

.NET Framework

C#

```
using System;
using System.IO;
using System.Text.RegularExpressions;

public class Recipe
{
    private static Regex _Regex = new Regex( ➥
"<[a-z:_][-a-z0-9._:]*((\s+[^>]+)*|/s*)/?>", RegexOptions.IgnoreCase );

    public void Run(string fileName)
    {
        String line;
        int lineNbr = 0;
        using (StreamReader sr = new StreamReader(fileName))
        {
            while(null != (line = sr.ReadLine()))
            {
                lineNbr++;
                if (_Regex.IsMatch(line))
                {
                    Console.WriteLine("Found match '{0}' at line {1}",
                        line,
                        lineNbr);
                }
            }
        }
    }

    public static void Main( string[] args )
    {
        Recipe r = new Recipe();
        r.Run(args[0]);
    }
}
```

Visual Basic .NET

```
Imports System
Imports System.IO
Imports System.Text.RegularExpressions
Public Class Recipe

    Private Shared _Regex As Regex = New Regex("<[a-z:_]➡
[-a-z0-9._:]*((\s+[^>]+)*|/s*)/?>")

    Public Sub Run(ByVal fileName As String)
        Dim line As String
        Dim lineNbr As Integer = 0
        Dim sr As StreamReader = File.OpenText(fileName)
        line = sr.ReadLine
        While Not line Is Nothing
            lineNbr = lineNbr + 1
            If _Regex.IsMatch(line) Then
                Console.WriteLine("Found match '{0}' at line {1}", _
                    line, _
                    lineNbr)
            End If
            line = sr.ReadLine
        End While
        sr.Close()
    End Sub

    Public Shared Sub Main(ByVal args As String())
        Dim r As Recipe = New Recipe
        r.Run(args(0))
    End Sub

End Class
```

VBScript

```
Dim fso,s,re,line,newstr
Set fso = CreateObject("Scripting.FileSystemObject")
Set s = fso.OpenTextFile(WScript.Arguments.Item(0), 1, True)
Set re = New RegExp
re.Pattern = "<[a-z:_][-a-z0-9._:]+((\s+[^>]+)*|/s*)/?>"
Do While Not s.AtEndOfStream
    line = s.ReadLine()
    lineNbr = lineNbr + 1
    If re.Test(line) Then
        WScript.Echo "Found match: '" & line & "' at line " & lineNbr
    End If
Loop
s.Close
```

How It Works

According to `http://www.w3.org/TR/REC-xml/`, an XML tag name must start with a letter, colon
(:), or underscore (_). Any character after that in the tag name can include a letter, digit, colon
(:), period (.), hyphen (-), or underscore (_). To match an XML tag name, use the following
expression:

`[a-z:_]`	a character class that matches a letter, colon, or underscore . . .
`[-a-z0-9._:]`	a character class that matches a dash, letter, digit, period, underscore, or colon . . .
`*`	found any number of times.

5-2. Finding an XML Attribute

This recipe allows you to find an XML attribute. Combine this recipe with recipe 5-1 to match XML tags and their attributes.

.NET Framework

C#

```
using System;
using System.IO;
using System.Text.RegularExpressions;

public class Recipe
{
    private static Regex _Regex = new Regex ( ➥
"(\s+[a-z:_][-a-z0-9._:]*=(""[^<&""]*""|'[^<&']*'))+", RegexOptions.IgnoreCase );

    public void Run(string fileName)
    {
        String line;
        int lineNbr = 0;
        using (StreamReader sr = new StreamReader(fileName))
        {
            while(null != (line = sr.ReadLine()))
            {
                lineNbr++;
                if (_Regex.IsMatch(line))
                {
                    Console.WriteLine("Found match '{0}' at line {1}",
                        line,
                        lineNbr);
                }
            }
        }
    }

    public static void Main( string[] args )
    {
        Recipe r = new Recipe();
        r.Run(args[0]);
    }
}
```

Visual Basic .NET

```
Imports System
Imports System.IO
Imports System.Text.RegularExpressions
Public Class Recipe

    Private Shared _Regex As Regex = New Regex(➥
"(\s+[a-z:_][-a-z0-9._:]*=(""[^&""]*""|'[^&']*'))+", RegexOptions.IgnoreCase)

    Public Sub Run(ByVal fileName As String)
        Dim line As String
        Dim lineNbr As Integer = 0
        Dim sr As StreamReader = File.OpenText(fileName)
        line = sr.ReadLine
        While Not line Is Nothing
            lineNbr = lineNbr + 1
            If _Regex.IsMatch(line) Then
                Console.WriteLine("Found match '{0}' at line {1}", _
                    line, _
                    lineNbr)
            End If
            line = sr.ReadLine
        End While
        sr.Close()
    End Sub

    Public Shared Sub Main(ByVal args As String())
        Dim r As Recipe = New Recipe
        r.Run(args(0))
    End Sub

End Class
```

VBScript

```
Dim fso,s,re,line,newstr
Set fso = CreateObject("Scripting.FileSystemObject")
Set s = fso.OpenTextFile(WScript.Arguments.Item(0), 1, True)
Set re = New RegExp
re.Pattern = "(\s+[a-z:_][-a-z0-9._:]*=(""[^&""]*""|'[^&']*'))+"
Do While Not s.AtEndOfStream
    line = s.ReadLine()
    lineNbr = lineNbr + 1
    If re.Test(line) Then
        WScript.Echo "Found match: '" & line & "' at line " & lineNbr
    End If
Loop
s.Close
```

How It Works

According to `http://www.w3.org/TR/REC-xml/`, the name of an XML attribute follows the same rules as a tag name in XML. The values of the attribute can contain anything except a less-than (<) sign, ampersand (&), and the quote character that's used around the attribute (either a single or double quote). The name of the XML tag is broken down in recipe 5-1, so the following focuses on what comes after the attribute name:

=	an equals sign, followed by . . .
(	a group that contains . . .
"	a double quote, followed by . . .
[^<&"]	a character class that matches anything except a less-than sign, ampersand, and double quote . . .
*	found any number of times . . .
"	a double quote . . .
|	or . . .
'	a single quote . . .
[^<&']	any character except a less-than sign, ampersand, or single quote . . .
*	found any number of times, then . . .
'	a single quote . . .
)	the end of the group.

5-3. Finding an HTML Attribute

This expression allows you to search for an HTML attribute. It ignores the text outside HTML tags. The examples here are looking for the summary attribute. The string <table summary="My table"> will match; <p>summary=""</p> won't match.

.NET Framework

C#

```
using System;
using System.IO;
using System.Text.RegularExpressions;

public class Recipe
{
    private static Regex _Regex = new Regex ( ➡
"<[^>\s]+(\s+[a-z]+(-[a-z]+)?(=(\"[^<&\"]*\"|'[^<&']*'|[^'\"<>\s]+)|[\s>]))+" );

    public void Run(string fileName)
    {
        String line;
        int lineNbr = 0;
        using (StreamReader sr = new StreamReader(fileName))
        {
            while(null != (line = sr.ReadLine()))
            {
                lineNbr++;
                if (_Regex.IsMatch(line))
                {
                    Console.WriteLine("Found match '{0}' at line {1}",
                        line,
                        lineNbr);
                }
            }
        }
    }

    public static void Main( string[] args )
    {
        Recipe r = new Recipe();
        r.Run(args[0]);
    }
}
```

Visual Basic .NET

```
Imports System
Imports System.IO
Imports System.Text.RegularExpressions
Public Class Recipe

    Private Shared _Regex As Regex = New Regex("<[^>\s]+➠
(\s+[a-z]+(-[a-z]+)?(=(""[^<&""]*""|'[^<&']*'|[^'""<>\s]+)|[\s>]))+")

    Public Sub Run(ByVal fileName As String)
        Dim line As String
        Dim lineNbr As Integer = 0
        Dim sr As StreamReader = File.OpenText(fileName)
        line = sr.ReadLine
        While Not line Is Nothing
            lineNbr = lineNbr + 1
            If _Regex.IsMatch(line) Then
                Console.WriteLine("Found match '{0}' at line {1}", _
                    line, _
                    lineNbr)
            End If
            line = sr.ReadLine
        End While
        sr.Close()
    End Sub

    Public Shared Sub Main(ByVal args As String())
        Dim r As Recipe = New Recipe
        r.Run(args(0))
    End Sub

End Class
```

How It Works

You can find a list of valid HTML attributes at http://www.w3.org/TR/html401/index/elements.html. All the attributes in this list have only the letters from a to z or a hyphen in them. At most, you'll find one hyphen. The regular expression used to match this is as follows:

[a-z]   the letters *a* through *z* . . .

+   found one or more times, followed by . . .

(a group that contains . . .

-        a hyphen, followed by . . .

[a-z]	the letters *a* through *z* . . .
+	found one or more times . . .
)	the end of the group . . .
?	that may be found at most once.

This first part of the regex, [a-z]+, will match attributes such as style and align. The second part adds an optional hyphen followed by more letters, which allows the regex to match attributes such as http-equiv.

The rest of the expression matches either a value that's separated from the attribute by an equals (=) sign or the end of the tag, since attributes in HTML can be without values. This regex is as follows:

(	a group that contains . . .
=	an equals sign, followed by . . .
(	a group that contains . . .
"	a double quote, followed by . . .
[^<&"]	a character class that matches anything except a less-than sign, ampersand, or double quote . . .
*	found any number of times, followed by . . .
"	a double quote . . .
|	or . . .
'	a single quote, followed by . . .
[^<&']	a character class that matches anything that isn't a less-than sign, ampersand, or single quote . . .
*	found any number of times . . .
'	a single quote . . .
|	or . . .
[^'""<>\s]	any character that isn't a single or double quote and isn't a less-than sign, greater-than sign, or whitespace . . .
+	found one or more times . . .
)	the end of the group . . .
|	or . . .
[\s>]	whitespace or a greater-than sign . . .
)	the end of the group.

Note In this example, I'm assuming that the text being fed to the expression is valid HTML. For instance, you can make this expression fail by sending in `<p> < summary="" > </p>`, which isn't valid HTML.

5-4. Removing an HTML Attribute

This expression allows you to remove an HTML attribute and its value altogether from an HTML tag. It doesn't do any validation to see if the tag is a real tag; in other words, it's assumed you're not worried about tags named <moo>, which isn't a valid HTML tag name.

.NET Framework

C#

```csharp
using System;
using System.IO;
using System.Text.RegularExpressions;

public class Recipe
{
    private static Regex _Regex = new Regex(
"(<[^"">]+|<[^>""]+(""[^""]*""[^""]*)*)\sstyle=(""[^&""]*""|'[^&']*')?")" );
    public void Run(string fileName)
    {
        String line;
        String newLine;
        using (StreamReader sr = new StreamReader(fileName))
        {
            while(null != (line = sr.ReadLine()))
            {
                newLine = _Regex.Replace(line, @"$1");
                Console.WriteLine("New string is: '{0}', original was: '{1}'",
                    newLine,
                    line);
            }
        }
    }

    public static void Main( string[] args )
    {
        Recipe r = new Recipe();
        r.Run(args[0]);
    }
}
```

Visual Basic .NET

```
Imports System
Imports System.IO
Imports System.Text.RegularExpressions
Public Class Recipe

    Private Shared _Regex As Regex = New
Regex("(<[^"">]+|<[^>""]+(""[^""]*""[^""]*)*)\sstyle=(""[^<&""]*""|'[^<&']*')?" )")

    Public Sub Run(ByVal fileName As String)
        Dim line As String
        Dim newLine As String
        Dim sr As StreamReader = File.OpenText(fileName)
        line = sr.ReadLine
        While Not line Is Nothing
            newLine = _Regex.Replace(line, "$1$2")
            Console.WriteLine("New string is: '{0}', original was: '{1}'", _
             newLine, _
             line)
            line = sr.ReadLine
        End While
        sr.Close()
    End Sub

    Public Shared Sub Main(ByVal args As String())
        Dim r As Recipe = New Recipe
        r.Run(args(0))
    End Sub

End Class
```

How It Works

This expression consists of five groups, which I'll break down and explain one at a time to make them a little easier to understand. The first group is (?<=<), which contains a look-behind that matches the beginning of a tag (<).

The second group, ([^/>]+), matches and captures anything between the start of the tag and before the next group. It makes sure the style attribute is inside a tag by matching only if the tag isn't closed by a greater-than sign between the time the tag opens and the style attribute begins.

The third group, (?:\sstyle=['""][^'""]+?['""]), matches the style attribute. (Refer to recipe 5-5 to see how a similar group breaks down.)

The fourth group is ([^/>]*), which matches and captures anything between the end of the style attribute and the fifth group. It differs from the second group only in its qualifier, because the * qualifier allows the attribute to be at the end of the tag. The second and fourth groups here capture text because the text will be used to reassemble the tag in the replacement expression $1$2.

The fifth and last group is a look-ahead that searches for the close of the tag. It looks for a greater-than sign that may optionally be preceded by a slash:

(?=   a positive look-ahead that contains . . .

/   a slash . . .

?   that may appear at most once, followed by . . .

>   a greater-than sign . . .

| or . . .

\s   whitespace . . .

)   the end of the positive look-ahead.

5-5. Adding an HTML Attribute

This recipe adds an HTML attribute to a tag. It makes sure the attribute isn't already in the tag. In this example, the tag is an h2 tag, and the attribute that's added is a class attribute.

.NET Framework

C#

```csharp
using System;
using System.IO;
using System.Text.RegularExpressions;

public class Recipe
{
    private static Regex _Regex = new Regex( @"(<h2)(?![^>]*\sclass=""[^<&""]*"")" )
    public void Run(string fileName)
    {
        String line;
        String newLine;
        using (StreamReader sr = new StreamReader(fileName))
        {
            while(null != (line = sr.ReadLine()))
            {
                newLine = _Regex.Replace(line, "$1 class=\"myclass\" ");
                Console.WriteLine("New string is: '{0}', original was: '{1}'",
                    newLine,
                    line);
            }
        }
    }

    public static void Main( string[] args )
    {
        Recipe r = new Recipe();
        r.Run(args[0]);
    }
}
```

Visual Basic .NET

```vbnet
Imports System
Imports System.IO
Imports System.Text.RegularExpressions
Public Class Recipe

    Private Shared _Regex As Regex = New Regex("(<h2)(?![^>]*\sclass=""[^<&""]*"")")
```

```
    Public Sub Run(ByVal fileName As String)
        Dim line As String
        Dim newLine As String
        Dim sr As StreamReader = File.OpenText(fileName)
        line = sr.ReadLine
        While Not line Is Nothing
            newLine = _Regex.Replace(line, "$1 class=""myclass"" ")
            Console.WriteLine("New string is: '{0}', original was: '{1}'", _
             newLine, _
             line)
            line = sr.ReadLine
        End While
        sr.Close()
    End Sub

    Public Shared Sub Main(ByVal args As String())
        Dim r As Recipe = New Recipe
        r.Run(args(0))
    End Sub

End Class
```

VBScript

```
Dim fso,s,re,line,newstr
Set fso = CreateObject("Scripting.FileSystemObject")
Set s = fso.OpenTextFile(WScript.Arguments.Item(0), 1, True)
Set re = New RegExp
re.Pattern = "(<h2)(?![^>]*\sclass="")[^<&""]*"")"
Do While Not s.AtEndOfStream
    line = s.ReadLine()
    newstr = re.Replace(line, "$1 class=""c1"" ")
    WScript.Echo "New string '" & newstr & "', original '" & line & "'"
Loop
s.Close
```

How It Works

This regex uses a negative look-ahead to make sure the class attribute doesn't already exist in the tag before adding a new one. The negative look-ahead group is as follows:

(?!	a negative look-ahead that contains . . .
[^>]	a character class that matches anything except a greater-than sign . . .
*	found any number of times, followed by . . .
\s	whitespace, followed by . . .
class=	a *c*, *l*, *a*, *s*, *s*, and equals sign, followed by . . .
"	a double quote, then . . .
[^<&"]	a character class that matches anything except a less-than sign, ampersand, or a double quote . . .
*	found any number of times, followed by . . .
"	a double quote . . .
)	the end of the negative look-ahead.

Variations

This regex as provided is picky about the types of quotes the class attribute uses. If you want to search for single quotes or no quotes at all, change the "[^<&"]*" bit of the regex to (""[^<&""]*""|'[^<&']*'|[^<>\s]+). See recipe 5-3 for details.

5-6. Removing Whitespace from HTML

You can use this recipe to remove whitespace between tags in HTML. For instance, given
<html>   <head>, this recipe will return <html><head>.

.NET Framework

C#

```
using System;
using System.IO;
using System.Text.RegularExpressions;

public class Recipe
{
    private static Regex _Regex = new Regex( @"(?<=>)\s+(?=</?)" );

    public void Run(string fileName)
    {
        String line;
        String newLine;
        using (StreamReader sr = new StreamReader(fileName))
        {
            while(null != (line = sr.ReadLine()))
            {
                newLine = _Regex.Replace(line, "");
                Console.WriteLine("New string is: '{0}', original was: '{1}'",
                    newLine,
                    line);
            }
        }
    }

    public static void Main( string[] args )
    {
        Recipe r = new Recipe();
        r.Run(args[0]);
    }
}
```

Visual Basic .NET

```
Imports System
Imports System.IO
Imports System.Text.RegularExpressions
Public Class Recipe

    Private Shared _Regex As Regex = New Regex("(?<=>)\s+(?=</?)")
```

```vb
Public Sub Run(ByVal fileName As String)
    Dim line As String
    Dim newLine As String
    Dim sr As StreamReader = File.OpenText(fileName)
    line = sr.ReadLine
    While Not line Is Nothing
        newLine = _Regex.Replace(line, "")
        Console.WriteLine("New string is: '{0}', original was: '{1}'", _
         newLine, _
         line)
        line = sr.ReadLine
    End While
    sr.Close()
End Sub

Public Shared Sub Main(ByVal args As String())
    Dim r As Recipe = New Recipe
    r.Run(args(0))
End Sub
```

End Class

How It Works

This expression searches for more than one occurrence of whitespace (\s+) that's surrounded by either > or <. If either is found, it assumes the whitespace is outside an HTML tag. The look-behind that searches for the > is as follows:

(?<=   a positive look-behind that contains . . .

>   a greater-than sign . . .

)   the end of the positive look-behind.

To find an opening of an HTML tag after whitespace, a look-ahead in front of \s+ matches the beginning of the next tag. Since the tag could be a closing tag, the regex has to be able to match < and </. The result is as follows:

(?=   the beginning of a positive look-ahead . . .

<   a less-than sign . . .

/   a slash . . .

?   that's optional . . .

)   the end of the positive look-ahead.

The replacement expression is "", an empty string, which deletes the whitespace matched by the regex \s+.

5-7. Escaping Characters for HTML

This recipe highlights a unique method of replacing certain characters in HTML with escape sequences.

.NET Framework

C#

```csharp
using System;
using System.IO;
using System.Text.RegularExpressions;

public class Recipe
{
    private static Regex _Regex = new Regex( @">(?![^><]+?\/?<)" );

    private string ReverseString(string s)
    {
        char[] array = s.ToCharArray();
        Array.Reverse(array);
        return new String(array);
    }

    public void Run(string fileName)
    {
        String line;
        String newLine;
        using (StreamReader sr = new StreamReader(fileName))
        {
            while(null != (line = sr.ReadLine()))
            {
                newLine = _Regex.Replace(ReverseString(line), ";tl&");
                Console.WriteLine("New string is: '{0}', original was: '{1}'",
                    ReverseString(newLine),
                    line);
            }
        }
    }

    public static void Main( string[] args )
    {
        Recipe r = new Recipe();
        r.Run(args[0]);
    }
}
```

Visual Basic .NET

```
Imports System
Imports System.IO
Imports System.Text.RegularExpressions
Public Class Recipe

    Private Shared _Regex As Regex = New Regex(">(?![^><]+?/?<)")

    Private Function ReverseString(s As String) As String
        Dim strArray As Char() = s.ToCharArray()
        Array.Reverse(strArray)
        Return New String(strArray)
    End Function

    Public Sub Run(ByVal fileName As String)
        Dim line As String
        Dim newLine As String
        Dim sr As StreamReader = File.OpenText(fileName)
        line = sr.ReadLine
        While Not line Is Nothing
            newLine = _Regex.Replace(line, ";tl&")
            Console.WriteLine("New string is: '{0}', original was: '{1}'", _
             newLine, _
             line)
            line = sr.ReadLine
        End While
        sr.Close()
    End Sub

    Public Shared Sub Main(ByVal args As String())
        Dim r As Recipe = New Recipe
        r.Run(args(0))
    End Sub

End Class
```

VBScript

```
Dim fso,s,re,line,newstr
Set fso = CreateObject("Scripting.FileSystemObject")
Set s = fso.OpenTextFile(WScript.Arguments.Item(0), 1, True)
Set re = New RegExp
re.Pattern = ">(?![^><]+?/?<)"
re.Global = True
Do While Not s.AtEndOfStream
    line = s.ReadLine()
```

```
    newstr = re.Replace(StrReverse(line), ";tl&")
    WScript.Echo "New string '" & StrReverse(newstr) & "', original '" & line & "'"
Loop
s.Close
```

How It Works

This one was a little tricky to put together, because in the recipe I needed to make sure the >
character didn't close an HTML tag. Without using back references to put the strings back into
the replacements, I was limited to using look-behinds. However, many implementations of
regular expressions, including all the implementations in this book, don't support variable-
length look-behinds. Since I didn't know how long an HTML tag could be, I needed to have
variable-length capability.

So I cheated—just a little. In this recipe, I used the languages' capabilities (I created a
custom function in C# and Visual Basic .NET, and I used StrReverse in VBScript) to reverse
the string, and then I attacked it with an expression, this time looking *ahead* to make sure the
character is after a full tag.

The group in this expression matches everything from the beginning of an HTML tag up
to a > that isn't inside an HTML tag. Broken down, the expression is as follows:

>   a greater-than sign . . .

(?!   a negative look-ahead that contains . . .

[^   a character class that *doesn't* include . . .

>   a greater-than sign . . .

<   or less-than sign . . .

+?   found one or more times but matching as little as possible . . .

/   a slash . . .

?   found zero or one time . . .

<   a less-than sign . . .

)   the end of the look-ahead.

5-8. Removing Whitespace from CSS

This expression removes the whitespace from inside the curly braces in CSS. Given a line such as p { font-family: Verdana, serif   ;   font-size: 10pt;   }, it will return p {font-family:Verdana, serif;font-size:10pt;}.

.NET Framework

C#

```csharp
using System;
using System.IO;
using System.Text.RegularExpressions;

public class Recipe
{
    private static Regex _Regex = new Regex( @"(?<=[:,;\w{])\s+(?=[}\w;,:])" );
    public void Run(string fileName)
    {
        String line;
        String newLine;
        using (StreamReader sr = new StreamReader(fileName))
        {
            while(null != (line = sr.ReadLine()))
            {
                newLine = _Regex.Replace(line, "");
                Console.WriteLine("New string is: '{0}', original was: '{1}'",
                    newLine,
                    line);
            }
        }
    }

    public static void Main( string[] args )
    {
        Recipe r = new Recipe();
        r.Run(args[0]);
    }
}
```

Visual Basic .NET

```vbnet
Imports System
Imports System.IO
Imports System.Text.RegularExpressions
Public Class Recipe
```

```
Private Shared _Regex As Regex = New Regex("(?<=[:;\w{])\s+(?=[}\w;:])")

Public Sub Run(ByVal fileName As String)
    Dim line As String
    Dim newLine As String
    Dim sr As StreamReader = File.OpenText(fileName)
    line = sr.ReadLine
    While Not line Is Nothing
        newLine = _Regex.Replace(line, "")
        Console.WriteLine("New string is: '{0}', original was: '{1}'", _
         newLine, _
         line)
        line = sr.ReadLine
    End While
    sr.Close()
End Sub

Public Shared Sub Main(ByVal args As String())
    Dim r As Recipe = New Recipe
    r.Run(args(0))
End Sub

End Class
```

How It Works

The look-behinds in this recipe (not supported in VBScript or JavaScript) look to the left of \s+ to see if a colon, a semicolon, a word character, or an opening curly brace appears. The look-behind is as follows:

(?<=   the beginning of a negative look-behind . . .

[:,;\w{]   a character class that includes a colon, a comma, a semicolon, \w, or a left brace . . .

)   the end of the negative look-behind.

The look-ahead matches the same thing (except for } instead of {). The look-ahead syntax is as follows:

(?=   the start of a positive look-ahead . . .

. . .   the inner expression . . .

)   the end of the positive look-ahead.

5-9. Finding Matching <script> Tags

This recipe demonstrates how to capture <script> tags and everything inside them.

.NET Framework

C#

```csharp
using System;
using System.IO;
using System.Text.RegularExpressions;

public class Recipe
{

    private static Regex _Regex =
        new Regex(@"<script language=""javascript"">(([^<""]|[^<]*<[^/][^<])*➡
(""[^""]*""([^<""]|[^<]*<[^/][^<])*)*)?</script>",
                RegexOptions.IgnoreCase | RegexOptions.Multiline);

    public void Run(string fileName)
    {
        String line;
        using (StreamReader sr = new StreamReader(fileName))
        {
            line = sr.ReadToEnd();
            foreach (Match m in _Regex.Matches(line))
            {
                Console.WriteLine("Found match '{0}'",
                    m.ToString());
            }
        }
    }

    public static void Main( string[] args )
    {
        Recipe r = new Recipe();
        r.Run(args[0]);
    }
}
```

Visual Basic .NET

```vbnet
Imports System
Imports System.IO
Imports System.Text.RegularExpressions
Public Class Recipe
```

```vbnet
    Private Shared _Regex As Regex = _
        New Regex("<script language=""javascript"">(([^<""]|[^<]*<[^/][^<])*➥
(""[^""]*""([^<""]|[^<]*<[^/][^<])*)*)?</script>", _
            RegexOptions.IgnoreCase Or RegexOptions.Multiline)

    Public Sub Run(ByVal fileName As String)
        Dim line As String
        Dim sr As StreamReader = File.OpenText(fileName)
        line = sr.ReadToEnd()
        If Not line Is Nothing
            For Each m As Match In _Regex.Matches(line)
                Console.WriteLine("Found match '{0}'", m.ToString())
            Next
        End If
        sr.Close()
    End Sub

    Public Shared Sub Main(ByVal args As String())
        Dim r As Recipe = New Recipe
        r.Run(args(0))
    End Sub

End Class
```

VBScript

```vbscript
Dim fso,s,re,line,matches,m
Set fso = CreateObject("Scripting.FileSystemObject")
Set s = fso.OpenTextFile(WScript.Arguments.Item(0), 1, True)
Set re = New RegExp
re.Pattern = "<script language=""javascript"">(([^<""]|[^<]*<[^/][^<])*(""[^""]*""➥
([^<""]|[^<]*<[^/][^<])*)*)?</script>"
re.IgnoreCase = True
re.MultiLine = True
re.Global = True
line = s.ReadAll()
Set matches = re.Execute(line)
For Each m in matches
    WScript.Echo "Found match:  '" & m.Value & "'"
Next
s.Close
```

How It Works

This regex works by looking for a few different conditions inside <script> tags. Of course, you can greatly reduce this regex just by using lazy qualifiers (such as *?), which match as little as possible. Using lazy qualifiers, the regex is simply `<script.*?</script>`. Not using lazy qualifiers, though, makes the regex significantly more difficult.

Inside the script tags, this regex looks for three conditions. The first is that a less-than sign or a double quote isn't found at all between the end of the opening tag and the beginning of the closing tag. This part is relatively straightforward:

`[^<"]`	any character that isn't a less-than sign or a double quote . . .
`*`	found any number of times.

The next condition that the regex searches for is whether a less-than sign exists. This can happen in script where a less-than sign is in a comparison, such as `i < 0`. Fortunately, there's no operator called `</`, so if a less-than sign is found, it can't be followed by a slash. The second condition checks for the following:

`(`	a group that contains . . .
`[^<]`	a character class that matches anything but a less-than sign . . .
`*`	found any number of times . . .
`<`	a less-than sign, followed by . . .
`[^/]`	any character except a slash . . .
`[^<]`	any character except a less-than sign . . .
`*`	found any number of times . . .
`)`	the end of the group . . .
`*`	where the group may appear any number of times.

The third condition checks to make sure that if any quotes are found in the string, they're closed before the ending script tag:

`. . .`	the first group, followed by . . .
`(`	a group that contains . . .
`"`	a double quote, followed by . . .
`[^"]`	a character class that matches anything that isn't a double quote . . .
`*`	found any number of times . . .
`"`	a double quote . . .
`. . .`	the group repeated again . . .
`)`	the end of the group . . .
`*`	where the group may be found any number of times.

This will allow several quoted strings within the script tags but will make sure the quotes are closed before the ending tag.

For the sake of simplicity, this regex doesn't do a couple of things—the point is to demonstrate the technique to get you started without being overwhelming. After you feel comfortable with the regex, you can modify it. For instance, aside from double quotes, you could change the regex to also check for single quotes. Also, you could modify the regex to look for HTML comments.

Variations

This recipe explicitly matches JavaScript script tags, but you can easily alter it to match any other script tag. If it's unimportant what type of script it is, you can modify the first part of the expression to say something such as `<script language=""((vb|j(ava)?)script""`. This will match JavaScript, JScript, and VBScript. To find even more ways to match the attribute, see recipe 5-3.

CHAPTER 6

■ ■ ■

Source Code

This chapter includes recipes you can use while writing software for tasks such as changing method names, finding globally unique identifiers (GUIDs), changing namespace names, and performing other tasks related to working with source code files.

The .NET Framework, through reflection, provides ways of finding method names in classes. Where possible, use APIs that have been provided to you from vendors—in theory, they've been tested and will give you functionality you don't have to build yourself.

The recipes in this chapter are intended to give you a good start in writing your own regular expressions that help you with coding tasks. For instance, one of the notions I've been experimenting with is using regexes to enforce corporate naming standards in conjunction with tools such as FxCop. For more information about FxCop, see the team page at `http://www.gotdotnet.com/team/fxcop`. Your usage may vary, which is why the regexes in this chapter are like food recipes—modify them to suit your tastes.

Caution In some of the recipes, I change method names and perform some other tasks that could be used for some light refactoring. Regular expressions can come in handy, but they aren't a substitute for getting the code right the first time.

6-1. Finding Code Comments

You can use this recipe to find comments in code. It will find the beginning of C, C++, C#, and single-line comments, but it will also ignore the beginning of comments if they're in double quotes.

.NET Framework

C#

```
using System;
using System.IO;
using System.Text.RegularExpressions;

public class Recipe
{
    private static Regex _Regex = new Regex( ➡
"^(?:[^\"]*(?:\"[^\"]*\"[^\"]*)?)*(?:/\\*|//)" );

    public void Run(string fileName)
    {
        String line;
        int lineNbr = 0;
        using (StreamReader sr = new StreamReader(fileName))
        {
            while(null != (line = sr.ReadLine()))
            {
                lineNbr++;
                if (_Regex.IsMatch(line))
                {
                    Console.WriteLine("Found match '{0}' at line {1}",
                        line,
                        lineNbr);
                }
            }
        }
    }

    public static void Main( string[] args )
    {
        Recipe r = new Recipe();
        r.Run(args[0]);
    }
}
```

Visual Basic .NET

```vbnet
Imports System
Imports System.IO
Imports System.Text.RegularExpressions
Public Class Recipe

    Private Shared _Regex As Regex = _
        New Regex("^(?:[^""]*(?:""[^""]*""[^""]*)?)*(?:/\*|//)")

    Public Sub Run(ByVal fileName As String)
        Dim line As String
        Dim lineNbr As Integer = 0
        Dim sr As StreamReader = File.OpenText(fileName)
        line = sr.ReadLine
        While Not line Is Nothing
            lineNbr = lineNbr + 1
            If _Regex.IsMatch(line) Then
                Console.WriteLine("Found match '{0}' at line {1}", _
                    line, _
                    lineNbr)
            End If
            line = sr.ReadLine
        End While
        sr.Close()
    End Sub

    Public Shared Sub Main(ByVal args As String())
        Dim r As Recipe = New Recipe
        r.Run(args(0))
    End Sub

End Class
```

VBScript

```vbscript
Dim fso,s,re,line,lineNbr
Set fso = CreateObject("Scripting.FileSystemObject")
Set s = fso.OpenTextFile(WScript.Arguments.Item(0), 1, True)
Set re = New RegExp
re.Pattern = "^(?:[^""]*(?:""[^""]*""[^""]*)?)*(?:/\*|//)"
lineNbr = 0
Do While Not s.AtEndOfStream
    line = s.ReadLine()
    lineNbr = lineNbr + 1
```

```
    If re.Test(line) Then
        WScript.Echo "Found match: '" & line & "' at line " & lineNbr
    End If
Loop
s.Close
```

How It Works

The first part of this expression, `^(?:[^"]*(?:"[^"]*"[^"]*)?)*`, makes sure the comment that's matched isn't inside quotes. It does this by making sure an even number of quotes appears before what could be a comment. If it finds an odd number of quotes before the start of the comment, you can assume the code is in comments. One issue with this expression is that it doesn't deal with escaped quotes on a line, so beware that escaped quotes such as `\"` will cause the comment to be undetected if the escaped quotes aren't matched. The following example will cause the comment to be ignored:

```
"I have a double quote: \"" /*This is my ignored comment */
```

Also, this regex doesn't take into account quotes spanning more than one line; if you think this is the case in your data, you can use the multiline option in regular expressions to span lines. See the "Syntax Overview" section in this book for more information about using the multiline option for searches.

This first part breaks down as follows:

`^`	the beginning of the line . . .
`(?:`	a noncapturing group that contains . . .
`[^"]`	a character class that isn't a double quote . . .
`*`	found any number of times . . .
`(?:`	another noncapturing group that contains . . .
`"`	a double quote . . .
`[^"]`	a character class that isn't a double quote . . .
`*`	found any number of times . . .
`"`	a double quote, followed by . . .
`[^"]`	a character class that isn't a double quote . . .
`*`	found any number of times . . .
`)`	the end of the noncapturing group . . .
`?`	where the whole group appears at most once . . .
`)`	the end of the outer noncapturing group . . .
`*`	found any number of times.

So, this expression is making sure that if a double quote is found, it's followed by one more that isn't followed by another one (thus, you get an even number of quotes). You can use this expression to start any other expression where you want to make sure it matches something that isn't inside quotes.

The second part of the expression is pretty straightforward and matches the comment itself. Here all you care about finding is the beginning of the comment—it doesn't matter what's inside it or how it ends at this point. All you know is that you've found the beginning of a comment that isn't in quotes—which is good enough for this search. The comment expression is as follows:

(?:	a noncapturing group that contains . . .
\/	a slash . . .
*	an asterisk . . .
|	or . . .
\/	a slash . . .
\/	another slash . . .
)	the end of a group.

This will match strings that start with /* or //.

6-2. Finding Lines with an Odd Number of Quotes

This recipe looks for lines with an odd number of quotes in a single line. I've found it incredibly useful to narrow down quote issues in shell scripts when syntax highlighting wasn't available to help me find unclosed quotes. This recipe matches the strings `Unclosed"`, which has an unclosed double quote, and `"\"this"`, which has an odd number of quotes.

This expression assumes it doesn't matter whether the quotes are escaped; it assumes only that an odd number of them is an issue.

.NET Framework

ASP.NET

```
<%@ Page Language="vb" AutoEventWireup="false" %>
<!DOCTYPE HTML PUBLIC "-//W3C//DTD HTML 4.0 Transitional//EN">
<html>
<head><title></title>
</head>
<body>
    <form Id="Form1" RunAt="server">
    <asp:TextBox id="txtInput" runat="server"></asp:TextBox>
    <asp:RegularExpressionValidator Id="revInput" RunAt="server"
        ControlToValidate="txtInput"
        ErrorMessage="Please enter a valid value"
        ValidationExpression='^[^"]*"([^"]*|([^"]*"[^"]*"[^"]*)*)$'>
    </asp:RegularExpressionValidator>
    <asp:Button Id="btnSubmit" RunAt="server" CausesValidation="True"
        Text="Submit"></asp:Button>
    </form>
</body>
```

C#

```csharp
using System;
using System.IO;
using System.Text.RegularExpressions;

public class Recipe
{
    private static Regex _Regex =
        new Regex( "^[^\"]*\"([^\"]*|([^\"]*\"[^\"]*\"[^\"]*)*)$" );

    public void Run(string fileName)
    {
        String line;
        int lineNbr = 0;
        using (StreamReader sr = new StreamReader(fileName))
        {
```

```csharp
        while(null != (line = sr.ReadLine()))
        {
            lineNbr++;
            if (_Regex.IsMatch(line))
            {
                Console.WriteLine("Found match '{0}' at line {1}",
                    line,
                    lineNbr);
            }
        }
    }
}

public static void Main( string[] args )
{
    Recipe r = new Recipe();
    r.Run(args[0]);
}
}
```

Visual Basic .NET

```vbnet
Imports System
Imports System.IO
Imports System.Text.RegularExpressions
Public Class Recipe

    Private Shared _Regex As Regex = _
        New Regex("^[^""]*""([^""]*|([^""]*""[^""]*""[^""]*)*)$")

    Public Sub Run(ByVal fileName As String)
        Dim line As String
        Dim lineNbr As Integer = 0
        Dim sr As StreamReader = File.OpenText(fileName)
        line = sr.ReadLine
        While Not line Is Nothing
            lineNbr = lineNbr + 1
            If _Regex.IsMatch(line) Then
                Console.WriteLine("Found match '{0}' at line {1}", _
                    line, _
                    lineNbr)
            End If
            line = sr.ReadLine
        End While
        sr.Close()
    End Sub
```

```
    Public Shared Sub Main(ByVal args As String())
        Dim r As Recipe = New Recipe
        r.Run(args(0))
    End Sub

End Class
```

VBScript

```
Dim fso,s,re,line,lineNbr
Set fso = CreateObject("Scripting.FileSystemObject")
Set s = fso.OpenTextFile(WScript.Arguments.Item(0), 1, True)
Set re = New RegExp
re.Pattern = "^[^""]*""([^""]*|([^""]*""[^""]*""[^""]*)*)$"
lineNbr = 0
Do While Not s.AtEndOfStream
    line = s.ReadLine()
    lineNbr = lineNbr + 1
    If re.Test(line) Then
        WScript.Echo "Found match: '" & line & "' at line " & lineNbr
    End If
Loop
s.Close
```

JavaScript

```
<html>
<head>
<title></title>
</head>
<body>
<form name="form1">
    <input type="textbox" name="txtInput" />
    <script type="text/javascript">
    function validate() {
        if (! document.form1.txtInput.value.match(➡
/^[^"]*"([^"]*|([^"]*"[^"]*"[^"]*)*)$/)) {
            alert("Please enter valid value!")
        } else {
            alert("Success!")
        }
    }
    </script>
    <input type="button" name="btnSubmit" onclick="validate()" value="Go" />
</form>
</body>
</html>
```

How It Works

It's best to go through this expression by breaking it down into a few parts. Overall, the purpose of the expression is to find a quote, and when it does, it makes sure the quote either isn't followed by another one at all or is followed by an even number of quotes. If it's the only one on the line, you'll assume it's mismatched. If it's followed by an even number of quotes, it's also mismatched because an odd number of them appears on the line.

Make sure the quote is found on a line with no other quote before it. (You want to start with a clean slate.) The expression breaks down as follows:

^	the beginning of the line . . .
[^"]	a character class that doesn't match a double quote . . .
*	found zero or more times . . .
"	a double quote.

The group that follows this part of the expression has two parts separated by the "or" operator, |:

[^"]	a character class that doesn't match a double quote . . .
*	found zero or more times.

Finally, the expression ([^"]*"[^"]*"[^"]*)* will look for an even number of quotes by saying the following:

(	a group that contains . . .
[^"]	a character class that isn't a quote . . .
*	found zero or more times . . .
"	a quote . . .
[^"]	a character class that isn't a quote . . .
*	found zero or more times (so the quote isn't closed) . . .
"	a quote . . .
[^"]	a character class that isn't a quote . . .
*	found zero or more times . . .
)	the end of the group . . .
*	where the group can repeat (this allows even numbers).

6-3. Reordering Method Parameters

You can use this recipe to change the order of parameters in a method. MyMethod(1, "mystring") becomes MyMethod("mystring", 1). In this case, MyMethod has only two parameters.

■Note This regex assumes the input is a single-line method call.

.NET Framework

C#

```
using System;
using System.IO;
using System.Text.RegularExpressions;

public class Recipe
{
    private static Regex _Regex =
        new Regex( @"\bMyMethod\s*\(\s*([^,]+|""[^""]*"")\s*,➡
\s*([^,]+|""[^""]*"")(?=\s*[,)])" );
    public void Run(string fileName)
    {
        String line;
        String newLine;
        using (StreamReader sr = new StreamReader(fileName))
        {
            while(null != (line = sr.ReadLine()))
            {
                newLine = _Regex.Replace(line, "MyMethod($2, $1");
                Console.WriteLine("New string is: '{0}', original was: '{1}'",
                    newLine,
                    line);
            }
        }
    }

    public static void Main( string[] args )
    {
        Recipe r = new Recipe();
        r.Run(args[0]);
    }
}
```

Visual Basic .NET

```
Imports System
Imports System.IO
Imports System.Text.RegularExpressions
Public Class Recipe

    Private Shared _Regex As Regex = _
        New Regex("\bMyMethod\s*\(\s*([^,]+|""[^""]*"")\s*,➡
\s*([^,]+|""[^""]*"")(?=\s*[,)])")

    Public Sub Run(ByVal fileName As String)
        Dim line As String
        Dim newLine As String
        Dim sr As StreamReader = File.OpenText(fileName)
        line = sr.ReadLine
        While Not line Is Nothing
            newLine = _Regex.Replace(line, "MyMethod($2, $1)")
            Console.WriteLine("New string is: '{0}', original was: '{1}'", _
             newLine, _
             line)
            line = sr.ReadLine
        End While
        sr.Close()
    End Sub

    Public Shared Sub Main(ByVal args As String())
        Dim r As Recipe = New Recipe
        r.Run(args(0))
    End Sub

End Class
```

VBScript

```
Dim fso,s,re,line,newstr
Set fso = CreateObject("Scripting.FileSystemObject")
Set s = fso.OpenTextFile(WScript.Arguments.Item(0), 1, True)
Set re = New RegExp
re.Pattern = " MyMethod\s*\(\s*([^,]+|""[^""]*"")\s*,➡
\s*([^,]+|""[^""]*"")(?=\s*[,)])"
Do While Not s.AtEndOfStream
    line = s.ReadLine()
    newstr = re.Replace(line, "MyMethod($2, $1)")
    WScript.Echo "New string '" & newstr & "', original '" & line & "'"
Loop
s.Close
```

JavaScript

```
<html>
<head>
<title></title>
</head>
<body>
<form name="form1">
    <input type="text" name="txtInput" />
    <div id="lblResult"></div>
    <script language="javascript">
        function replace() {
            document.getElementById('lblResult').innerHTML = ➥
document.form1.txtInput.value.replace(/\bMyMethod\s*\(\s*([^,]+|\"[^\"]*\")\s*,➥
\s*([^,]+|\"[^\"]*\")(?=\s*[,)])/, " MyMethod($2, $1");
        }
    </script>
    <input type="button" name="btnSubmit" onclick="replace()" value="Go" />
</form>
</body>
</html>
```

How It Works

Since \s* is used quite a bit in this regex to match any amount of whitespace, I'll skip it in order to focus on the regex that matches the variable inside the parentheses. This regex will match a variable name, assuming that the variable name includes anything up to a comma. The regex will also match a quoted string. This regex is [^,]+|\"[^\"]*\", which breaks down as follows:

[^,]	a character class that matches anything except a comma . . .
+	found one or more times . . .
|	or . . .
"	a double quote, followed by . . .
[^"]	a character class that matches anything that isn't a double quote . . .
*	found any number of times, followed by . . .
"	a double quote.

The first and second groups are captured and put back into the replacement string with the back references $1 and $2.

6-4. Changing a Method Name

You can use this recipe to change the name of a method in source code. MyMethod becomes
MyNewMethod.

.NET Framework

C#

```
using System;
using System.IO;
using System.Text.RegularExpressions;

public class Recipe
{
    private static Regex _Regex = new Regex( @"\bMyMethod\s*\(" );
    public void Run(string fileName)
    {
        String line;
        String newLine;
        using (StreamReader sr = new StreamReader(fileName))
        {
            while(null != (line = sr.ReadLine()))
            {
                newLine = _Regex.Replace(line, @"MyNewMethod(");
                Console.WriteLine("New string is: '{0}', original was: '{1}'",
                    newLine,
                    line);
            }
        }
    }

    public static void Main( string[] args )
    {
        Recipe r = new Recipe();
        r.Run(args[0]);
    }
}
```

Visual Basic .NET

```
Imports System
Imports System.IO
Imports System.Text.RegularExpressions
Public Class Recipe

    Private Shared _Regex As Regex = New Regex("\bMyMethod\s*\(")
```

```vb
    Public Sub Run(ByVal fileName As String)
        Dim line As String
        Dim newLine As String
        Dim sr As StreamReader = File.OpenText(fileName)
        line = sr.ReadLine
        While Not line Is Nothing
            newLine = _Regex.Replace(line, "MyNewMethod(")
            Console.WriteLine("New string is: '{0}', original was: '{1}'", _
             newLine, _
             line)
            line = sr.ReadLine
        End While
        sr.Close()
    End Sub

    Public Shared Sub Main(ByVal args As String())
        Dim r As Recipe = New Recipe
        r.Run(args(0))
    End Sub

End Class
```

VBScript

```vb
Dim fso,s,re,line,newstr
Set fso = CreateObject("Scripting.FileSystemObject")
Set s = fso.OpenTextFile(WScript.Arguments.Item(0), 1, True)
Set re = New RegExp
re.Pattern = "\bMyMethod\s*\("
Do While Not s.AtEndOfStream
    line = s.ReadLine()
    newstr = re.Replace(line, "MyNewMethod(")
    WScript.Echo "New string '" & newstr & "', original '" & line & "'"
Loop
s.Close
```

JavaScript

```html
<html>
<head>
<title></title>
</head>
<body>
<form name="form1">
    <input type="text" name="txtInput" />
    <div id="lblResult"></div>
    <script language="javascript">
```

```
        function replace() {
            document.getElementById('lblResult').innerHTML = ➥
document.form1.txtInput.value.replace(/\bMyMethod\s*\(/, "MyNewMethod(");
        }
    </script>
    <input type="button" name="btnSubmit" onclick="replace()" value="Go" />
</form>
</body>
</html>
```

How It Works

This expression simply looks for the method name, making sure it's a new word (so it doesn't mistakenly match something such as YourAndMyMethod).

\b	a word boundary . . .
. . .	the method name . . .
\s	whitespace . . .
*	found zero or more times . . .
\(	an open parenthesis.

6-5. Removing Inline Comments

This recipe allows you to remove inline, C#-style comments that start with /* and end with */. The string int i = 0; /*define i here */ becomes int i = 0;.

.NET Framework

C#

```csharp
using System;
using System.IO;
using System.Text.RegularExpressions;

public class Recipe
{
    private static Regex _Regex = new Regex( @"/\*.*?\*/" );
    public void Run(string fileName)
    {
        String line;
        String newLine;
        using (StreamReader sr = new StreamReader(fileName))
        {
            while(null != (line = sr.ReadLine()))
            {
                newLine = _Regex.Replace(line, "");
                Console.WriteLine("New string is: '{0}', original was: '{1}'",
                    newLine,
                    line);
            }
        }
    }

    public static void Main( string[] args )
    {
        Recipe r = new Recipe();
        r.Run(args[0]);
    }
}
```

Visual Basic .NET

```vbnet
Imports System
Imports System.IO
Imports System.Text.RegularExpressions
Public Class Recipe

    Private Shared _Regex As Regex = New Regex("/\*.*?\*/")
```

```vbnet
Public Sub Run(ByVal fileName As String)
    Dim line As String
    Dim newLine As String
    Dim sr As StreamReader = File.OpenText(fileName)
    line = sr.ReadLine
    While Not line Is Nothing
        newLine = _Regex.Replace(line, "")
        Console.WriteLine("New string is: '{0}', original was: '{1}'", _
         newLine, _
         line)
        line = sr.ReadLine
    End While
    sr.Close()
End Sub

Public Shared Sub Main(ByVal args As String())
    Dim r As Recipe = New Recipe
    r.Run(args(0))
End Sub

End Class
```

VBScript

```vbscript
Dim fso,s,re,line,newstr
Set fso = CreateObject("Scripting.FileSystemObject")
Set s = fso.OpenTextFile(WScript.Arguments.Item(0), 1, True)
Set re = New RegExp
re.Pattern = "/\*.*?\*/"
Do While Not s.AtEndOfStream
    line = s.ReadLine()
    newstr = re.Replace(line, "")
    WScript.Echo "New string '" & newstr & "', original '" & line & "'"
Loop
s.Close
```

JavaScript

```html
<html>
<head>
<title></title>
</head>
<body>
<form name="form1">
    <input type="text" name="txtInput" />
    <div id="lblResult"></div>
    <script language="javascript">
```

```
        function replace() {
            document.getElementById('lblResult').innerHTML = ➡
document.form1.txtInput.value.replace(/\/\*.*?\*\//, "");
        }
    </script>
    <input type="button" name="btnSubmit" onclick="replace()" value="Go" />
</form>
</body>
</html>
```

How It Works

The expression uses a lazy qualifier, *?, to match as little as possible. The expression matches the following:

\/	a slash . . .
*	a literal asterisk . . .
.	any character . . .
*?	found zero, one, or many times matching as little as possible . . .
*	a literal asterisk starting the close of the comment . . .
\/	a closing slash.

This allows a comment to be replaced by a zero-length string, which removes the comment from the line.

Variations

It may be desirable to remove extra whitespace around the inline comment. Add \s* at the beginning and the end of the regex to tell it to also remove any whitespace characters it finds immediately surrounding the comment: \s*/*.*?*/\s*.

Also, you may full well want to skip replacing comments that are found within strings. To do this, add the pattern ^([^"]|([^"]*"[^"]*"[^"]*)+) in front of the regex to ensure an even number of quotes is found before the expression. For more information about this, see recipe 6-1 and the similar recipes 1-17 and 6-2.

6-6. Commenting Out Code

This simple expression comments out code by replacing the beginning of the line with comments. It's most useful in editors that allow regular expressions to be used.

.NET Framework

C#

```csharp
using System;
using System.IO;
using System.Text.RegularExpressions;

public class Recipe
{
    private static Regex _Regex = new Regex( @"^(?!//)" );
    public void Run(string fileName)
    {
        String line;
        String newLine;
        using (StreamReader sr = new StreamReader(fileName))
        {
            while(null != (line = sr.ReadLine()))
            {
                newLine = _Regex.Replace(line, @"//");
                Console.WriteLine("New string is: '{0}', original was: '{1}'",
                    newLine,
                    line);
            }
        }
    }

    public static void Main( string[] args )
    {
        Recipe r = new Recipe();
        r.Run(args[0]);
    }
}
```

Visual Basic .NET

```vbnet
Imports System
Imports System.IO
Imports System.Text.RegularExpressions
Public Class Recipe

    Private Shared _Regex As Regex = New Regex("^(?!//)")
```

```
    Public Sub Run(ByVal fileName As String)
        Dim line As String
        Dim newLine As String
        Dim sr As StreamReader = File.OpenText(fileName)
        line = sr.ReadLine
        While Not line Is Nothing
            newLine = _Regex.Replace(line, "//")
            Console.WriteLine("New string is: '{0}', original was: '{1}'", _
             newLine, _
             line)
            line = sr.ReadLine
        End While
        sr.Close()
    End Sub

    Public Shared Sub Main(ByVal args As String())
        Dim r As Recipe = New Recipe
        r.Run(args(0))
    End Sub

End Class
```

VBScript

```
Dim fso,s,re,line,newstr
Set fso = CreateObject("Scripting.FileSystemObject")
Set s = fso.OpenTextFile(WScript.Arguments.Item(0), 1, True)
Set re = New RegExp
re.Pattern = "^(?!//)"
Do While Not s.AtEndOfStream
    line = s.ReadLine()
    newstr = re.Replace(line, "//")
    WScript.Echo "New string '" & newstr & "', original '" & line & "'"
Loop
s.Close
```

How It Works

The expression is simply ^(?!//), which is a line anchor that matches the beginning of the line but doesn't swallow any characters followed by a negative look-ahead. The replacement expression is //, which adds two forward slashes and a space to the beginning of each line.

The negative look-ahead is as follows:

(?!   a negative look-ahead that contains . . .

//   two slashes . . .

)   the end of the negative look-ahead.

The negative look-ahead verifies that the beginning of the line doesn't already start with a comment.

Variations

To make this regex work with VB-style and VBScript-style comments, just substitute occurrences of // with '.

6-7. Matching Variable Names

This recipe allows you to match variable names that comply to JScript and JavaScript naming rules, where a variable must start with either a letter or an underscore and can contain after that a letter, underscore, or digit.

.NET Framework

C#

```
using System;
using System.IO;
using System.Text.RegularExpressions;

public class Recipe
{
    private static Regex _Regex = new Regex( @"^[a-z_][a-z0-9_]+$",
        RegexOptions.IgnoreCase );
    public void Run(string fileName)
    {
        String line;
        int lineNbr = 0;
        using (StreamReader sr = new StreamReader(fileName))
        {
            while(null != (line = sr.ReadLine()))
            {
                lineNbr++;
                if (_Regex.IsMatch(line))
                {
                    Console.WriteLine("Found match '{0}' at line {1}",
                        line,
                        lineNbr);
                }
            }
        }
    }

    public static void Main( string[] args )
    {
        Recipe r = new Recipe();
        r.Run(args[0]);
    }
}
```

Visual Basic .NET

```
Imports System
Imports System.IO
Imports System.Text.RegularExpressions
Public Class Recipe

    Private Shared _Regex As Regex = _
        New Regex("^[a-z_][a-z0-9_]+$", RegexOptions.IgnoreCase)

    Public Sub Run(ByVal fileName As String)
        Dim line As String
        Dim lineNbr As Integer = 0
        Dim sr As StreamReader = File.OpenText(fileName)
        line = sr.ReadLine
        While Not line Is Nothing
            lineNbr = lineNbr + 1
            If _Regex.IsMatch(line) Then
                Console.WriteLine("Found match '{0}' at line {1}", _
                    line, _
                    lineNbr)
            End If
            line = sr.ReadLine
        End While
        sr.Close()
    End Sub

    Public Shared Sub Main(ByVal args As String())
        Dim r As Recipe = New Recipe
        r.Run(args(0))
    End Sub

End Class
```

VBScript

```
Dim fso,s,re,line,newstr
Set fso = CreateObject("Scripting.FileSystemObject")
Set s = fso.OpenTextFile(WScript.Arguments.Item(0), 1, True)
Set re = New RegExp
re.Pattern = "^[a-z_][a-z0-9_]+$"
re.IgnoreCase = True
Do While Not s.AtEndOfStream
    line = s.ReadLine()
```

```
    lineNbr = lineNbr + 1
    If re.Test(line) Then
        WScript.Echo "Found match: '" & line & "' at line " & lineNbr
    End If
Loop
s.Close
```

JavaScript

```html
<html>
<head>
<title></title>
</head>
<body>
<form name="form1">
    <input type="textbox" name="txtInput" />
    <script type="text/javascript">
    function validate() {
        if (! document.form1.txtInput.value.match(/^[a-z_][a-z0-9_]+$/)) {
            alert("Please enter valid value!")
        } else {
            alert("Success!")
        }
    }
    </script>
    <input type="button" name="btnSubmit" onclick="validate()" value="Go" />
</form>
</body>
</html>
```

How It Works

This regex uses character classes to specify the ranges of letters or numbers that can occur in the match. The regex is as follows:

^	the beginning of the line, followed by . . .
[a-z_]	a character class that matches the letters *a* through *z* or an underscore . . .
[a-z0-9_]	a character class that matches the letters *a* through *z*, zero through nine, or an underscore . . .
+	found one or more times, followed by . . .
$	the end of the line.

Variations

Alternatively, you can replace the digit range 0-9 with the \d character class. Also, [a-z] will match only the lowercase letters *a* through *z*. If you'd like to match uppercase or lowercase letters, use the RegexOptions.Ignorecase option in C# and Visual Basic .NET, IgnoreCase = True in VBScript, or the i option in JavaScript. See the "Syntax Overview" section of this book for more information.

6-8. Searching for Variable Declarations

This recipe allows you to search for a variable declaration in C#. This expression is smart enough to look for a declaration that isn't in comments. The declaration that's searched for in this example is int myvar—you don't know whether it's public or private, so the expression looks for one or none.

.NET Framework

C#

```csharp
using System;
using System.IO;
using System.Text.RegularExpressions;

public class Recipe
{
    private static Regex _Regex =
        new Regex( @"^(?:(?:(?!\/\/|\/\/\*).)*|➥
(?:(?!\/\/\*).)*\/\/\*.*?\*\/(?:(?!\/\/\*).)*)(public|private)?➥
\s+int\s+myvar\s+=" );

    public void Run(string fileName)
    {
        String line;
        int lineNbr = 0;
        using (StreamReader sr = new StreamReader(fileName))
        {
            while(null != (line = sr.ReadLine()))
            {
                lineNbr++;
                if (_Regex.IsMatch(line))
                {
                    Console.WriteLine("Found match '{0}' at line {1}",
                        line,
                        lineNbr);
                }
            }
        }
    }

    public static void Main( string[] args )
    {
        Recipe r = new Recipe();
        r.Run(args[0]);
    }
}
```

Visual Basic .NET

```
Imports System
Imports System.IO
Imports System.Text.RegularExpressions
Public Class Recipe

    Private Shared _Regex As Regex = _
New Regex("^(?:(?:(?!\/\/|\/\/\*).)*|➡
(?:(?!\/\/\*).)*\/\/\*.*?\*\/(?:(?!\/\/\*).)*)(public|private)?➡
\s+int\s+myvar\s+=")

    Public Sub Run(ByVal fileName As String)
        Dim line As String
        Dim lineNbr As Integer = 0
        Dim sr As StreamReader = File.OpenText(fileName)
        line = sr.ReadLine
        While Not line Is Nothing
            lineNbr = lineNbr + 1
            If _Regex.IsMatch(line) Then
                Console.WriteLine("Found match '{0}' at line {1}", _
                    line, _
                    lineNbr)
            End If
            line = sr.ReadLine
        End While
        sr.Close()
    End Sub

    Public Shared Sub Main(ByVal args As String())
        Dim r As Recipe = New Recipe
        r.Run(args(0))
    End Sub

End Class
```

VBScript

```
Dim fso,s,re,line,lineNbr
Set fso = CreateObject("Scripting.FileSystemObject")
Set s = fso.OpenTextFile(WScript.Arguments.Item(0), 1, True)
Set re = New RegExp
re.Pattern = "^(((?!\/\/\/|\/\/\*).)*|((?!\/\/\*).)*\/\/\*.*?\*\/((?!\/\/\*).)*)➡
(public|private)?\s+int\s+myvar\s+="
lineNbr = 0
Do While Not s.AtEndOfStream
    line = s.ReadLine()
    lineNbr = lineNbr + 1
```

```
        If re.Test(line) Then
            WScript.Echo "Found match: '" & line & "' at line " & lineNbr
        End If
Loop
s.Close
```

JavaScript

```
<html>
<head>
<title></title>
</head>
<body>
<form name="form1">
    <input type="textbox" name="txtInput" />
    <script type="text/javascript">
    function validate() {
        if (! document.form1.txtInput.value.match(➥
/^(((?!\/\/|\/\*).)*|((?!\/\*).)*\/\*.*?\*\/((?!\/\*).)*)➥
(public|private)?\s+int\s+myvar\s+=/)) {
            alert("Please enter valid value!")
        } else {
            alert("Success!")
        }
    }
    </script>
    <input type="button" name="btnSubmit" onclick="validate()" value="Go" />
</form>
</body>
</html>
```

How It Works

The bulk of this expression makes sure the declaration isn't found inside a comment. This part of the expression is ^(?:(?:(?!\/\/|\/*).)*|(?:(?!\/*).)*\/*.*?*\/(?:(?!\/*).)*), which I'll break into smaller parts so you can digest it a little easier. It consists of two parts separated by the "or" operator, |. The first part is (?:(?!\/\/|\/*).)*, and the second is (?:(?!\/*).)*\/*.*?*\/(?:(?!\/*).)*).

■**Note** Multiline variable declarations aren't included in the results of this expression.

The first group makes sure the line doesn't have // or /* somewhere before the declaration. The second group says, "If it does have /* before it, make sure there's */ somewhere after it and not another opening comment." The first group breaks down as follows:

(?:	a noncapturing group that contains . . .
(?!	a negative look-ahead with . . .
//	two slashes . . .
|	or . . .
/*	a slash and a literal asterisk . . .
)	the end of the negative look-ahead . . .
.	any character . . .
)	the end of the noncapturing group . . .
*	found zero, one, or many times.

This expression will make sure the line doesn't contain // or /* in front of the declaration. The second group, separated by the "or" operator, makes sure that if a /* sequence is found, it ends with a */ sequence before the declaration and makes sure no other /* sequence is found again before the declaration. The following is that expression, broken down:

(?:	a noncapturing group that contains . . .
(?!	a negative look-ahead with . . .
/*	a /* combination . . .
)	the end of the negative look-ahead . . .
.	any character . . .
)	the end of the noncapturing group . . .
*	zero, one, or many times . . .
/*	an comment opening /* . . .
.	any character . . .
*?	found zero, one, or many times (but as few as possible) . . .
*/	a */ combination . . .
(?:	a noncapturing group . . .
(?!	a negative look-ahead . . .
/*	a /* combination . . .
)	the end of the negative look-ahead . . .
.	any character . . .
)	the end of the noncapturing group . . .

*	zero, one, or many times . . .
)	the end of the noncapturing group.

After you're sure the declaration isn't found inside comments, you can search for the declaration. That part of the expression is as follows:

(	a group that contains . . .
public	the characters p, u, b, l, i, and c . . .
|	or . . .
private	the characters p, r, i, v, a, t, and e . . .
)	the end of the group . . .
\s	whitespace . . .
+	found one or many times . . .
int	i, n, and t . . .
\s	whitespace . . .
+	found one or many times . . .
myvar	the variable name . . .
\s	whitespace . . .
+	found one or more times . . .
=	an equals sign.

This is all the expression cares about for the variable declaration—it knows enough at this point to tell that a variable is being declared and set to something.

6-9. Searching for Words Within Comments

You can use this recipe to search for the first word in a code comment. The regex will match //
TODO, ' TODO and also /* TODO */.

.NET Framework

C#

```csharp
using System;
using System.IO;
using System.Text.RegularExpressions;

public class Recipe
{
    private static Regex _Regex = new Regex( @"(/\*|//|')\s*TODO" );

    public void Run(string fileName)
    {
        String line;
        int lineNbr = 0;
        using (StreamReader sr = new StreamReader(fileName))
        {
            while(null != (line = sr.ReadLine()))
            {
                lineNbr++;
                if (_Regex.IsMatch(line))
                {
                    Console.WriteLine("Found match '{0}' at line {1}",
                        line,
                        lineNbr);
                }
            }
        }
    }

    public static void Main( string[] args )
    {
        Recipe r = new Recipe();
        r.Run(args[0]);
    }
}
```

Visual Basic .NET

```
Imports System
Imports System.IO
Imports System.Text.RegularExpressions
Public Class Recipe

    Private Shared _Regex As Regex = New Regex("(/\*|//|')\s*TODO")

    Public Sub Run(ByVal fileName As String)
        Dim line As String
        Dim lineNbr As Integer = 0
        Dim sr As StreamReader = File.OpenText(fileName)
        line = sr.ReadLine
        While Not line Is Nothing
            lineNbr = lineNbr + 1
            If _Regex.IsMatch(line) Then
                Console.WriteLine("Found match '{0}' at line {1}", _
                    line, _
                    lineNbr)
            End If
            line = sr.ReadLine
        End While
        sr.Close()
    End Sub

    Public Shared Sub Main(ByVal args As String())
        Dim r As Recipe = New Recipe
        r.Run(args(0))
    End Sub

End Class
```

VBScript

```
Dim fso,s,re,line,lineNbr
Set fso = CreateObject("Scripting.FileSystemObject")
Set s = fso.OpenTextFile(WScript.Arguments.Item(0), 1, True)
Set re = New RegExp
re.Pattern = "(/\*|//|')\s*TODO"
lineNbr = 0
Do While Not s.AtEndOfStream
    line = s.ReadLine()
    lineNbr = lineNbr + 1
    If re.Test(line) Then
        WScript.Echo "Found match: '" & line & "' at line " & lineNbr
    End If
Loop
s.Close
```

How It Works

In this example, the first word found in the comment is *TODO*, which if used would provide similar functionality to the Task List in Visual Studio .NET. A possible use is to make an NAnt task that performs this search on source files before compiling.

The following are the details:

(the beginning of a group that contains . . .

/*   the beginning of a multiline comment (/*) . . .

| or . . .

//   the beginning of a single-line comment . . .

| or . . .

'   the beginning of a VB-style comment . . .

)   the end of the group . . .

\s   whitespace, followed by . . .

*   found any number of times, followed by . . .

TODO   up to the word you're trying to find.

6-10. Finding .NET Namespaces

You can use this recipe to find namespaces in .NET that are groups of names delimited by a period (.). The name can start with a letter or underscore and after that contain a letter, number, or underscore.

.NET Framework

C#

```csharp
using System;
using System.IO;
using System.Text.RegularExpressions;

public class Recipe
{
    private static Regex _Regex =
        new Regex( @"^([a-z_][a-z0-9_]+)(\.[a-z_][a-z0-9_]+)*$",
RegexOptions.IgnoreCase );

    public void Run(string fileName)
    {
        String line;
        int lineNbr = 0;
        using (StreamReader sr = new StreamReader(fileName))
        {
            while(null != (line = sr.ReadLine()))
            {
                lineNbr++;
                if (_Regex.IsMatch(line))
                {
                    Console.WriteLine("Found match '{0}' at line {1}",
                        line,
                        lineNbr);
                }
            }
        }
    }

    public static void Main( string[] args )
    {
        Recipe r = new Recipe();
        r.Run(args[0]);
    }
}
```

Visual Basic .NET

```vbnet
Imports System
Imports System.IO
Imports System.Text.RegularExpressions
Public Class Recipe

    Private Shared _Regex As Regex = _
        New Regex("^([a-z_][a-z0-9_]+)(\.[a-z_][a-z0-9_]+)*$", ➠
RegexOptions.IgnoreCase)

    Public Sub Run(ByVal fileName As String)
        Dim line As String
        Dim lineNbr As Integer = 0
        Dim sr As StreamReader = File.OpenText(fileName)
        line = sr.ReadLine
        While Not line Is Nothing
            lineNbr = lineNbr + 1
            If _Regex.IsMatch(line) Then
                Console.WriteLine("Found match '{0}' at line {1}", _
                    line, _
                    lineNbr)
            End If
            line = sr.ReadLine
        End While
        sr.Close()
    End Sub

    Public Shared Sub Main(ByVal args As String())
        Dim r As Recipe = New Recipe
        r.Run(args(0))
    End Sub

End Class
```

VBScript

```vbscript
Dim fso,s,re,line,lineNbr
Set fso = CreateObject("Scripting.FileSystemObject")
Set s = fso.OpenTextFile(WScript.Arguments.Item(0), 1, True)
Set re = New RegExp
re.Pattern = "^([a-z_][a-z0-9_]+)(\.[a-z_][a-z0-9_]+)*$"
re.IgnoreCase = True
lineNbr = 0
Do While Not s.AtEndOfStream
    line = s.ReadLine()
```

```
        lineNbr = lineNbr + 1
        If re.Test(line) Then
            WScript.Echo "Found match: '" & line & "' at line " & lineNbr
        End If
Loop
s.Close
```

JavaScript

```
<html>
<head>
<title></title>
</head>
<body>
<form name="form1">
    <input type="textbox" name="txtInput" />
    <script type="text/javascript">
    function validate() {
        if (! document.form1.txtInput.value.match(➥
/^([a-z_][a-z0-9_]+)(.[a-z_][a-z0-9_]+)*$/)) {
            alert("Please enter valid value!")
        } else {
            alert("Success!")
        }
    }
    </script>
    <input type="button" name="btnSubmit" onclick="validate()" value="Go" />
</form>
</body>
</html>
```

How It Works

Recipe 6-7 highlighted a similar regex that matches variable names. The key difference in this regex is the second group, which matches other names separated from the previous one by a period (.).

The second group breaks down as follows:

(	a group containing . . .
\.	a literal period, followed by . . .
[a-z_][a-z0-9_]+	the regex discussed in recipe 6-7 . . .
)	the end of the group . . .
*	where this group can be found any number of times.

6-11. Finding Hexadecimal Numbers

This recipe will limit the input to numbers and letters that are valid for hexadecimal representations.

.NET Framework

C#

```csharp
using System;
using System.IO;
using System.Text.RegularExpressions;

public class Recipe
{
    private static Regex _Regex = new Regex( @"^[0-9a-f]+$",
        RegexOptions.IgnoreCase );

    public void Run(string fileName)
    {
        String line;
        int lineNbr = 0;
        using (StreamReader sr = new StreamReader(fileName))
        {
            while(null != (line = sr.ReadLine()))
            {
                lineNbr++;
                if (_Regex.IsMatch(line))
                {
                    Console.WriteLine("Found match '{0}' at line {1}",
                        line,
                        lineNbr);
                }
            }
        }
    }

    public static void Main( string[] args )
    {
        Recipe r = new Recipe();
        r.Run(args[0]);
    }
}
```

Visual Basic .NET

```
Imports System
Imports System.IO
Imports System.Text.RegularExpressions
Public Class Recipe

    Private Shared _Regex As Regex = New Regex("^[0-9a-f]+$", _
        RegexOptions.IgnoreCase)

    Public Sub Run(ByVal fileName As String)
        Dim line As String
        Dim lineNbr As Integer = 0
        Dim sr As StreamReader = File.OpenText(fileName)
        line = sr.ReadLine
        While Not line Is Nothing
            lineNbr = lineNbr + 1
            If _Regex.IsMatch(line) Then
                Console.WriteLine("Found match '{0}' at line {1}", _
                    line, _
                    lineNbr)
            End If
            line = sr.ReadLine
        End While
        sr.Close()
    End Sub

    Public Shared Sub Main(ByVal args As String())
        Dim r As Recipe = New Recipe
        r.Run(args(0))
    End Sub

End Class
```

VBScript

```
Dim fso,s,re,line,lineNbr
Set fso = CreateObject("Scripting.FileSystemObject")
Set s = fso.OpenTextFile(WScript.Arguments.Item(0), 1, True)
Set re = New RegExp
re.Pattern = "^[0-9a-f]+$"
re.IgnoreCase = True
lineNbr = 0
Do While Not s.AtEndOfStream
    line = s.ReadLine()
    lineNbr = lineNbr + 1
    If re.Test(line) Then
        WScript.Echo "Found match: '" & line & "' at line " & lineNbr
```

```
    End If
Loop
s.Close
```

JavaScript

```
<html>
<head>
<title></title>
</head>
<body>
<form name="form1">
    <input type="textbox" name="txtInput" />
    <script type="text/javascript">
    function validate() {
        if (! document.form1.txtInput.value.match(/^[0-9a-f]+$/i)) {
            alert("Please enter valid value!")
        } else {
            alert("Success!")
        }
    }
    </script>
    <input type="button" name="btnSubmit" onclick="validate()" value="Go" />
</form>
</body>
</html>
```

How It Works

This recipe uses a simple character class to limit the input to digits and the letters *a* through *f*:

^	the beginning of the line, followed by . . .
[0-9a-f]	a character class that matches the digits zero through nine and the letters *a* through *f* . . .
+	found one or more times . . .
$	the end of the line.

Alternatively, you can replace 0-9 in the character class with \d.

6-12. Finding GUIDs

You can use this recipe to find GUID/UUID numbers in the format specified at http://
en.wikipedia.org/wiki/GUID. Matches are 9e2da810-784a-4d2f-aee7-77c4bab9fe0c and
f8d0edf1-34f2-43ec-bf41-dd34ce4b8467.

.NET Framework

C#

```
using System;
using System.IO;
using System.Text.RegularExpressions;

public class Recipe
{
    private static Regex _Regex =
        new Regex ( "^([0-9a-f]{8}(-[0-9a-f]{4}){3}-[0-9a-f]{12}|➡
[0-9a-f]{32})$", RegexOptions.IgnoreCase );

    public void Run(string fileName)
    {
        String line;
        int lineNbr = 0;
        using (StreamReader sr = new StreamReader(fileName))
        {
            while(null != (line = sr.ReadLine()))
            {
                lineNbr++;
                if (_Regex.IsMatch(line))
                {
                    Console.WriteLine("Found match '{0}' at line {1}",
                        line,
                        lineNbr);
                }
            }
        }
    }

    public static void Main( string[] args )
    {
        Recipe r = new Recipe();
        r.Run(args[0]);
    }
}
```

Visual Basic .NET

```
Imports System
Imports System.IO
Imports System.Text.RegularExpressions
Public Class Recipe

    Private Shared _Regex As Regex = _
        New Regex("^([0-9a-f]{8}(-[0-9a-f]{4}){3}-[0-9a-f]{12}|➡
[0-9a-f]{32})$", RegexOptions.IgnoreCase)

    Public Sub Run(ByVal fileName As String)
        Dim line As String
        Dim lineNbr As Integer = 0
        Dim sr As StreamReader = File.OpenText(fileName)
        line = sr.ReadLine
        While Not line Is Nothing
            lineNbr = lineNbr + 1
            If _Regex.IsMatch(line) Then
                Console.WriteLine("Found match '{0}' at line {1}", _
                    line, _
                    lineNbr)
            End If
            line = sr.ReadLine
        End While
        sr.Close()
    End Sub

    Public Shared Sub Main(ByVal args As String())
        Dim r As Recipe = New Recipe
        r.Run(args(0))
    End Sub

End Class
```

VBScript

```
Dim fso,s,re,line,lineNbr
Set fso = CreateObject("Scripting.FileSystemObject")
Set s = fso.OpenTextFile(WScript.Arguments.Item(0), 1, True)
Set re = New RegExp
re.Pattern = "^([0-9a-f]{8}(-[0-9a-f]{4}){3}-[0-9a-f]{12}|[0-9a-f]{32})$"
re.IgnoreCase = True
lineNbr = 0
Do While Not s.AtEndOfStream
    line = s.ReadLine()
```

```
        lineNbr = lineNbr + 1
        If re.Test(line) Then
            WScript.Echo "Found match: '" & line & "' at line " & lineNbr
        End If
Loop
s.Close
```

JavaScript

```
<html>
<head>
<title></title>
</head>
<body>
<form name="form1">
    <input type="textbox" name="txtInput" />
    <script type="text/javascript">
    function validate() {
        if (! document.form1.txtInput.value.match(➡
/^([0-9a-f]{8}(-[0-9a-f]{4}){3}-[0-9a-f]{12}|[0-9a-f]{32})$/i)) {
            alert("Please enter valid value!")
        } else {
            alert("Success!")
        }
    }
    </script>
    <input type="button" name="btnSubmit" onclick="validate()" value="Go" />
</form>
</body>
</html>
```

How It Works

This recipe is built upon the hexadecimal-matching regex shown in recipe 6-11 but uses the format specified at http://en.wikipedia.org/wiki/GUID to make sure the GUID is complete. I'll break the recipe down here, focusing on the parts other than the character class:

[. . .]	the character class that matches hexadecimal numbers . . .
{8}	found eight times exactly, followed by . . .
(	a group that contains . . .
-	a hyphen, which separates the parts, followed by . . .
[. . .]	the character class . . .
{4}	found exactly four times . . .
)	the end of the group . . .

{3}   which is found exactly three times, followed by . . .

-           a hyphen, then . . .

[. . .]   the character class . . .

{12}   found exactly 12 times.

This regex also matches the GUID if it doesn't have the dashes in it, such as 2355d96bca624cb5b1405c33119d88dd. It does this simply with the following:

| or . . .

[. . .]   the same character class . . .

{32}   found exactly 32 times.

6-13. Setting a SQL Owner

This handy recipe inserts an owner on stored procedures in a script where there's no owner. This can be especially useful in large scripts where you may have forgotten to assign an owner to the objects. It won't add an owner if there's already one assigned. For example, the following line:

```
CREATE PROCEDURE MYPROC
```

becomes the following:

```
CREATE PROCEDURE [dbo].[MYPROC]
```

.NET Framework

C#

```
using System;
using System.IO;
using System.Text.RegularExpressions;

public class Recipe
{
    private static Regex _Regex =
        new Regex( @"(CREATE\s+PROCEDURE\s+)(?!(?:\w+|\[\w+\])\.)➥
(\w+|\[\w+\])", RegexOptions.IgnoreCase);
    public void Run(string fileName)
    {
        String line;
        String newLine;
        using (StreamReader sr = new StreamReader(fileName))
        {
            while(null != (line = sr.ReadLine()))
            {
                newLine = _Regex.Replace(line, "$1[dbo].$2");
                Console.WriteLine"New string is: '{0}', original was: '{1}'",
                    newLine,
                    line);
            }
        }
    }

    public static void Main( string[] args )
    {
        Recipe r = new Recipe();
        r.Run(args[0]);
    }
}
```

Visual Basic .NET

```
Imports System
Imports System.IO
Imports System.Text.RegularExpressions
Public Class Recipe

    Private Shared _Regex As Regex = _
        New Regex("(CREATE\s+PROCEDURE\s+)(?!(?:\w+|\[\w+\])\.)➥
(\w+|\[\w+\])", RegexOptions.IgnoreCase)

    Public Sub Run(ByVal fileName As String)
        Dim line As String
        Dim newLine As String
        Dim sr As StreamReader = File.OpenText(fileName)
        line = sr.ReadLine
        While Not line Is Nothing
            newLine = _Regex.Replace(line, "$1[dbo].$2")
            Console.WriteLine("New string is: '{0}', original was: '{1}'", _
             newLine, _
             line)
            line = sr.ReadLine
        End While
        sr.Close()
    End Sub

    Public Shared Sub Main(ByVal args As String())
        Dim r As Recipe = New Recipe
        r.Run(args(0))
    End Sub

End Class
```

VBScript

```
Dim fso,s,re,line,newstr
Set fso = CreateObject("Scripting.FileSystemObject")
Set s = fso.OpenTextFile(WScript.Arguments.Item(0), 1, True)
Set re = New RegExp
re.Pattern = "(CREATE\s+PROCEDURE\s+)(?!(?:\w+|\[\w+\])\.)(\w+|\[\w+\])"
re.IgnoreCase = True
Do While Not s.AtEndOfStream
    line = s.ReadLine()
    newstr = re.Replace(line, "$1[dbo].$2")
    WScript.Echo "New string '" & newstr & "', original '" & line & "'"
Loop
s.Close
```

How It Works

The usefulness of this expression comes from the negative look-ahead, (?!, which allows the expression to check to make sure there isn't already an existing owner. If there isn't, the expression makes the replacement. The owner's name can be wrapped in brackets or not, and for the purposes of this expression you can assume that the database restricts the characters in an owner's name to word characters.

The main part of the expression that contains this logic is as follows:

(?!	the beginning of a negative look-ahead . . .
(?:	a noncapturing group that contains . . .
\w	a word character . . .
+	found one or more times . . .
|	or . . .
\[	a literal opening bracket, followed by . . .
\w	a word character . . .
+	found one or more times . . .
\]	a literal closing bracket . . .
)	the end of the noncapturing group, followed by . . .
\.	a literal period, then . . .
)	the end of the negative look-ahead.

This looks for a user, and if it finds one, the expression doesn't match and no replacement is made. The expression is prevented from adding owners to objects where it has already found an owner.

6-14. Validating Pascal Case Names

The recipe validates names that are in Pascal case (sometimes called *upper camel case*) such as MyVariable and HelloWorld.

.NET Framework

ASP.NET

```
<%@ Page Language="vb" AutoEventWireup="false" %>
<!DOCTYPE HTML PUBLIC "-//W3C//DTD HTML 4.0 Transitional//EN">
<html>
<head><title></title>
</head>
<body>
    <form Id="Form1" RunAt="server">
    <asp:TextBox id="txtInput" runat="server"></asp:TextBox>
    <asp:RegularExpressionValidator Id="revInput" RunAt="server"
        ControlToValidate="txtInput"
        ErrorMessage="Please enter a valid value"
      ValidationExpression='^([A-Z][a-z]+)+$'>
    </asp:RegularExpressionValidator>
    <asp:Button Id="btnSubmit" RunAt="server" CausesValidation="True"
        Text="Submit"></asp:Button>
    </form>
</body>
```

C#

```csharp
using System;
using System.IO;
using System.Text.RegularExpressions;

public class Recipe
{
    private static Regex _Regex = new Regex( "^([A-Z][a-z]+)+$" );

    public void Run(string fileName)
    {
        String line;
        int lineNbr = 0;
        using (StreamReader sr = new StreamReader(fileName))
        {
            while(null != (line = sr.ReadLine()))
            {
                lineNbr++;
                if (_Regex.IsMatch(line))
                {
```

```csharp
                    Console.WriteLine("Found match '{0}' at line {1}",
                        line,
                        lineNbr);
                }
            }
        }
    }

    public static void Main( string[] args )
    {
        Recipe r = new Recipe();
        r.Run(args[0]);
    }
}
```

Visual Basic .NET

```vbnet
Imports System
Imports System.IO
Imports System.Text.RegularExpressions
Public Class Recipe

    Private Shared _Regex As Regex = New Regex("^([A-Z][a-z]+)+$")

    Public Sub Run(ByVal fileName As String)
        Dim line As String
        Dim lineNbr As Integer = 0
        Dim sr As StreamReader = File.OpenText(fileName)
        line = sr.ReadLine
        While Not line Is Nothing
            lineNbr = lineNbr + 1
            If _Regex.IsMatch(line) Then
                Console.WriteLine("Found match '{0}' at line {1}", _
                    line, _
                    lineNbr)
            End If
            line = sr.ReadLine
        End While
        sr.Close()
    End Sub

    Public Shared Sub Main(ByVal args As String())
        Dim r As Recipe = New Recipe
        r.Run(args(0))
    End Sub

End Class
```

VBScript

```
Dim fso,s,re,line,lineNbr
Set fso = CreateObject("Scripting.FileSystemObject")
Set s = fso.OpenTextFile(WScript.Arguments.Item(0), 1, True)
Set re = New RegExp
re.Pattern = "^([A-Z][a-z]+)+$"
lineNbr = 0
Do While Not s.AtEndOfStream
    line = s.ReadLine()
    lineNbr = lineNbr + 1
    If re.Test(line) Then
        WScript.Echo "Found match: '" & line & "' at line " & lineNbr
    End If
Loop
s.Close
```

JavaScript

```
<html>
<head>
<title></title>
</head>
<body>
<form name="form1">
    <input type="textbox" name="txtInput" />
    <script type="text/javascript">
    function validate() {
        if (! document.form1.txtInput.value.match(/^([A-Z][a-z]+)+$/)) {
            alert("Please enter valid value!")
        } else {
            alert("Success!")
        }
    }
    </script>
    <input type="button" name="btnSubmit" onclick="validate()" value="Go" />
</form>
</body>
</html>
```

How It Works

You can match Pascal case, which is a convention where names are run together and each name begins with a capital letter, by searching for groups of any number of lowercase letters that follow an uppercase letter. The regular expression breaks down as follows:

^	the beginning of the line, followed by . . .
(	a group that contains . . .
[A-Z]	the letters *A* through *Z* (uppercase), followed by . . .
[a-z]	the letters *a* through *z* (lowercase) . . .
+	found one or more times . . .
)	the end of the group . . .
+	where the group is found one or more times . . .
$	the end of the line.

Variations

If you want to match numbers as well as lowercase letters after an uppercase one, you have a couple of choices. For instance, you might want to limit the numbers to appear only at the end of the substring. This requires a little more work than just adding \d to the [a-z] character class. Instead, go with [A-Z][a-z]*[a-z\d]. That specifies a capital letter at the beginning, any lowercase letters in the middle, and either a lowercase letter or a digit at the end.

You may want to match other naming conventions, such as all-uppercase names or camel-case names. Camel-case names begin with a lowercase letter, but after that they include uppercase letters, followed by lowercase letters, where words are run together. Examples of camel case are firstName, middleInitial, and addressLine1.

To match camel-case names, modify the regex slightly to specify that it needs to start with one or more lowercase letters: ^[a-z]([A-Z][a-z]+)*$.

All-uppercase names are easier, but perhaps you want to specify groups of one or more capital letters joined by underscores—a common naming convention still found in a lot of databases and in constant names. For instance, to match EMPLOYEE_TABLE, use ^[A-Z]+(_[A-Z]+)*$.

6-15. Changing Null Comparisons

You can use this recipe to swap null evaluations in tests. Some programming shops by convention write their null comparisons like this:

```
if ( null == myvar )
```

instead of like this:

```
if ( myvar == null )
```

This recipe makes the latter look like the former. The reason why some programmers use this convention is to avoid accidentally assigning a value to null by using = instead of == in the comparison. The compiler will produce an error if the code looks like this:

```
if ( null = myvar )
```

But it won't necessarily produce an error if the code looks like this:

```
if ( myvar = null )
```

.NET Framework

C#

```csharp
using System;
using System.IO;
using System.Text.RegularExpressions;

public class Recipe
{
    private static Regex _Regex = new Regex( @"\(\s*(.+)\s*([=!]=)\s*null\s*\)" );
    public void Run(string fileName)
    {
        String line;
        String newLine;
        using (StreamReader sr = new StreamReader(fileName))
        {
            while(null != (line = sr.ReadLine()))
            {
                newLine = _Regex.Replace(line, @"(null $2 $1)");
                Console.WriteLine("New string is: '{0}', original was: '{1}'",
                    newLine,
                    line);
            }
        }
    ]

    public static void Main( string[] args )
    {
```

```
        Recipe r = new Recipe();
        r.Run(args[0]);
    }
}
```

Visual Basic .NET

```vbnet
Imports System
Imports System.IO
Imports System.Text.RegularExpressions
Public Class Recipe

    Private Shared _Regex As Regex = New Regex("\(\s*(.+)\s*([=!]=)\s*null\s*\)")

    Public Sub Run(ByVal fileName As String)
        Dim line As String
        Dim newLine As String
        Dim sr As StreamReader = File.OpenText(fileName)
        line = sr.ReadLine
        While Not line Is Nothing
            newLine = _Regex.Replace(line, "(null $2 $1)")
            Console.WriteLine("New string is: '{0}', original was: '{1}'", _
             newLine, _
             line)
            line = sr.ReadLine
        End While
        sr.Close()
    End Sub

    Public Shared Sub Main(ByVal args As String())
        Dim r As Recipe = New Recipe
        r.Run(args(0))
    End Sub

End Class
```

VBScript

```vbscript
Dim fso,s,re,line,newstr
Set fso = CreateObject("Scripting.FileSystemObject")
Set s = fso.OpenTextFile(WScript.Arguments.Item(0), 1, True)
Set re = New RegExp
re.Pattern = "\(\s*(.+)\s*([=!]=)\s*null\s*\)"
Do While Not s.AtEndOfStream
    line = s.ReadLine()
    newstr = re.Replace(line, "(null $2 $1)")
    WScript.Echo "New string '" & newstr & "', original '" & line & "'"
Loop
s.Close
```

JavaScript

```html
<html>
<head>
<title></title>
</head>
<body>
<form name="form1">
    <input type="text" name="txtInput" />
    <div id="lblResult"></div>
    <script language="javascript">
        function replace() {
            document.getElementById('lblResult').innerHTML = ➥
document.form1.txtInput.value.replace➥
(/\(\s*(.+)\s*([=!]=)\s*null\s*\)/, "(null $2 $1)");
        }
    </script>
    <input type="button" name="btnSubmit" onclick="replace()" value="Go" />
</form>
</body>
</html>
```

How It Works

Two groups in this expression capture the comparison operator and the variable name. The word *null* isn't important to capture because you can put it back into the replacement expression. The search expression is as follows:

\(	an open parenthesis . . .
\s	whitespace . . .
*	found zero, one, or many times . . .
(	a group that contains . . .
.	any character . . .
+	found one or more times . . .
)	the end of the group . . .
\s	whitespace . . .
*	found zero or more times . . .
(	a second group . . .
[!=]	a character class that can contain ! or =, followed by . . .
=	a second equals sign . . .
)	the end of the second group . . .

\s	whitespace . . .
*	found zero or more times . . .
null	the word *null* . . .
\s	whitespace . . .
*	zero, one, or many times . . .
\)	the closing parenthesis.

The first group will capture the comparison operator, which can be either != or ==. This needs to be captured in a group because it can vary among matches. Since the character class is qualified with a ?, which will make the character class optional, the group will also capture assignments that include a single =.

The second group is the variable name itself, which is put back into the replacement expression with the second back reference, $2.

6-16. Changing .NET Namespaces

This recipe demonstrates how to change a namespace name. The "How It Works" section explains why this operation isn't as straightforward as recipe 1-6, which shows you how to replace words.

.NET Framework

C#

```csharp
using System;
using System.IO;
using System.Text.RegularExpressions;

public class Recipe
{
    private static Regex _Regex = new Regex( @"(?<=\s)OldNameSpace(?=\.)" );
    public void Run(string fileName)
    {
        String line;
        String newLine;
        using (StreamReader sr = new StreamReader(fileName))
        {
            while(null != (line = sr.ReadLine()))
            {
                newLine = _Regex.Replace(line, @"NewNameSpace");
                Console.WriteLine("New string is: '{0}', original was: '{1}'",
                    newLine,
                    line);
            }
        }
    }

    public static void Main( string[] args )
    {
        Recipe r = new Recipe();
        r.Run(args[0]);
    }
}
```

Visual Basic .NET

```vb
Imports System
Imports System.IO
Imports System.Text.RegularExpressions
Public Class Recipe
```

```vbnet
    Private Shared _Regex As Regex = New Regex("(?<=\s)OldNameSpace(?=\.)")

    Public Sub Run(ByVal fileName As String)
        Dim line As String
        Dim newLine As String
        Dim sr As StreamReader = File.OpenText(fileName)
        line = sr.ReadLine
        While Not line Is Nothing
            newLine = _Regex.Replace(line, "NewNameSpace")
            Console.WriteLine("New string is: '{0}', original was: '{1}'", _
             newLine, _
             line)
            line = sr.ReadLine
        End While
        sr.Close()
    End Sub

    Public Shared Sub Main(ByVal args As String())
        Dim r As Recipe = New Recipe
        r.Run(args(0))
    End Sub

End Class
```

VBScript

```vbscript
Dim fso,s,re,line,newstr
Set fso = CreateObject("Scripting.FileSystemObject")
Set s = fso.OpenTextFile(WScript.Arguments.Item(0), 1, True)
Set re = New RegExp
re.Pattern = "(^|\s)OldNameSpace(?=\.)"
Do While Not s.AtEndOfStream
    line = s.ReadLine()
    newstr = re.Replace(line, "$1NewNameSpace")
    WScript.Echo "New string '" & newstr & "', original '" & line & "'"
Loop
s.Close
```

JavaScript

```html
<html>
<head>
<title></title>
</head>
<body>
<form name="form1">
    <input type="text" name="txtInput" />
```

```
    <div id="lblResult"></div>
    <script language="javascript">
        function replace() {
            document.getElementById('lblResult').innerHTML = ➡
document.form1.txtInput.value.replace(/([^\s])OldNameSpace(?=\.)/, ➡
"$1NewNameSpace");
        }
    </script>
    <input type="button" name="btnSubmit" onclick="replace()" value="Go" />
</form>
</body>
</html>
```

How It Works

This recipe uses look-behinds in the .NET versions to replace a namespace. The reason why you can't use the standard \b word anchor is that a period is a word boundary character. That's why this recipe uses the look-behind that looks specifically for whitespace.

The search expression is as follows:

(?<=   a positive look-behind that includes . . .

\s   whitespace . . .

)   the end of the positive look-behind . . .

. . .   the old namespace name, followed by . . .

(?=   a positive look-ahead that includes . . .

\.   a literal period . . .

)   the end of the positive look-ahead.

6-17. Removing Whitespace in Method Calls

You can use this regular expression to eliminate extra whitespace found after an opening parenthesis and before a closing parenthesis. For instance, the following:

```
MyMethod( var1, var2   )
```

becomes the following:

```
MyMethod(var1, var2)
```

.NET Framework

C#

```csharp
using System;
using System.IO;
using System.Text.RegularExpressions;

public class Recipe
{
    private static Regex _Regex = new Regex( @"(?<=\()\s+|\s+(?=\))" );
    public void Run(string fileName)
    {
        String line;
        String newLine;
        using (StreamReader sr = new StreamReader(fileName))
        {
            while(null != (line = sr.ReadLine()))
            {
                newLine = _Regex.Replace(line, "");
                Console.WriteLine("New string is: '{0}', original was: '{1}'",
                    newLine,
                    line);
            }
        }
    }

    public static void Main( string[] args )
    {
        Recipe r = new Recipe();
        r.Run(args[0]);
    }
}
```

Visual Basic .NET

```vbnet
Imports System
Imports System.IO
Imports System.Text.RegularExpressions
Public Class Recipe

    Private Shared _Regex As Regex = New Regex("(?<=\()\s+|\s+(?=\))")

    Public Sub Run(ByVal fileName As String)
        Dim line As String
        Dim newLine As String
        Dim sr As StreamReader = File.OpenText(fileName)
        line = sr.ReadLine
        While Not line Is Nothing
            newLine = _Regex.Replace(line, "")
            Console.WriteLine("New string is: '{0}', original was: '{1}'", _
             newLine, _
             line)
            line = sr.ReadLine
        End While
        sr.Close()
    End Sub

    Public Shared Sub Main(ByVal args As String())
        Dim r As Recipe = New Recipe
        r.Run(args(0))
    End Sub

End Class
```

How It Works

This recipe searches for whitespace that can be either preceded by an opening parenthesis or followed by a closing parenthesis. To avoid replacing the parentheses, it uses look-arounds to make sure they exist. The regex is in two parts, separated by the "or" operator, |. The first part is as follows:

(?<=	the beginning of a positive look-behind that contains . . .
\(	a literal opening parenthesis, followed by . . .
)	the end of the positive look-behind, then . . .
\s	whitespace . . .
+	found one or more times.

The second part is as follows:

\s   whitespace . . .

+   found one or more times . . .

(?=   a positive look-ahead that looks for . . .

\)   a literal closing parenthesis . . .

)   the end of the positive look-ahead.

Although VBScript and JavaScript both support look-aheads, they don't support look-behinds.

Variations

This recipe is fairly simple, but it could be easily combined with others in this book to do more complicated matching, such as making sure the replacement happens only outside quotes and outside comments (see recipes 6-8 and 6-9).

6-18. Parsing Command-Line Arguments

This recipe allows you to obtain command-line arguments from a string. It assumes that the input is a command with arguments that can begin either with a forward slash or with a hyphen. You can separate the argument names from their optional values using either a colon or an equals sign, such as the following:

```
mycommand.exe /myarg:value
mycommand.exe -myarg=value
```

.NET Framework

C#

```csharp
using System;
using System.IO;
using System.Text.RegularExpressions;

public class Recipe
{
    private static Regex _Regex =
        new Regex( @"\s+[-/](?<arg>[a-z0-9?]+)([:=](?<val>[^\s"]+|"[^"]*"))?",
            RegexOptions.IgnoreCase );

    public void Run(string fileName)
    {
        String line;
        int lineNbr = 0;
        using (StreamReader sr = new StreamReader(fileName))
        {
            while(null != (line = sr.ReadLine()))
            {
                lineNbr++;
                foreach (Match m in _Regex.Matches(line))
                {
                    Console.WriteLine("Found match '{0}' at line {1}",
                        m.Result("${arg} with value ${val}"),
                        lineNbr);
                }
            }
        }
    }

    public static void Main( string[] args )
    {
        Recipe r = new Recipe();
        r.Run(args[0]);
    }
}
```

Visual Basic .NET

```
Imports System
Imports System.IO
Imports System.Text.RegularExpressions
Public Class Recipe

    Private Shared _Regex As Regex = New Regex("\s+[-/]➡
(?<arg>[a-z0-9?]+)([:=](?<val>[^\s"]+|"[^"]*"))?", RegexOptions.IgnoreCase)

    Public Sub Run(ByVal fileName As String)
        Dim line As String
        Dim lineNbr As Integer = 0
        Dim sr As StreamReader = File.OpenText(fileName)
        line = sr.ReadLine
        While Not line Is Nothing
            lineNbr = lineNbr + 1
            Dim m As Match
            For Each m In _Regex.Matches(line)
                Console.WriteLine("Found match '{0}' at line {1}", _
                    m.Result("${arg} with value ${val}"), _
                    lineNbr)
            Next m
            line = sr.ReadLine
        End While
        sr.Close()
    End Sub

    Public Shared Sub Main(ByVal args As String())
        Dim r As Recipe = New Recipe
        r.Run(args(0))
    End Sub

End Class
```

How It Works

This recipe finds parameters that are split from each other by whitespace. The parameter is set off by either a forward slash or a hyphen, and each parameter is separated from its value by either a colon or an equals sign. The regex is as follows:

\s	whitespace . . .
+	found one or more times, followed by . . .
[-/]	a character class that matches either a hyphen or a forward slash . . .
(?<arg>	a named group named *arg* that contains . . .

[a-z0-9?]   a character class that matches the letters *a* through *z*, the numbers zero through nine, and a question mark . . .

+   found one or more times . . .

)   the end of the named group.

The previous part of the regex matches the name of the parameter. The next part of the expression matches the optional value, which is separated from the argument by a colon or an equals sign:

(a group that contains . . .

[:=]   a character class that includes a colon or an equals sign . . .

(?<val>   a group named *val* that contains . . .

[^\s"]   a character class that matches anything that *isn't* whitespace or a double quote . . .

+   found one or more times . . .

| or . . .

"   a double quote, followed by . . .

[^"]   a character class that matches anything that isn't a double quote . . .

*   found any number of times . . .

"   a double quote . . .

)   the end of the named group . . .

)   the end of the outer group . . .

?   where the group is found at most one time.

6-19. Finding Words in Curly Braces

You can use this recipe to find values that reside inside curly braces. Similar to the
`String.Format` method in .NET, it will ignore even numbers of braces doubled up as
literal braces. Therefore, it will match {value} but not {{value}}.

.NET Framework

C#

```
using System;
using System.IO;
using System.Text.RegularExpressions;

public class Recipe
{
    private static Regex _Regex = new Regex( "(?!<{)((({{)*(){(?<val>[^}]+)" );

    public void Run(string fileName)
    {
        String line;
        int lineNbr = 0;
        using (StreamReader sr = new StreamReader(fileName))
        {
            while(null != (line = sr.ReadLine()))
            {
                lineNbr++;
                foreach (Match m in _Regex.Matches(line))
                {
                    Console.WriteLine("Found match '{0}' at line {1}",
                        m.Result("${val}"),
                        lineNbr);
                }
            }
        }
    }

    public static void Main( string[] args )
    {
        Recipe r = new Recipe();
        r.Run(args[0]);
    }
}
```

Visual Basic .NET

```vbnet
Imports System
Imports System.IO
Imports System.Text.RegularExpressions
Public Class Recipe

    Private Shared _Regex As Regex = New Regex("(?!<{)((({)*{)(?<val>[^}]+)")

    Public Sub Run(ByVal fileName As String)
        Dim line As String
        Dim lineNbr As Integer = 0
        Dim sr As StreamReader = File.OpenText(fileName)
        line = sr.ReadLine
        While Not line Is Nothing
            lineNbr = lineNbr + 1
            Dim m As Match
            For Each m In _Regex.Matches(line)
                Console.WriteLine("Found match '{0}' at line {1}", _
                    m.Result("${val}"), _
                    lineNbr)
            Next m
            line = sr.ReadLine
        End While
        sr.Close()
    End Sub

    Public Shared Sub Main(ByVal args As String())
        Dim r As Recipe = New Recipe
        r.Run(args(0))
    End Sub

End Class
```

VBScript

```vbscript
Dim fso,s,re,line,lineNbr,m,matches
Set fso = CreateObject("Scripting.FileSystemObject")
Set s = fso.OpenTextFile(WScript.Arguments.Item(0), 1, True)
Set re = New RegExp
re.Pattern = "((({)*{)(?!{)([^}]+)"
lineNbr = 0
Do While Not s.AtEndOfStream
    line = s.ReadLine()
    lineNbr = lineNbr + 1
```

```
    Set matches = re.Execute(line)
    For Each m In matches
        WScript.Echo "Found match: '" & m.Value & "' at line " & lineNbr
    Next
Loop
s.Close
```

How It Works

At first, you might be tempted to look for just {[^}]+} as an expression and be done with it. The problem with doing that is that if the value inside curly braces is inside escaped (doubled-up) curly braces, this regex will falsely identify that as a match.

The solution is to look for an odd number of curly braces surrounding the value. The value is anything that isn't a curly brace (in this example, that includes escaped ones). That's just [^}]+. The part of the regex that matches an odd number of opening braces is a little more complex:

(the beginning of a group that contains . . .

({{)   a group with two braces in it . . .

*   found any number of times, followed by . . .

{   a single curly brace . . .

)   the end of the group . . .

(?!   the beginning of a negative look-ahead that contains . . .

{   a single curly brace . . .

)   the end of the negative look-ahead.

At this point, the regex will match an odd number of opening braces. After that, anything that's not a closing curly brace is part of the value, which is [^}]+.

6-20. Parsing Visual Basic .NET Declarations

You can use this recipe to parse Visual Basic .NET declarations, such as the following:

```
Dim myString As String
```

For more complete matching, use this recipe with recipe 6-7 to be more thorough when matching variable names.

.NET Framework

C#

```csharp
using System;
using System.IO;
using System.Text.RegularExpressions;

public class Recipe
{
    private static Regex _Regex =
        new Regex( @"^\s*Dim\s+(?<var>\w+)\s+As\s+(?<type>[\w.]+)",
            RegexOptions.IgnoreCase );

    public void Run(string fileName)
    {
        String line;
        using (StreamReader sr = new StreamReader(fileName))
        {
            while(null != (line = sr.ReadLine()))
            {
                if (_Regex.IsMatch(line))
                {
                    Console.WriteLine("Found variable:  '{0}'; type: '{1}'",
                        _Regex.Match(line).Result("${var}"),
                        _Regex.Match(line).Result("${type}"));
                }
            }
        }
    }

    public static void Main( string[] args )
    {
        Recipe r = new Recipe();
        r.Run(args[0]);
    }
}
```

Visual Basic .NET

```
Imports System
Imports System.IO
Imports System.Text.RegularExpressions
Public Class Recipe

    Private Shared _Regex As Regex = _
        New Regex("^\s*Dim\s+(?<var>\w+)\s+As\s+(?<type>[\w.]+)", _
            RegexOptions.IgnoreCase)

    Public Sub Run(ByVal fileName As String)
        Dim line As String
        Dim newLine As String
        Dim sr As StreamReader = File.OpenText(fileName)
        line = sr.ReadLine
        While Not line Is Nothing
            If _Regex.IsMatch(line) = True Then
                Console.WriteLine("Found variable:  '{0}'; type: '{1}'", _
                    _Regex.Match(line).Result("${var}"), _
                    _Regex.Match(line).Result("${type}"))
            End If
            line = sr.ReadLine
        End While
        sr.Close()
    End Sub

    Public Shared Sub Main(ByVal args As String())
        Dim r As Recipe = New Recipe
        r.Run(args(0))
    End Sub

End Class
```

VBScript

```
Dim fso,s,re,line,newstr
Set fso = CreateObject("Scripting.FileSystemObject")
Set s = fso.OpenTextFile(WScript.Arguments.Item(0), 1, True)
Set re = New RegExp
re.Pattern = "^\s*Dim\s+(\w+)\s+As\s+([\w.]+)"
re.IgnoreCase = True
Do While Not s.AtEndOfStream
    line = s.ReadLine()
    If re.Test(line) = True Then
        newstr = re.Replace(line, "Found variable: '$1'; type: '$2'")
```

6-20 ■ PARSING VISUAL BASIC .NET DECLARATIONS

```
        WScript.Echo newstr
    End If
Loop
s.Close
```

JavaScript

```
<html>
<head>
<title></title>
</head>
<body>
<form name="form1">
    <input type="text" name="txtInput" />
    <div id="lblResult"></div>
    <script language="javascript">
        function replace() {
            document.getElementById('lblResult').innerHTML = ➥
document.form1.txtInput.value.replace(/^\s*Dim\s+(\w+)\s+As\s+([\w.]+)/i, ➥
"Found variable: '$1'; type: '$2'");
        }
    </script>
    <input type="button" name="btnSubmit" onclick="replace()" value="Go" />
</form>
</body>
</html>
```

How It Works

This expression searches for a `Dim` declaration. The first part of the expression searches for the word *Dim*, followed by at least one space to separate it from the variable name:

^	the beginning of the line, followed by . . .
\s	whitespace . . .
*	found any number of times, followed by . . .
Dim	*D*, *i*, and *m* . . .
\s	whitespace . . .
+	found at least once.

The variable name here is matched by using \w, which matches the letters *A* through *Z*, the letters *a* through *z*, zero through nine, and an underscore. I've done this just to make this expression easier to follow—see recipe 6-7 for an example of being more exact with variable names. Here's the expression broken down:

(?<var>	a group named *var* that contains . . .
\w	a word character . . .
+	found one or more times . . .
)	the end of the named group, followed by . . .
\s	whitespace . . .
+	found one of more times.

Next comes the word *As* and at least one space to separate it from the type name:

As	*A*, *s*, followed by . . .
\s	whitespace . . .
+	found one or more times.

Finally, the type name is identified by a named group in the .NET Framework examples, as shown here:

(?<type>	a group named *type* that contains . . .
[\w.]	a word character or a period (which will loosely match a type name) . . .
+	found one or more times . . .
)	the end of the named group.

Like the variable name, the type match can be altered to be a closer match (see recipe 6-7 and recipe 6-10 for examples). This one will work on code that can be compiled, because the compiler has already checked to make sure your variable and type names are valid.

6-21. Parsing INI Files

You can use this recipe to parse keys and values in INI files. Although you could implement this functionality with different commands (such as `String.Split` in .NET), this recipe has the ability to also make sure the line isn't commented out.

.NET Framework

C#

```csharp
using System;
using System.IO;
using System.Text.RegularExpressions;

public class Recipe
{
    private static Regex _Regex =
        new Regex( @"^(?<key>[^#=]+)\s*=\s*(?<value>[^#]*)\s*" );

    public void Run(string fileName)
    {
        String line;
        using (StreamReader sr = new StreamReader(fileName))
        {
            while(null != (line = sr.ReadLine()))
            {
                if (_Regex.IsMatch(line))
                {
                    Console.WriteLine("Found key:  '{0}'; value: '{1}'",
                        _Regex.Match(line).Result("${key}"),
                        _Regex.Match(line).Result("${value}"));
                }
            }

        }
    }

    public static void Main( string[] args )
    {
        Recipe r = new Recipe();
        r.Run(args[0]);
    }
}
```

Visual Basic .NET

```
Imports System
Imports System.IO
Imports System.Text.RegularExpressions
Public Class Recipe

    Private Shared _Regex As Regex = _
        New Regex("^(?<key>[^#=]+)\s*=\s*(?<value>[^#]*)\s*")

    Public Sub Run(ByVal fileName As String)
        Dim line As String
        Dim lineNbr As Integer = 0
        Dim sr As StreamReader = File.OpenText(fileName)
        line = sr.ReadLine
        While Not line Is Nothing
            If _Regex.IsMatch(line) = True Then
                Console.WriteLine("Found key:  '{0}'; value: '{1}'", _
                    _Regex.Match(line).Result("${key}"), _
                    _Regex.Match(line).Result("${value}"))
            End If
            line = sr.ReadLine
        End While
        sr.Close()
    End Sub

    Public Shared Sub Main(ByVal args As String())
        Dim r As Recipe = New Recipe
        r.Run(args(0))
    End Sub

End Class
```

VBScript

```
Dim fso,s,re,line,lineNbr
Set fso = CreateObject("Scripting.FileSystemObject")
Set s = fso.OpenTextFile(WScript.Arguments.Item(0), 1, True)
Set re = New RegExp
re.Pattern = "^(?<key>[^#=]+)\s*=\s*(?<value>[^#]*)\s*"
lineNbr = 0
Do While Not s.AtEndOfStream
    line = s.ReadLine()
    If re.Test(line) = True Then
        newstr = re.Replace(line, "Found key: '$1'; value: '$2'")
        WScript.Echo newstr
    End If
Loop
s.Close
```

JavaScript

```
<html>
<head>
<title></title>
</head>
<body>
<form name="form1">
    <input type="textbox" name="txtInput" />
    <script type="text/javascript">
    function validate() {
        if (! document.form1.txtInput.value.match(/^(?<key>[^#=]+)\s*=\s*➥
(?<value>[^#]*)\s*/)) {
            alert("Please enter valid value!")
        } else {
            alert("Success!")
        }
    }
    </script>
    <input type="button" name="btnSubmit" onclick="validate()" value="Go" />
</form>
</body>
</html>
```

How It Works

The only differences between the .NET versions and the scripting versions of the recipe is that the .NET versions take advantage of named groups to easily access the results of the match. The scripting version is broken down here, starting with the part of the regex recipe that matches the key (everything up to the first = and not commented out):

^	the beginning of the line, followed by . . .
(	a group that contains . . .
[^#=]	a character class that matches anything except a pound sign or equals sign . . .
+	found one or more times . . .
)	the end of the group . . .
\s	whitespace . . .
*	found any number of times . . .
=	an equals sign.

The next part of the regex captures the value, starting at the first character that isn't white-space:

\s	whitespace . . .
*	found any number of times, followed by . . .
(	a group that contains . . .
[^#]	any character that isn't a comment character . . .
*	found any number of times . . .
)	the end of the group, followed by . . .
\s	whitespace . . .
*	found any number of times.

6-22. Parsing .NET Compiler Output

This recipe extracts the name, line number, and character position where a compiler error occurred when compiling .NET files with csc.exe and vbc.exe.

.NET Framework

C#

```csharp
using System;
using System.IO;
using System.Text.RegularExpressions;

public class Recipe
{
    private static Regex _Regex = new Regex( ➥
@"^(?<path>[A-Za-z]:\\[^/:*?""<>|]+)\((?<line>\d+),(?<pos>\d+)\):");

    public void Run(string fileName)
    {
        String line;
        using (StreamReader sr = new StreamReader(fileName))
        {
            while(null != (line = sr.ReadLine()))
            {
                if (_Regex.IsMatch(line))
                {
                    Console.WriteLine("Error in file:  '{0}' at ➥
line '{1}', position '{2}'",
                        _Regex.Match(line).Result("${path}"),
                        _Regex.Match(line).Result("${line}"),
                        _Regex.Match(line).Result("${pos}"),
);
                }
            }
        }
    }

    public static void Main( string[] args )
    {
        Recipe r = new Recipe();
        r.Run(args[0]);
    }
}
```

Visual Basic .NET

```
Imports System
Imports System.IO
Imports System.Text.RegularExpressions
Public Class Recipe

    Private Shared _Regex As Regex = _
        New Regex("^(?<path>[A-Za-z]:\\[^/:*?""""<>|]+)\((?<line>\d+),(?<pos>\d+)\):")

    Public Sub Run(ByVal fileName As String)
        Dim line As String
        Dim lineNbr As Integer = 0
        Dim sr As StreamReader = File.OpenText(fileName)
        line = sr.ReadLine
        While Not line Is Nothing
            If _Regex.IsMatch(line) = True Then
                Console.WriteLine("Error in file:  '{0}' at line '{1}', ➡
position '{2}'", _
                    _Regex.Match(line).Result("${path}"), _
                    _Regex.Match(line).Result("${line}"), _
                    _Regex.Match(line).Result("${pos}"), _
)
            End If
            line = sr.ReadLine
        End While
        sr.Close()
    End Sub

    Public Shared Sub Main(ByVal args As String())
        Dim r As Recipe = New Recipe
        r.Run(args(0))
    End Sub

End Class
```

How It Works

When a compiler error is thrown by csc.exe or vbc.exe, each error is prefixed with the path of the source code file along with the line on which the error occurred and the line position of the error. The line and position are separated by commas and enclosed in parentheses right after the path name. The regex, broken down, is as follows:

^	the beginning of the line, followed by . . .
(?<path>	a group named path that contains . . .
[A-Za-z]:\\	the drive letter (see recipe 2-7) . . .

`[^/:*?""<>|]`	any character that isn't an invalid character in a filename (see recipe 2-9) . . .
`+`	found one or more times . . .
`)`	the end of the named group . . .
`\(`	a literal opening parenthesis, followed by . . .
`(?<line>`	a group named line that contains . . .
`\d`	a digit . . .
`+`	found one or more times . . .
`)`	the end of the group named *line* . . .
`,`	a comma . . .
`(?<pos>`	a group named *pos* . . .
`\d`	a digit . . .
`+`	found one or more times . . .
`)`	the end of the group named *pos* . . .
`\)`	a literal closing parenthesis . . .
`:`	a colon.

■ **Note** This exact format of this output changes in any new version of the compilers—their outputs don't conform to any sort of output standards.

6-23. Parsing the Output of dir

This recipe allows you to parse the output of the dir command to grab the names of directories and display their time stamps.

Note Certain options change the format of the dir output. This recipe assumes the output is the standard dir command on Windows 2000, Windows XP, and Windows NT, with no additional options passed to it.

.NET Framework

C#

```csharp
using System;
using System.IO;
using System.Text.RegularExpressions;

public class Recipe
{
    private static Regex _Regex = new Regex( @"^(?<ts>\d{2}/\d{2}/\d{4}➥
\s+\d{2}:\d{2}\s+[AP]M)\s+((?<type>\<DIR\>)\s+)?(?<name>[-\w\s.]+)$" );

    public void Run(string fileName)
    {
        String line;
        using (StreamReader sr = new StreamReader(fileName))
        {
            while(null != (line = sr.ReadLine()))
            {
                if (_Regex.IsMatch(line))
                {
                    Console.WriteLine("Found directory:  '{0}' with ➥
timestamp: '{1}'",
                        _Regex.Match(line).Result("${name}"),
                        _Regex.Match(line).Result("${ts}"));
                }
            }
        }
    }

    public static void Main( string[] args )
    {
        Recipe r = new Recipe();
        r.Run(args[0]);
    }
}
```

Visual Basic .NET

```
Imports System
Imports System.IO
Imports System.Text.RegularExpressions
Public Class Recipe

    Private Shared _Regex As Regex = New Regex("^(?<ts>\d{2}/\d{2}/\d{4}➡
\s+\d{2}:\d{2}\s+[AP]M)\s+((?<type>\<DIR\>)\s+)?(?<name>[-\w\s.]+)$")

    Public Sub Run(ByVal fileName As String)
        Dim line As String
        Dim newLine As String
        Dim sr As StreamReader = File.OpenText(fileName)
        line = sr.ReadLine
        While Not line Is Nothing
            If _Regex.IsMatch(line) = True Then
                Console.WriteLine("Found directory:  '{0}' with timestamp: '{1}'", _
                    _Regex.Match(line).Result("${name}"), _
                    _Regex.Match(line).Result("${ts}"))
            End If
            line = sr.ReadLine
        End While
        sr.Close()
    End Sub

    Public Shared Sub Main(ByVal args As String())
        Dim r As Recipe = New Recipe
        r.Run(args(0))
    End Sub

End Class
```

VBScript

```
Dim fso,s,re,line,newstr
Set fso = CreateObject("Scripting.FileSystemObject")
Set s = fso.OpenTextFile(WScript.Arguments.Item(0), 1, True)
Set re = New RegExp
re.Pattern = "^(\d{2}/\d{2}/\d{4}\s+\d{2}:\d{2}\s+[AP]M)\s+➡
((\<DIR\>)\s+)?([-\w\s.]+)$"
Do While Not s.AtEndOfStream
    line = s.ReadLine()
    If re.Test(line) = True Then
        newstr = re.Replace(line, "Found directory: '$4' with timestamp: '$1'")
        WScript.Echo newstr
    End If
Loop
s.Close
```

How It Works

This regex consists of a couple of named groups that grab parts of the output of the `dir` command. In the .NET examples in this recipe, named groups make the matches more accessible later. In the VBScript example, back references print the results.

The first group, shown here, parses the time stamp from the output:

`(?<ts>`	a group named *ts* that contains . . .
`. . .`	the regex that matches the date and time . . .
`)`	the end of the named group, followed by . . .
`\s`	whitespace . . .
`+`	found one or more times.

The second group, named *type* in the .NET Framework examples, matches `<DIR>`:

`(`	a group that contains . . .
`(?<type>`	a named group with . . .
`<DIR>`	<, *D*, *I*, *R*, and > . . .
`)`	the end of the named group . . .
`\s`	whitespace . . .
`+`	found one or more times . . .
`)`	the end of the group . . .
`?`	that may be found at most once.

The last group matches the name of the directory. The matching is loose because the output is a command that's printing existing directory names, which is significantly different from user input. Because the directories have already been created, they must contain valid characters. If the data were instead free-form text, the regex would need to be more thorough.

`(?<name>`	a group called *name* that contains . . .
`[-\w\s.]`	a character class that matches a word character, whitespace, or period . . .
`+`	found one or more times . . .
`)`	the end of the group . . .
`$`	the end of the line.

6-24. Setting the Assembly Version

This recipe allows you to replace the default assembly version number that's located in the AssemblyInfo.cs or AssemblyInfo.vb file in projects created by Microsoft Visual Studio .NET. This recipe searches for lines that look like the following:

```
[assembly: AssemblyVersion("1.0.* ")]
<Assembly: AssemblyVersion("1.0.*")>
```

.NET Framework

C#

```csharp
using System;
using System.IO;
using System.Text.RegularExpressions;

public class Recipe
{
    private static Regex _Regex =
        new Regex(@"(?<=[[<]assembly: assemblyversion\("")1\.0\.\*(?="")",
            RegexOptions.IgnoreCase);
    public void Run(string fileName)
    {
        String line;
        String newLine;
        using (StreamReader sr = new StreamReader(fileName))
        {
            while(null != (line = sr.ReadLine()))
            {
                newLine = _Regex.Replace(line, "2.1.123.1234");
                Console.WriteLine("New string is: '{0}', original was: '{1}'",
                    newLine,
                    line);
            }
        }
    }

    public static void Main( string[] args )
    {
        Recipe r = new Recipe();
        r.Run(args[0]);
    }
}
```

Visual Basic .NET

```vbnet
Imports System
Imports System.IO
Imports System.Text.RegularExpressions
Public Class Recipe

    Private Shared _Regex As Regex = _
        New Regex("(?<=[[<]assembly: assemblyversion\("")1\.0\.\*(?=""))")

    Public Sub Run(ByVal fileName As String)
        Dim line As String
        Dim newLine As String
        Dim sr As StreamReader = File.OpenText(fileName)
        line = sr.ReadLine
        While Not line Is Nothing
            newLine = _Regex.Replace(line, "2.1.123.1234")
            Console.WriteLine("New string is: '{0}', original was: '{1}'", _
             newLine, _
             line)
            line = sr.ReadLine
        End While
        sr.Close()
    End Sub

    Public Shared Sub Main(ByVal args As String())
        Dim r As Recipe = New Recipe
        r.Run(args(0))
    End Sub

End Class
```

VBScript

```vbscript
Dim fso,s,re,line,newstr
Set fso = CreateObject("Scripting.FileSystemObject")
Set s = fso.OpenTextFile(WScript.Arguments.Item(0), 1, True)
Set re = New RegExp
re.Pattern = "([[<]assembly: assemblyversion\("")1\.0\.\*(?=""))"
Do While Not s.AtEndOfStream
    line = s.ReadLine()
    newstr = re.Replace(line, "$12.1.123.1234")
    WScript.Echo "New string '" & newstr & "', original '" & line & "'"
Loop
s.Close
```

How It Works

I've used this recipe in a custom NAnt task to replace the version located in the `AssemblyInfo.cs` and `AssemblyInfo.vb` files with the current build version. The recipe is fairly simple, varying here between the .NET and scripting versions because VBScript doesn't support look-behinds:

`(?<=`	a positive look-behind that contains . . .
`[[<]`	a character class that matches either a left bracket or a less-than sign, followed by . . .
`assembly: assemblyversion`	the `AssemblyVersion` attribute . . .
`\(`	a literal opening parenthesis . . .
`"`	a double quote . . .
`)`	the end of the positive look-behind, followed by . . .
`1\.0\.\*`	the default version number, with the periods and asterisk escaped . . .
`(?=`	a positive look-ahead that contains . . .
`"`	a double quote . . .
`)`	the end of the positive look-ahead.

When the replacement is done, whatever is matched by the look-arounds is left alone, so the only thing that's modified is `1.0.*`.

The VBScript version is only slightly different. Since negative look-behinds aren't supported in VBScript, the expression must capture the text up to the version number and then put it back with the `$1` back reference in the replacement string.

6-25. Matching Qualified Assembly Names

This recipe allows you to verify the format of fully qualified assembly names. You can use it where a user must enter an assembly name into a user interface. This recipe puts together many of the concepts shown in this chapter, such as matching namespace names and matching hexadecimal numbers.

.NET Framework

C#

```csharp
using System;
using System.IO;
using System.Text.RegularExpressions;

public class Recipe
{
    private static final string nameSpaceRe =
        @"(?<ns>[a-z_][a-z\d_]+(\.[a-z_][a-z\d_]+)*)";
    private static final string typeRe =
        @"(?<t>[a-z_][a-z\d_]+(\.[a-z_][a-z\d_]+)*)";
    private static final string verRe = @"(?<v>Version=(\d+\.){3}\d+)";
    private static final string cultureRe = "(?<c>Culture=[^,]+)";
    private static final string tokenRe =
        @"(,\s*(?<pkt>PublicKeyToken=([a-f\d]{16}|null)))?";
    private static Regex _Regex =
        new Regex(String.Format(@"^{0},\s*{1},\s*{2},\s*{3}{4}"
            nameSpaceRe,
            typeRe,
            verRe,
            cultureRe,
            tokenRe), RegexOptions.IngoreCase);

    public void Run(string fileName)
    {
        String line;
        int lineNbr = 0;
        using (StreamReader sr = new StreamReader(fileName))
        {
            while(null != (line = sr.ReadLine()))
            {
                lineNbr++;
                foreach (Match m in _Regex.Matches(line))
                {
                    Console.WriteLine("Found match '{0}' at line {1}",
                        m.Result("${1}"),
                        lineNbr);
```

```csharp
                }
            }
        }
    }

    public static void Main( string[] args )
    {
        Recipe r = new Recipe();
        r.Run(args[0]);
    }
}
```

Visual Basic .NET

```vbnet
Imports System
Imports System.IO
Imports System.Text.RegularExpressions
Public Class Recipe

    Private Const nameSpaceRe As String = _
        "(?<ns>[a-z_][a-z\d_]+(\.[a-z_][a-z\d_]+)*)"
    Private Const typeRe As String = "(?<t>[a-z_][a-z\d_]+(\.[a-z_][a-z\d_]+)*)"
    Private Const verRe As String = "(?<v>Version=(\d+\.){3}\d+)"
    Private Const cultureRe As String = "(?<c>Culture=[^,]+)"
    Private Const tokenRe As String = _
        "(,\s*(?<pkt>PublicKeyToken=([a-f\d]{16}|null)))?"

    Private Shared _Regex As Regex = New Regex( _
    String.Format("^{0},\s*{1},\s*{2},\s*{3}{4}" _
            nameSpaceRe, _
            typeRe, _
            verRe, _
            cultureRe, _
            tokenRe), RegexOptions.IgnoreCase)

    Public Sub Run(ByVal fileName As String)
        Dim line As String
        Dim lineNbr As Integer = 0
        Dim sr As StreamReader = File.OpenText(fileName)
        line = sr.ReadLine
        While Not line Is Nothing
            lineNbr = lineNbr + 1
            Dim m As Match
            For Each m In _Regex.Matches(line)
                Console.WriteLine("Found match '{0}' at line {1}", _
                    m.Result("${1}"), _
                    lineNbr)
```

```
            Next m
            line = sr.ReadLine
        End While
        sr.Close()
    End Sub

    Public Shared Sub Main(ByVal args As String())
        Dim r As Recipe = New Recipe
        r.Run(args(0))
    End Sub

End Class
```

How It Works

Each part of this recipe should look familiar, because this recipe builds upon other recipes in this book. I've added each part in a named group for easy extraction. You can see the namespace and type name parts in more detail in recipe 6-10. You can understand the `PublicKeyToken` value, which is optional or can be null in this regex, by taking a look at recipe 6-11, which explains hexadecimal numbers.

The version and culture parts are relatively new, although the version part simply matches three groups of digits separated by periods followed by a final group of digits, which allows it to match numbers such as `1.0.121.1213` and `0.12.213.212`. The culture part simply takes everything up to the next delimiter, which is a comma in fully qualified assembly names.

Index

^   *line anchor—the beginning of the line*

1-1, 1-9, 1-12, 1-17, 1-21, 2-1, 2-5, 2-6, 2-7, 3-5, 3-6, 3-7, 3-8, 4-1, 4-2, 4-5, 4-7, 4-9, 4-10, 4-13, 4-14, 4-15, 4-16, 4-17, 4-18, 4-19, 4-20, 4-21, 4-22, 6-6, 6-7, 6-8, 6-10, 6-11, 6-12, 6-14, 6-20, 6-21, 6-22, 6-23

$ *line anchor—the end of the line*

1-9, 1-11, 1-13, 1-26, 3-3, 3-4, 4-1, 4-2, 4-5, 4-7, 4-9, 4-10, 4-13, 4-14, 4-15, 4-16, 4-17, 4-20, 4-22, 6-2, 6-7, 6-10, 6-11, 6-12, 6-14, 6-23

(...)   *expression group—captures matches and allows qualifiers and ranges to be applied to a group of expressions*

1-3, 1-4, 1-10, 1-11, 1-16, 2-6, 3-1, 4-1, 4-2, 4-3, 4-5, 4-8, 4-10, 4-11, 4-12, 4-13, 4-14, 4-15, 4-20, 4-22, 5-1, 5-2, 5-3, 5-4, 5-9, 6-2, 6-3, 6-9, 6-10, 6-12, 6-13, 6-14, 6-15, 6-18, 6-19, 6-24, 6-25

{}   *range qualifier—specifies the number of occurrences for previous expression*

1-9, 2-3, 3-7, 3-8, 4-1, 4-2, 4-3, 4-4, 4-5, 4-8, 4-9, 4-10, 4-12, 4-13, 4-14, 4-15, 4-17, 6-12, 6-23, 6-25

*   *qualifier—zero or more*

1-1, 1-7, 1-9, 1-11, 1-17, 1-24, 1-26, 2-2, 3-1, 3-3, 3-4, 3-5, 4-5, 4-8, 4-11, 4-20, 5-1, 5-2, 5-3, 5-4, 5-5, 5-9, 6-1, 6-2, 6-3, 6-4, 6-8, 6-9, 6-10, 6-15, 6-18, 6-19, 6-20, 6-21, 6-22, 6-24, 6-25

\+   *qualifier—one or more*

1-3, 1-10, 1-11, 1-14, 1-15, 2-1, 2-2, 2-4, 2-5, 2-8, 2-9, 2-10, 3-1, 3-2, 3-5, 3-6, 4-4, 4-5, 4-7, 4-18, 4-19, 4-20, 5-1, 5-2, 5-3, 5-4, 5-6, 5-7, 5-8, 6-3, 6-7, 6-8, 6-10, 6-11, 6-13, 6-14, 6-15, 6-17, 6-18, 6-19, 6-20, 6-21, 6-22, 6-23, 6-25

?   *qualifier—zero or one time*

1-4, 2-6, 4-1, 4-2, 4-5, 4-10, 4-12, 4-15, 4-16, 4-17, 4-21, 4-22, 5-1, 5-3, 5-4, 5-6, 5-7, 5-9, 6-1, 6-5, 6-8, 6-18, 6-23, 6-25

[...]   *character class—matches one single character*

1-5, 1-9, 2-1, 2-2, 2-7, 2-8, 4-1, 4-2, 4-3, 4-7, 4-10, 4-11, 4-13, 4-15, 4-16, 4-19, 4-20, 5-1, 5-2, 5-3, 5-8, 6-3, 6-7, 6-10, 6-11, 6-12, 6-13, 6-14, 6-15, 6-18, 6-20, 6-22, 6-23, 6-24, 6-25

forums.apress.com
FOR PROFESSIONALS BY PROFESSIONALS™

JOIN THE APRESS FORUMS AND BE PART OF OUR COMMUNITY. You'll find discussions that cover topics of interest to IT professionals, programmers, and enthusiasts just like you. If you post a query to one of our forums, you can expect that some of the best minds in the business—especially Apress authors, who all write with *The Expert's Voice*™—will chime in to help you. Why not aim to become one of our most valuable participants (MVPs) and win cool stuff? Here's a sampling of what you'll find:

DATABASES
Data drives everything.

Share information, exchange ideas, and discuss any database programming or administration issues.

INTERNET TECHNOLOGIES AND NETWORKING
Try living without plumbing (and eventually IPv6).

Talk about networking topics including protocols, design, administration, wireless, wired, storage, backup, certifications, trends, and new technologies.

JAVA
We've come a long way from the old Oak tree.

Hang out and discuss Java in whatever flavor you choose: J2SE, J2EE, J2ME, Jakarta, and so on.

MAC OS X
All about the Zen of OS X.

OS X is both the present and the future for Mac apps. Make suggestions, offer up ideas, or boast about your new hardware.

OPEN SOURCE
Source code is good; understanding (open) source is better.

Discuss open source technologies and related topics such as PHP, MySQL, Linux, Perl, Apache, Python, and more.

PROGRAMMING/BUSINESS
Unfortunately, it is.

Talk about the Apress line of books that cover software methodology, best practices, and how programmers interact with the "suits."

WEB DEVELOPMENT/DESIGN
Ugly doesn't cut it anymore, and CGI is absurd.

Help is in sight for your site. Find design solutions for your projects and get ideas for building an interactive Web site.

SECURITY
Lots of bad guys out there—the good guys need help.

Discuss computer and network security issues here. Just don't let anyone else know the answers!

TECHNOLOGY IN ACTION
Cool things. Fun things.

It's after hours. It's time to play. Whether you're into LEGO® MINDSTORMS™ or turning an old PC into a DVR, this is where technology turns into fun.

WINDOWS
No defenestration here.

Ask questions about all aspects of Windows programming, get help on Microsoft technologies covered in Apress books, or provide feedback on any Apress Windows book.

HOW TO PARTICIPATE:
Go to the Apress Forums site at **http://forums.apress.com/**.
Click the New User link.